Charles McGraw

Charles McGraw

*Biography of a Film
Noir Tough Guy*

ALAN K. RODE

with a foreword by Jim Steranko

McFarland & Company, Inc., Publishers
Jefferson, North Carolina, and London

Frontispiece: Charles McGraw

Library of Congress Cataloguing-in-Publication Data

Rode, Alan K., 1954–
Charles McGraw : biography of a film noir tough guy /
Alan K. Rode ; with a foreword by Jim Steranko.
p.   cm.
Includes bibliographical references and index.

ISBN 13: 978-0-7864-3167-0
illustrated case binding : 50# alkaline paper

1. McGraw, Charles, 1914–1980.   2. Motion picture actors
and actresses—United States—Biography.   I. Title.
PN2287.M5457R63   2008   791.4302'8092—dc22 [B]   2007028633

British Library cataloguing data are available

On the cover: Charles McGraw (author's collection);
background ©2007 Shutterstock

Manufactured in the United States of America

McFarland & Company, Inc., Publishers
Box 611, Jefferson, North Carolina 28640
www.mcfarlandpub.com

For Millie

Acknowledgments

There are many people to thank for assisting and encouraging me with this book. If I am remiss in expressing my gratitude to any individual on these pages, please accept my sincerest apologies in advance.

The word "interview" is a generic term used to describe the varying degrees of communications I had with many different people about Charles McGraw. From a conversation behind a stage curtain at a film festival, an email response, a brief telephone call, a letter or an extended series of discussions, I am supremely appreciative and honored by everyone who took the time to communicate with me:

Julie Adams, Theodore Bikel, Jules Dassin, the late Richard Fleischer (one of the kindest gentleman in Hollywood, who gave me an extended interview and encouraged me over three years ago; he is sorely missed), Richard Erdman, John Ericson, Nicole Carter Forsythe (who considerately passed along her husband John's comments), Betty Garrett, Gordon Gebert, Susan Gordon, Johnny Grant, Farley Granger, Barbara Hale, Earl Holliman, McGraw's great friend Bobby Hoy, L.Q Jones (the one and only "Sheriff"!), Mickey Knox, Michael McGreevey, Dick Martin, Terry Minton, Lindsley Parsons Jr., Joseph Pevney, Paul Picerni, Stanley Rubin (may we all have many more dinners at Le Petit Four), Mark Schucart at the Los Angeles Department of Coroner, Jean Simmons, Jim Steranko, Warren Stevens, Joan Taylor, Peggy Webber and Jacqueline White.

Two women made hugely significant contributions to my effort to chronicle the life and times of Charles McGraw; this book wouldn't have been possible without them.

Jill Julia McGraw candidly shared her memories about her mother and father as well as growing up as a movie actor's daughter in Hollywood. She also generously gave me several personal family photos, some of which are in this book. I sincerely hope that Jill finds the peace and contentment that has eluded her for so long.

Millie Black opened her home and heart to me and became one of my dearest friends. In addition to contributing many items from her personal collection of photographs, clippings and memorabilia for this book, she was a witty raconteur who loved to recount her life over seven decades in Hollywood and the years spent with Charles McGraw. She patiently answered all of my questions, some of which addressed memories unpleasant to recall. Despite her own personal challenges, Millie joyously brought to life a period of our popular culture that is rapidly becoming consigned solely to books and movies.

Many of the numerous documents reviewed for this book were made available to me by some distinguished archival institutions. My thanks to the following institutions and their estimable staffs:

Barbara Hall and staff at the Margaret Herrick Library of the Academy of Motion Picture Arts and Sciences. I am particularly indebted to Barbara for allowing me access to some of Richard Brooks' papers on *In Cold Blood* before they had been reviewed and archived by the Academy.

Lauren Buisson and staff at the Special Collections department of the UCLA Library. Many thanks to Lauren for supporting my review of numerous RKO production files and script boxes.

Ned Comstock at the USC Film and Television Library. Like so many other film writers and historians, I owe a great debt to the unending enthusiasm and helpfulness of Ned, who always seemed to find what I asked for, and would send me surprises in the mail that I had long forgotten about.

The Louis B. Mayer Library at the American Film Institute that allowed me to review their unique collection of *The Flash*, the house organ newspaper of RKO Radio Studios.

The New York Public Library at Lincoln Center.

I am also most grateful to selected institutions in Akron, Ohio, McGraw's boyhood home:

David Spurlock, Bill Luton and Norma Hill at the *Akron Beacon Journal* who provided important news clippings on McGraw from their archival morgue.

Sue Gutman, Records Technician for Akron Public Schools.

John V. Miller, Director of Archival Services at the University of Akron, selflessly dedicated himself to responding to my requests for McGraw's college transcripts and provided me with various photos—including several he arranged to have taken of McGraw's boyhood house—and newspaper clippings about McGraw's family.

I greatly appreciate the assistance of the Los Angeles Police Department, particularly Brenda Benton at L.A.P.D. Media Relations, for assisting me in my effort to contact retired L.A.P.D. officer Terry Minton, who willingly relived with me his memories of McGraw's tragic death.

For those friends and colleagues who assisted me so many specific ways:

The late Michael Fitzgerald, who helped connect me with Jackie White Anderson and left life's stage way too early.

Tom Weaver. Tom has interviewed and written about more vintage film people than anyone on Planet Earth. He was unceasingly supportive in providing contact information, editing acumen and humorous encouragement.

Gordon Gates, whose resourcefulness and assistance in tracking down McGraw's television shows, including the entire 39 episodes of *The Adventures of Falcon,* was unparalleled.

My close friend and colleague at the Film Noir Foundation and "Noir City" Film Festival, Eddie Muller, "The Czar of Noir," whose books and good work remain an inspiration. Eddie reviewed my original proposal for this book and provided me with insightful advice.

Lee Server, a great biographer and writer of popular culture who offered me his advice and unstinting encouragement.

Arthur Lyons, my friend, author of many fine books, and host of *The Palm Springs Film Noir Festival*, who regularly phoned to compare notes on our individual writing projects.

Claire and Donovan Brandt, and the rest of the gang at Eddie Brandt's Saturday Matinee, who came up with nearly all of the obscure McGraw films while we became summer barbecue buddies.

Jim Steranko, who informed me I wasn't alone in my admiration of Charles McGraw. Our numerous communications developed into a friendship that resulted in the excellent foreword that Jim composed for this book.

The one and only James Ellroy for his kind consideration in contributing the back cover blurb for this book. For specific assistance and encouragement: Michael Hayde, Fred Rappaport, Karen Burroughs Hannsbery, Stone Wallace, Janine Basinger, Phillippe Garnier, Stephanie Madison (eternal thanks for refusing to allow me to procrastinate), Anita Carson, Hal Lane, John Hagner, Michael Hyatt, Matt Kennedy, Del Harvey (my supportive friend and colleague at Filmmonthly.com), Michael Barnum, Philip Crawford, Don Malcolm, Foster Hirsch, Scott Thompson and John O'Dowd.

La Familia. My mother, father, brother David and my late grandparents, where the love of movies and actors began around the dinner table before I could walk comfortably and continues anew. For my wife Jemma, for her unstinting support in tolerating a husband who spent interminable hours either on a computer or watching films and old television programs in a room surrounded by Charles McGraw movie posters. Few femme fatales would have dared to take this task on. Thanks, Hug.

I would be remiss if I didn't close where so much of this book nearly five years ago. A Saturday afternoon spent in Los Angeles with my "comrade in noir" "Dark Marc" Dolezal. Marc drove out with me to visit Adele Jergens and then insisted on the way back that we still had time to find "McGraw's house" in the dusk of an early evening. It was a journey that eventually resulted in much of what resides within these pages.

Table of Contents

Acknowledgments   vii

Foreword: The McGraw Role No One Knows (by Jim Steranko)   1

Prologue: Not Ready for His Close-Up   3

  1. Child of the Heartland   7

  2. Young Thespian   12

  3. Hungry During the Golden Era   18

  4. What Did You Do in the War, Charlie?   22

  5. Bright Boy Gets a Break   27

  6. The Watershed Year   32

  7. The Lion Goes Black   43

  8. In Demand   48

  9. The Capital of Noir   57

10. The Other Side of the Hill   66

11. "Not Enough (Blood) to Suit Me"   71

12. The Certifiable Howard Hughes   77

13. The Sleeper That Almost Wasn't   82

14. Missing the Brass Ring   92

15. RKO Studios as Andersonville   100

16. Freelance Actor   104

17. Small-Screen Evolution   107

18. "Where Do We Get Such Men..."   112

19. Family Tensions   119

20. Character Actor   124

21. *Spartacus*   132

22. "Good Evening"   138

23. Golden Age Dissolution   145

24. A Glorious Time   149

25. Single Actor, Needs Work   155

26. Cold-Blooded Comeback   157

27. Last Hurrah   163

28. Means of Descent   170

29. Last Call   179

30. A Noir-Stained Legacy   184

Critical Filmography   191

Television Credits   197

Chapter Notes   199

Sources   203

Index   209

Foreword: The McGraw Role No One Knows

by Jim Steranko

Is it my imagination or is there a note of irony in the fact that so many of yesterday's leading men have vanished from the public consciousness, while certain actors who supported them on the big screen have not only remained cultural favorites, but often become cult icons?

Contemporary filmgoers would have difficulty identifying a legion of stars that were capable of opening movies in their day, such as Charles Boyer, Herbert Marshall, Pat O'Brien, Farley Granger, Ray Milland, Franchot Tone, Dennis Morgan, Dane Clark, Leslie Howard, Robert Walker, David Niven, and George Brent, among others. Conversely, a host of character actors, including John Carradine, Edward Everett Horton, James Gleason, Ward Bond, William Demarest, Jack Elam, S.Z. Sakall, Mike Mazurki, and Sydney Greenstreet have considerably more recognizability, if not by name, then by face, than their movie-star associates.

Charles McGraw falls into the latter category, but, unlike many who revisited the *same* role throughout their careers, he not only played the dramatic spectrum, he specialized in character polarity, often portraying either the most dedicated cops or the most sadistic killers (similar to Cagney, Bogart, and Robinson). Sometimes he was top-billed; sometimes not, but he was always memorable — and sometimes unforgettable. That face, that voice, that arsenal of mannerisms. He was like a scar that never completely healed, a mark left on the marrow of cinema — and the souls of audiences, as well.

No wonder he came to mind when I cast a white-knuckle antihero a few decades ago, not in film, but in another authentic American art form — the comics.

When I accepted the assignment to take over *Nick Fury, Agent of S.H.I.E.L.D.*, Marvel Comics' four-color 007 facsimile, the series was shambling through creative purgatory, charted by a knot of writers and artists who (with the exception of Jack Kirby) apparently didn't know or didn't care about its direction — or, more appropriately, its *lack* of direction.

I felt I could turn that quality to my advantage. Because the character and his motivations were so lackluster and ill-defined, the opportunity existed to recast Fury into an entity I could understand, easily articulate, and, ultimately, dramatize. The raw material was drawn from Marvel's World War II series *Sgt. Fury and His Howling Commandoes*, but transitioning an unshaven, wrinkle-suited, cigar-chomping non-com into the director of America's top-secret spy organization *without modification* was too absurd, even for comics.

Under my influence, he became trimmer, more sophisticated, and maybe even a cut more dangerous. Fury swapped his stogie for a cheroot, decorated his pad in Danish Modern, and began wearing Ivy League suits. He suddenly got gray at the temples and I actually had him shave his stubble on camera, a visual statement that expressed the suppression of his previous incarnation and confirmed his transformation into a contemporary action warrior. Garbed in a black leather zipsuit and armed with a new cache of caustic comebacks, Fury became cooler than Connery.

One of the shortcuts I used in writing dialogue for fictional characters was to cast them (in my mind's eye — or ear, in this case) as prominent film actors; so, rather than inventing the rhythms of their voices, the idiosyncrasies of their inflections, and the nature of their delivery, I used real-life models with which I was reasonably familiar — and perhaps the audience was, too.*

I might have used Charles Bronson, Kirk Douglas, James Coburn, or other cinematic tough-guys upon which to build my matrix, but instead opted for one of my favorite character actors: Charles McGraw. Whether playing heroes or villains, he was always as hard-boiled as they came, always just as ready to shut anyone up with a backhand slap as with a warning. His vocal delivery neatly summed up everything he brought to the screen: a predatory growl as harrowing as that of a cornered tiger's, bristling with menace, and suggesting a penchant for violence beyond that of his blunt, granite features. Sometimes there was even a harsh, metallic quality in his timbre, like that of a Sonovox voice amplifier. Something beyond human. Perhaps something even *less* than human.

The voice of Charles McGraw personified what I felt Fury was all about. His was the voice I heard as I wrote him into the S.H.I.E.L.D. saga. His voice was the core of the character, the point at which every adventure began and ended.

Like so many of his cinematic comrades, McGraw and company will undoubtedly continue to impact contemporary culture, as long as there are those of us, such as Alan Rode, the author of this well-researched and revealing biography, who are enriched by their efforts.

---

*Yes, Virginia, I know perceiving such a point would be positively subliminal, but nothing ventured, nothing gained. I once explained this device to Stan Lee and discovered he did something similar, at least while imagining the voice of the Fantastic Four's Ben Grimm aka the Thing. When Stan wrote the character, he patterned dialogue on the speech patterns of Brooklynesque comedian Jimmy Durante.

Jim Steranko, one of the most controversial figures in pop culture, has been the editor and publisher of the international magazine Prevue, the writer and artist of S.H.I.E.L.D., Captain America, and X-Men for Marvel. As a filmmaker he has collaborated with Steven Spielberg, George Lucas, and Francis Coppola. His work has been shown at more than 250 exhibitions worldwide, including such venues as the Louvre.

Prologue: Not Ready for His Close-Up

The zenith of the hellacious Los Angeles summer came early at the end of July 1980. The sun broiled the low-hanging smog with dead air, turning the San Fernando Valley into a pressure cooker. After four consecutive days of greater than 100 degree temperatures recorded at Burbank Airport, the mercury spiked at 107 on Tuesday, the 29th of July — a new record.

By early evening, the firmament morphed into a pastel haze accompanied by the thematic hum of rush hour traffic from the 101 Freeway. The chiaroscuro sky provided a perfect backdrop for the L.A.P.D. prowl car that glided to the curb and parked behind the ambulance.

The police officer exited the car and made his way through a knot of rubbernecking neighbors congregated by the driveway gate. There was nobody within to protect, only the next of kin and the taxpayers to serve.

At first glance, the scene outside the small house conjured up memories of Billy Wilder's classic Hollywood gothic, *Sunset Boulevard*. A closer examination revealed pronounced differences.

No newsreel or television cameras were at the ready and Erich von Stroheim wasn't present to call "Action!" The address wasn't in sylvan Beverly Hills. The quiet North Hollywood neighborhood was an appendage of nearby Studio City.

The decedent wasn't a bullet-ridden William Holden floating in a swimming pool either. The corpse inside the house was that of the film actor, Charles McGraw. A striking-looking Eurasian woman cried and embraced McGraw's body until gently restrained by another lady, the owner of the residence. The sobbing woman was the actor's ex-wife and the woman comforting her had lived with McGraw during the preceding thirteen years.

A dual bereavement scene at ground zero of his own demise was characteristic of Charles McGraw's tumultuous existence. The actor enjoyed a rip-snorting finale whether it was on a movie set or, better yet, a punchline shared with friends in a local barroom. No one would be laughing over this tragic denouement, though. No matter how many times McGraw might have perished as a baddie on screen, nobody who worked on a show with this veteran pro could have anticipated such a macabre finale.

Nobody in the movies was like Charles McGraw. He embodied a unique screen persona that conveyed serious business. The actor specialized in playing men of authority and action. His résumé of over 130 feature films and television episodes included numerous memorable performances. To his fellow thespians, McGraw was known as "an actor's actor": a ranked heavyweight performer who just missed grabbing the brass ring of authentic Hollywood stardom. The youthful McGraw had the blue eyes, the striking screen presence and certainly the acting chops to match a Douglas or Lancaster, but it didn't happen for him.

3

Instead, McGraw settled in for a long run as a successful character actor, usually playing a tough-as-nails cinematic hard case. There was talk about Supporting Oscar nods for his work in *The Bridges at Toko-Ri* and *Spartacus*, but again, it never happened. He didn't let up and stayed in demand for over three decades. Who else would they have used besides McGraw to play Robert Blake's father for *In Cold Blood* (1967), for God's sake?

Early on in his career, McGraw etched a permanent cinematic niche with his singular portrayals of cops and heavies in film noir pictures of the late '40s and early '50s. He had a brief fling with stardom while at RKO with leading roles in a collection of unique "B" crime films including *The Threat* (1949), *Armored Car Robbery* (1950), *Roadblock* (1951) and the classic *The Narrow Margin* (1952). The actor became synonymous with blunt portrayals of hard-boiled crooks and coppers; McGraw and noir went together like ham and eggs. His distinctive visage, ominously looming out of a darkened doorway during the opening minutes of *T-Men* (1947) and cast in menacing profile while walking towards the diner in *The Killers* (1946), was one of the most iconic visual touchstones of the film noir style during the genre's classic period. For movie aficionados who favor the damp pavement of film noir's dark streets, Charles McGraw was where the rubber met the road.

Ultimate noir prose stylist James Ellroy believes that McGraw is the visual template for the prototype L.A.P.D. Robbery-Homicide dick from the 1950s. Little wonder. A raincoat tightly lashed around a broad chest, the fedora brim shading a flint-rock face, a cigarette dangling from a clenched jaw.

His guttural rasp of a voice, reminiscent of broken china plates grating around in a burlap sack, was complemented by an intimidating, laser-like glare and a taciturn demeanor that verged on being closed captioned for the hearing impaired. McGraw's brusque noir characterizations are comparable in technique to Thelonious Monk's splayed fingers beating his unique jazz stylings into submission on the piano ivories. The title of Monk's identifying theme "Straight, No Chaser" exemplified McGraw's artistic and personal bent for over half a century.

I discovered Charles McGraw's treasure trove of hard-edged noir films while watching movies on television during the 1960s. McGraw became my cinematic touchstone. Not quite a star or a household name, but always distinctive, he was the actor that remained memorable after the final credits rolled. McGraw made toughness and malevolence authentic. That voice! I remember being entranced watching him in *Spartacus* at the local movie theatre. Even to a young kid, the sprawling spectacle lost a lot of its excitement after Kirk Douglas drowned McGraw in what appeared to be a vat of chunky beef vegetable soup. To this day, McGraw's guttural riposte to Douglas before their final grapple "No talking in the kitchen, slave" makes me inexplicably smile.

Years later, I wondered what ever happened to McGraw after noticing him on an old television program. I started watching more of his films, partly to satisfy my long-term fascination with movies that are now called film noir, partly to discover more about a favorite actor.

I found out that McGraw died under tragic and obscure circumstances in 1980. I needed to know more ... and more ... and then more again. This book is essentially the outcome of a durable fascination with Charles McGraw and film noir that assumed epic proportions.

While no actor in Hollywood conveyed implacable resolve with finer clarity on screen, the fluency of the authentic McGraw offscreen was found to be a good deal fuzzier.

McGraw deliberately cultivated an image steeped in fiction. The typical Hollywood pabulum, as dished by studio biographers, movie press agents and newspaper columnists, included additional dollops of fantasy when churning out his bios. McGraw was alternately born in Ireland, Ohio, the Far East and New York City. He was a middleweight prizefighter with 20 professional bouts, the actor led Boy Scouts on hikes through the Hollywood Hills on weekends, he was a police reporter for the *Brooklyn Eagle*, McGraw was wounded during World War II with Patton's army in France. And so on....

McGraw's companion, Mildred "Millie" Black, who was at his side during the final years, recalled listening to McGraw relate several fairy tales about his war service to a press agent once. When she queried him afterward about why he lied, the actor responded: "That's what they want to hear."

During my search for the authentic Charles McGraw, truth, fiction, and a dearth of factual information congealed into a confusing texture of paradoxical character layers. At least Captain Ahab knew who he was looking for. Imagine the remote stranger who was always remembered as the life of the party.

Most of the people who knew him are gone and a totally focused picture of the inner McGraw would be impossible to achieve in any event. He was an enigmatic man; conversely sociable but reserved, open, yet wary, cock-of-the-walk confident on screen but anxious on the set. From his long-term marriage, the relationship with his only child, available documentation from the past and the recollections of his surviving friends and co-workers; there is as much here as could be found and as much as could be told.

From a historical perspective, McGraw's film career straddled the dual eras of Old and New Hollywood. He made his screen debut in 1942 when the town was ruled by studio moguls who, despite their excesses, certainly knew how to make great movies. McGraw worked steadily till the film industry reached its commercial nadir, when an oil company would buy Paramount Studios and add their name under the time-honored mountain logo.

Charles McGraw worked with many of the legendary stars, directors and celebrities in Hollywood including Howard Hughes, Robert Mitchum, Alfred Hitchcock, Burt Lancaster, Richard Brooks, Kirk Douglas and Stanley Kramer. His career was concurrent to the industry's transition from the studio assembly line to independent film production and television. He witnessed the premature finale of RKO Studios as a major filmmaking entity, the dissolution of movie censorship and the disappearance of the Western as a primal American film genre. Many of these characters, events and associated aspects of cinematic popular culture are scrutinized herein with Charles McGraw cast in a distinctive role as a historical tour guide from the classic film noir era to postmodern Hollywood.

There are other chronological intersections from the life of Charles McGraw: the Great Depression, the famed Group Theatre in New York City, Hollywood during World War II with the Sunset Strip as a glamorous state of mind, the destructive Blacklist period, and the small town milieu of Studio City in the San Fernando Valley when the town had a stoplight, five or six bars and a horde of thirsty cowboys and stuntmen from Republic Studios. Many of these latter accounts include a lesser known cast of characters, notably Millie Black, who arrived in Hollywood the same year as McGraw and lived with him during the final thirteen years of his life. One cannot relate McGraw's life and times in Hollywood without telling Millie's story as well.

Finally, it is all about Charlie. With the notable exception of his wife, hardly anyone who knew the adult McGraw more than slightly called him anything other than Charlie. His name reflected a wire-brush demeanor that was relentlessly working class. McGraw was the antithesis of the Hollywood actor-celebrity syndrome. He hated pretentiousness and considered his chosen vocation that of a service trade that demanded a high level of performance. An actor had to be prepared and know his craft. To deliver his lines faultlessly and iteratively no matter how many hours were spent waiting around the set for a call or holding court in a bar the night before. For McGraw, getting the work done right was always the bottom line. Like an artisan who strived to be well-rounded, one of his few professional regrets was that he never became a skilled stuntman.

What could have been and what was for Charles McGraw is aptly summed up by one of his more trenchant film noir lines. As a cop at a loss for words to comfort his dead partner's wife in *Armored Car Robbery*, McGraw murmured in his rasping growl, "Tough break, Marsha." Perfect. Even though it was a hell of a career, it could have been so much more for Charlie with a couple of decent breaks. But a successful career in the movies doesn't account for the daily reality outside the start and stop times on the studio call sheet. McGraw's existence encompassed a major segment of American film history and possessed a great deal of professional accomplishment and fun-loving verve. But there were also the inner demons and nihilism that became central to his being. In the end, he composed his own dark epitaph. Charles McGraw's life became an authentic film noir story.

1

Child of the Heartland

Charles McGraw's foremost role was that of a pugnacious Irish scrapper. A robust customer who adhered to a personal moral code and never gave in when he thought he was right. While the personality traits possessed a considerable degree of accuracy, the shamrock lineage was a fable. Charlie's Irish ancestry, like his adopted surname of McGraw, was an assumed performance with a very long run. In reality, the tough character of cinematic urban streets had familial roots that originated in the American heartland.

Frank P. Butters tried his hand at a number of different trades as a young man and traveled the western United States in search of his fortune at the beginning of the twentieth century. Butters, born in 1886, could trace his descendants back to the *Mayflower* and was an apocryphal late nineteenth century American. Several letters from Butters to his family during his formative years are reflective of a genuine Horatio Alger trying to make his mark in the West of a century ago that retained many attributes of the American frontier. He bounced around California for awhile, worked as a teamster and got swept up in a gold strike while in northern Nevada. The young hostler wrote to his parents, "The gold fever is drying out the claim that I get if I get any at all ... will be 320 acres of ranchland and be a farmer."[1] In a scenario reminiscent of a hard-bitten Anthony Mann Western, the anticipated gold strike didn't materialize and young Frank Butters never got the ranchland. Whether he was swindled or just lost out on a dodge is unknown. Butters might have returned home empty-handed, but he proved to be a much more upbeat and resilient character than some of the cinematic hard-luck cases portrayed in Westerns nearly half a century later.

After he wooed and married Beatrice Crisp, a young immigrant from England, the Butters resided in Des Moines, Iowa, where their only child, Charles, was born on May 10, 1914. Butters parlayed his tradesman skills into a job with B.F. Goodrich Inc. In 1919, Goodrich transferred him to Akron, Ohio. The couple lived at several addresses before buying a house on 326 Cleveland Street, adjacent to downtown Akron, in the early 1920s. The elder Butters had chosen wisely. Due to the burgeoning rubber industry, Akron was the fastest growing city in the United States. During the decade of 1910 to 1920, the city's population exploded from 69,000 to 210,000.

Charles Butters enjoyed a boyhood that was reportedly active and typical. He was a registered Boy Scout for the year ending February 1927. He later worked as an usher at the Strand Theatre in downtown Akron while in high school. His friends and schoolmates called him "Chick." The young son was the apple of his father's eye, and the boy revered the elder Butters, who would eventually leave Goodrich and have long-term professional success as a skilled independent bricklayer and contractor. Charles was a dutiful son but, as he grew older, he became wary around his mother. According to McGraw's daughter, Beatrice Crisp was a relentless Methodist who affected laced-up whale-bone corsets while being fixated on eternal damnation as the inevitable outcome of Charlie's typical juvenile escapades.

Charles Butters attended Mason Elementary and then Akron Central High School, a mile and a half walk from the family home. As a student, young Charles was indifferently average; good

at physical education and civics, average at economics, history and English, less so in geometry. By the time he graduated in January 1932 (the Akron school system had two graduating classes per year in those days), over one-quarter of the country's workforce was unemployed, manufacturing output was less than half of 1929 levels and over a third of the country's 25,000 banks had shuttered their doors. A social safety net of government assistance was essentially non-existent. One worked at any job that could be found and relied on family and close friends. The Horatio Alger cliché that sustained the senior Butters and his nineteenth century generation was severely buffeted during the Great Depression but endured nevertheless. A man prospered based on a combination of work ethic, initiative and talent. Luck was usually the residue of design. The alternatives were to exist on the bum or starve. American culture hadn't successfully marketed our contemporary (twenty-first century) notion that poverty or lack of self-esteem are approved excuses for criminality and failure.

Charles Butters as a young boy (courtesy Mildred Black).

The economic calamity of the Depression stimulated a restless migration of young men across the country. The America of the 1930s possessed the underpinnings of infrastructure that supported the mass movement of people in cars, busses and the dominant railroads. Thousands of young men left home and took to the road looking for work and freedom. Charlie Butters was no exception. As an only child, he was better off than most, but the teenager was ready for bold undertakings. After being regaled by his father's adventures as a young man out West, Charlie yearned to explore what actor Sydney Greenstreet described in the film *The Maltese Falcon* as "the whole, wide, sweet world" that lay outside of Northern Ohio.

Charlie, his friend, Charles Ferguson and Ferguson's older brother Donald opted for adventure with pay: The three young men signed on for service on the New York–India run for the Roosevelt Line. The trio took a bus to New York City and signed aboard the freighter *Tampa*, presently docked in Brooklyn. The *Tampa* would be sailing to Ceylon to pick up bulk rubber cargo for delivery back to the Goodyear factory in Akron. There was probably an "Akron connection" that arranged the passage, quite possibly engineered by the elder Butters, that enabled the adventurous trio to make this journey The six-month deployment included port calls at Gibraltar, Cairo, Bombay, Calcutta and Rangoon.

"We got a big thrill at looking for the first time at the New York skyline,"[2] Charles scribbled in his diary when he arrived in New York to register and check aboard his ship in Brooklyn. He wrote further about initially exploring the pleasures of New York:

> ... went to Times Square, Bwdy and the Bowery. Went to a 15 cent show in the bowery and then took a Brooklyn subway back to the ship. Met two dames sitting on the running board of an Ohio Ford,

326 Cleveland Street, Akron, Ohio. Charles McGraw's boyhood home (built in 1917), where he lived until hitchhiking to New York City in 1935. The house remains occupied — note the satellite television dish (courtesy John V. Miller, University of Akron Archival Services).

talked to them until their boyfriends came. Signed coastwise articles at noon. Put "Shorty the Greek" in bed after he passed out on some extra shots of bad moonshine.[3]

The following night, the trio went to see Bing Crosby sing on Broadway. Charles was absolutely knocked out by Times Square and the Great White Way; the Akronian had never seen anything like it. The New York idyll for the three boys was brief. The *Tampa* got underway for Port Said, Egypt, on March 5, 1932. After a couple of days of terse "seasick" entries, Charles' diary abruptly ended as he settled into the routine of shipboard life. The extended foreign sojourn was a seminal life event for young Butters. After taking in the diverse pleasures and sobering realities of the outside world on his own terms, he matured rapidly from a home-grown kid to a confident young man. McGraw would embellish his merchant seaman adventure to press agents and reporters later on in Hollywood. His trip became expanded to multiple journeys and tours of duty in the Merchant Marine. One version even had the young American being marooned in India until rescued and sent home by the American Consulate.

Despite the subsequent embroidery, Charlie's seaward adventures remained an influence in his professional life when he composed and mailed this registered letter to his Studio City residence over two decades later in 1953:

To whom it may concern

I hereby state that I have conceived and now preparing a treatment on a projected T.V. series to be entitled *Tramp Freighter* or *Ticket to Anywhere*. This to be the chronicles in which the Captain of said vessel, becomes involved in the more wicked, but glamorous ports throughout the world."[4]

Unfortunately, there is no record of a treatment or script exploring the actor's interesting concept. One can easily visualize McGraw starring in an episodic television show as a rough-

University of Akron Campus in 1934, two years after McGraw attended for one semester (courtesy John V. Miller, University of Akron Archival Services).

hewn skipper, rigged out in weathered nautical garb, conning his cargo freighter into varied foreign intrigue.

The *Akron Beacon Journal* hailed Charles Butters and the Ferguson brothers' July 1932 homecoming to Ohio as the "return of the prodigals"[5] to the bosom of future Midwestern prosperity. Although the news article stated that Charlie would attend the University of Akron, his college career lasted exactly one semester and four courses. The courses were generic and his grades reflected scholastic indifference: Speech: C; Problems with Citizenship: D; Spanish: D; Rhetoric: D; ROTC: B; and Physical Training: "excused for this year."[6] Charlie bounced around at different jobs (including tire curer at Goodrich) before settling for work as a messenger at the Dime Savings Bank at the Flatiron Building in downtown Akron where his uncle, Raymond Brownsword, was the head teller. The younger Butters became increasingly restless, certainly more so than when he initially left home on his shipboard adventure.

World traveler Charlie's dissatisfied return to his hometown was reminiscent of a cogent slice of counsel that actor Sam Jaffe provided to star Sterling Hayden after pulling their jewelry heist in *The Asphalt Jungle* (1950). Hayden emphatically expresses his desire to return to the family farm in Kentucky with his share of the robbery swag, declining Jaffe's invitation to accompany him to Mexico City to chase "beautiful young girls." The sage master criminal Doc Riedenschneider (Jaffe) tries to advise his younger accomplice:

> Listen Dix, You can always go home and when you do, it's nothing. Believe me, I've done it. Nothing.[7]

Akron Central High School graduating class photograph of January 1932. Charlie is the back row, seventh from the left, the last one in the first doorway. The back of the photograph is signed by various friends and faculty including a teacher's entry to "her worst student" (photograph courtesy Mildred Black).

Charles Butters had seen the world and, while he was not afraid of tough work, hitting the books in school, inhaling noxious fumes inside a hot tire factory or twiddling his thumbs in a bank teller's cage simply wasn't going to cut it for him. Akron was home, but eventually was nothing with a future tied to it. After two and a half years of spinning his wheels, it was time to move on.

It isn't clear where he acquired his initial drive to become an actor. Certainly he became entranced with motion pictures, particularly those of hoofer Dick Powell, during high school days while working as an usher at the Strand Theatre. McGraw stated over two decades afterwards that he acquired the acting bug in 1935, but wasn't sure why:

I don't know what gave me the urge to become an actor ... I can remember having the ambition to be a dancer when I saw vaudeville performers at Keith's Palace. But I just don't know what inspired me to be an actor.[8]

What was evident was that young Charles Butters remained enchanted by his brief exposure to the excitement of New York. He was ready to return to the big city and explore things more thoroughly. At length, he shook his father's hand, kissed his fretting mother goodbye and hitchhiked from Ohio to the Great White Way in the spring of 1935.

2

Young Thespian

At the time of McGraw's arrival in New York City, the Depression had reached its somber apogee. People were still selling apples on street corners. Soup kitchens, breadlines and beggars skulking around Times Square were facts of life. Disease and hunger culled the streets of the most unfortunate, especially during the winter months. Robert Mitchum, who survived on the bum to arrive in L.A.'s Union Station on a freight car in 1933, recalled the body count of the brutal New York winter during the Depression: "You'd find 'em [bodies] under the subway steps … huddled up and gone."[9]

Although young Charles lived an austere existence in New York, he was insulated from the worst of the times. He left Ohio with a grubstake and his parents periodically sent money to their only son. McGraw was young and fit. Even during the Depression, there was usually some type of work that could be drummed up by a young comer. He waited tables, shoveled snow, tended bar and did any type of labor in order to eke out a living.

An iterative press story from these early New York days was that McGraw turned to boxing in order to make ends meet. According to one press release issued by Universal in conjunction with the actor's appearance in *Joe Butterfly* (1957), the young Butters "fought 19 amateur and 20 professional bouts in the middleweight class."[10] While there are some early, faded photos of McGraw in boxing garb and anything is possible (New York State amateur boxing records list a 'Charley Butters' with a 1940 record of 0–1–0), the colorful pugilistic background was a prime example of one of the many tall tales that McGraw enjoyed dispensing years later in Hollywood. Although the actor's penchant for brawling inside the ring might have been exaggerated, he wasn't totally averse to fisticuffs. The youngster's Midwestern ambivalence was quickly cured into a hidebound demeanor by the rough-and-tumble sidewalks of New York.

Veteran Hollywood actor-director Joseph Pevney remembers the twenty-three-year-old Charles McGraw as belligerent. The two men met as aspiring actors in a New England theatrical company in 1937. The future film director observed the youthful thespian getting into a fistfight with an established actor in the stock company. Nearly seventy years later, Pevney wryly recalled; "Charlie got his clock cleaned."[11]

The consequences of McGraw's pugilistic dustups were usually superfluous when it came to actual physical damage. Although the actor was more of an arguer than a fighter, backing down was viewed as a sign of weakness. What amounted to fighting for most people was often Charlie's way of testing strangers and getting acquainted. McGraw would typically end up buying a drink for the person that he previously traded swings with. According to Millie Black, Charlie became acquainted with her sister's husband after they squared off in the alley behind Keith's Bar next to Republic Studios. The men subsequently became fast friends. Bobby Hoy, a stuntman and character actor who would become a close McGraw pal in Hollywood, averred that Charlie was no great shakes as a barroom brawler. Hoy recalled that after one barroom altercation turned physical and a rare victory occurred, McGraw phoned one of his key cronies, stuntman Johnny Daheim, from O'Brien's Bar in Studio City at closing time to brag about his conquest. "Hey Johnny," rasped the actor triumphantly. "Bet on me, I'm on a winning streak!"[12]

Charlie primarily spent his time in New York City hanging around the theatre district, both stage doors and agencies, trying to force a break. Around this time, he discarded the burlesque-sounding surname Butters and borrowed the name Crisp from his mother.

The aspiring thespian hung out with other struggling actors and eventually caught on in a play titled *The Jazz Age* that opened in Ivoryton, Connecticut in the summer of 1937. The play bowed on Broadway in the fall of that year. The story that was trotted out later for a studio biography was that he went to a rehearsal with a roommate who was an actor and ended up getting chosen to read for the part rather than his friend — not a totally unlikely occurrence.

By whatever circumstances, McGraw won the role, played a boxer and garnered positive notices. *Variety* commented, "The realistic fight scene in *Jazz Age*, by the way, sent Charles Crisp to the doctor's twice … once for eight stitches in his scalp."[13] After his stitches in time, Charlie moved on to other stock productions, including *Boy Meets Girl and Dead End.*

Charlie's big break came later the same year when the young actor caught the eye of legendary Group Theatre director Harold Clurman. A note from stage director Michael Gordon was sent to young Crisp requesting that he appear at the 11:00 a.m. rehearsal of the Group Theatre's production of *Golden Boy* on Friday, October 22, 1937 at the Belasco Theatre on 44th Street. Charlie was tapped for the part of Drake and quickly became an integral part of one of America's most talented and revolutionary theatrical companies.

Golden Boy was written by Clifford Odets, the self-styled, charismatic spokesman of the proletariat. Odets' playwriting success during the 1930s can only be described as spectacular. At one point, the playwright had five productions playing in different Broadway theatres simultaneously. No one in American cultural life during the Depression possessed a more unerring sense of the mood of the times (and how to tap into it) than Odets. His latest play would mirror his own conflicted status as a playwright and screenwriter.

Joe Bonaparte, the protagonist in *Golden Boy,* is torn between the big money offered by pro boxing and pursuing his career as a violinist. The character's dilemma was analogous to Odets' back-and-forth career between lush paydays as a Hollywood screenwriter and a crusader for social justice along the Great White Way. Although the playwright's early fame and fortune would fade out like a giant, dying star, his success during the 1930s was unprecedented for a playwright and *Golden Boy* was another hit.

The cast of *Golden Boy* was headed by Luther Adler and Frances Farmer and also included John Garfield, Lee J. Cobb, Art Smith, Roman Bohnen, Morris Carnovsky, his wife Phoebe Brand, Elia Kazan, Martin Ritt, Howard Da Silva and Karl Malden. All of these performers ended up in Hollywood within the next five years with varying degrees of success. Odets had written *Golden Boy* specifically for John Garfield as Bonaparte, but Group Theatre politics intervened and Luther Adler got the lead role (a gross injustice). Fed up, Garfield left the Group for Hollywood and became a major movie star at Warner Brothers almost immediately. Elia Kazan's legendary renown as a film director began later, during the postwar period.

Many of the actors in the cast became close friends during the decade of the Group's existence (1931–1941). The company was largely composed of social progressives who tilted leftward. Some of them simply jumped on the prevailing political bandwagon because of the passion of their friends and, in Garfield's case, their spouses. More than a few became Communist party members during the depths of disillusionment during the Depression.

Many constituents of this talented ensemble had their relationships with one another either strengthened or destroyed due to the harrowing choices forced upon them by the Blacklist period that began in the late 1940s. Clifford Odets, Lee J. Cobb, and Elia Kazan informed on their comrades to the House of Un-American Activities Committee. According to actor Jeff Corey, who was blacklisted, Cobb reputedly paid $25,000 to have his testimony kept secret, but "they double-crossed him."[14] From the opening night ensemble, Morris Carnovsky, Brand, Martin Ritt, Art Smith and Howard Da Silva were all blacklisted. Two of the original *Golden Boy* cast members died during the Blacklist period: Roman Bohnen dropped dead of a heart attack while performing at the Actor's Lab in 1949 with a similar malady felling John Garfield three years later.

Although an ardent New Dealer, McGraw stayed clear from overt political activism. He was an arguer, not a joiner. More pointedly, Charlie was leery about putting his name on things and never became a petition signer (a habit that would later cause so much trouble for many of his Group Theatre fellows). Another aspect of his personality that inadvertently helped him steer clear of the Blacklist was his propensity for holding something back in many of his personal relationships. Charlie would have innumerable pals, drinking buddies, and working friends, but few if any intimates. For a relentlessly social man, McGraw was often viewed as a loner, both in his early theatrical days and later on in Hollywood. Despite his lack of interest in politics and inward nature, McGraw also proved to be lucky. Even though the actor would appear to be immune from the taint of the Blacklist, it turned out that only by the merest of hairsbreadths did Charlie miss being tarred. The sword of official Damocles would be poised over McGraw by the FBI only seven years after *Golden Boy* with his confidential files remaining hidden from public view for nearly six decades.

The Group Theatre was closer to its end than the beginning by the time *Golden Boy* opened. Charlie was nonetheless immersed in a cauldron of acting innovation, talent and expertise that permanently influenced his work. McGraw paid his professional dues, working diligently with some of the brightest acting teachers associated with the Group Theatre, notably Roman Bohnen and Art Smith, who went on to be the guiding lights of the Actor's Lab in Hollywood during the 1940s. While the young actor was a quick study on script (he could memorize pages of dialogue rapidly), he also learned how to assume the personality and motivations of the character he was playing as part of mastering the craft of a professional actor.

Nearly four decades later, veteran director William Witney recalled McGraw's mastery of the acting craft during a guest shot on an episode of *The Virginian* that Witney helmed in 1963:

> All those old actors that trod the boards.... There was no bullshit with 'em ... I remember Charlie McGraw being up for a part in a *Virginian*, a character named "Big Jim." Charlie wasn't that big, he was 5'10", 5'11". So the producer said, "Jeez, I don't know. The name of the character is Big Jim." And Charlie said, "*You* write some 'Big Jim' dialogue for me and I'll become 'Big Jim!'" Well, [McGraw] got the part and he did a hell of a job in the picture, I'll tell you that![15]

McGraw reputedly worked as a hoofer in dime-a-dance joints back in Akron and during his initial threadbare days in New York City. Whether aided by his reputed boxing talent or his skill as a dancer, Charlie's movements and timing on stage were smoothly impeccable. He never had to look down to hit his marks and his delivery of dialogue became polished. One of the greatest tributes to an actor was that he didn't appear to be acting. McGraw was relentlessly authentic on stage.

Off stage, Charlie became friendly with a fellow performer in the company, Harry Bratsberg. Bratsberg, who hailed from Detroit, Michigan, would later change his professional surname to Morgan while enjoying a career in films and television (modern audiences immediately recall Harry Morgan as Colonel Potter on TV's *M*A*S*H*) that prospered for over six decades. A closer pal was actor Bert Conway, who had a small role in the play. Conway, the son of vaude-

Aboard the *Woodrow Wilson* in 1938, bound for England with the cast of *Golden Boy*: 1. Elia Kazan, 2. Harold Bloomgarden, 3. Harry Bratsburg (Morgan), X. McGraw. (Courtesy Mildred Black)

villians, was also the assistant stage manager. He stayed friends with Charlie much later out in Hollywood.

Charlie's personal habits became reminiscent of a Damon Runyon character of the Roaring Twenties. Never an indiscriminate skirt chaser, he was a gentleman around the ladies and extended himself to help a fellow thespian or pal. McGraw gravitated to the milieu of the neighborhood saloon. This predilection was a relaxing routine that hadn't yet morphed into a destructively permanent habit. If McGraw was something of a natural as an actor, he was even more at home in the convivial, usually masculine atmosphere of the taproom. He actually honed his craft by holding court at the bar, telling jokes, stories and putting on performances. The bar was a comfort zone of ambience that McGraw always sought out. One of the actor's photos from a 1959 vacation in England included a snapshot of the King Charles Pub where the visiting monarch from Studio City no doubt paid a visit. McGraw's wife once remarked that if Charlie was in a plane crash in the Sahara Desert, he would simply brush himself off and stroll into the nearest bar to have a beer, get acquainted with the locals and then ask directions.

Golden Boy garnered favorable notices and Charlie, who had a small but important part, was singled out for praise ("Charles Crisp ... contributes a beautiful bit"[16]). After a seven-month run on Broadway, Charlie traveled with the company on the ocean liner *President Harding* in 1938 over to London, England for a run at the West End's St James Theatre. Charlie enjoyed the trip. He played volleyball with Harry Bratsberg, Elia Kazan and others while at sea. Once in England, Charlie contrived to stay much longer than the scheduled three-month run of the play.

The youthful American loved England. The acting tradition handed down from the original Bard appealed to his sense of history and the straightforwardness of the working class struck him as appropriately down-to-earth and friendly. The 25-year-old actor habitually took his lunch and dinner along with pints of stout in a back-box pub named The Golden Lion, adjacent to the St. James Theatre on Kings Street where *Golden Boy* was playing. Tilting pints with

a local tobacconist named "Burbey" Burstein, Charlie sought to partner with the Englishman to obtain the British rights to take *Golden Boy* on the road around the provinces. While Burstein sent telegrams to New York to obtain the rights from the Group Theatre, Crisp recruited a company of English actors and started rehearsals. The entire scheme fell apart when negotiations for the rights became "insurmountable."[17] Charlie was significantly disappointed not just for the failed opportunity but because he had fallen deeply in love and wanted desperately to remain in England.

Freda Choy Kitt, daughter of Julia McCarthy and Frank Choy-Kitt, had her occupation listed in most of McGraw's studio biographies as a "Parisian hat designer."[18] One intimate sniffed that McGraw met his wife while she was working in a West End Chinese restau-

Inscribed: "To my Mother and Father, Charles." Rear of photo annotated: "Railroads on Parade, 1940 Worlds Fair in New York City."

rant. That occupational venue would be highly unlikely. Freda was cultured, graceful and delicate. No matter what her background or where the initial meeting place was, McGraw was captivated with the striking Eurasian woman.

"My mother looked exactly like Ava Gardner," averred Jill Julia McGraw, the couple's only child. Perhaps not quite Ava, but Freda was a beautiful woman. She spent time in a convent as a young girl and McGraw was her first serious boyfriend. She was smitten with the young actor whom she always would refer to as "Charles" in a soft but precise English accent. The youthful McGraw, a strikingly good-looking man with piercing blue eyes, cut a graceful figure both on stage and in person. The couple married on October 12, 1938, and traveled to the U.S. together when the war broke out in 1939.

Back in New York City, the newlyweds struggled to make ends meet. There were a few plays such as *Night of January 16th*, a 1939 murder mystery written by a young Ayn Rand that played at the Shubert Theatre in Brooklyn. Although there were universally favorable notices such as one that praised Crisp's performance as "excellent,"[19] the short-term theatrical runs were only a means to an end.

The New York World's Fair of 1939–1940 provided an interim employment opportunity for the nascent actor. A chronological musical play about the history of American railroads was the centerpiece of this hopeful exposition located in the rural environs of Flushing Meadows, Queens, more than two decades before the arrival of New York Mets. *Railroads on Parade* combined a 17-acre static display with a Kurt Weill–composed paean to railroading that the fair program trumpeted:

Dramatic musical extravaganza with cast of 250!
Fifteen thrilling scenes of Drama, Music and Comedy with 50 horses and 20 locomotives on the world's largest stage![20]

Betty Garrett appeared with McGraw in *Railroads on Parade* during the entire run and recalled the experience 66 years later:

Charlie and I worked together for two years on *Railroads on Parade.* The stage for the show was a block long and was by a railroad yard. In one of the sequences, a canal boat would arrive. Charlie was the captain of the canal boat and he would lift me up and we would all choreograph to the tune "16 Miles on the Erie Canal." Charlie and I had time to talk during the show. I remembered him as a jolly person always.[21]

Appearing in four performances daily, McGraw took home $30 per week. *Railroads on Parade* kept him going till the fair closed down in October 1940. Charlie worked wherever possible, but the parts were inconsistent and, more critically, there were no break-out opportunities from secondary roles as heavies. Due to the frequent theatrical employment gaps, McGraw was becoming better known in some New York circles as a part-time bartender rather than an actor.

There was a greater sense of urgency towards earning a steady living when Freda and Charlie welcomed the birth of their daughter Jill on September 11, 1941. After a turn in Orson Welles' revival of *Native Son* in 1942, where he made friends with boxer-actor Canada Lee, McGraw decided to try his luck in Hollywood.

3

Hungry During the Golden Era

While the war mobilization was beginning to lift the economic veil of the Depression away in most of the country, the film industry in Hollywood had remained a viable economic beacon that attracted artistic talent from all over the world. The studios were on full-time scavenger hunt for talent, hiring (and firing) writers, actors and producer and directorial personnel while developing strategies to cope with some of their marquee talent slipping away due to military service.

By October of 1942, over 10 percent of studio employees were in uniform, and war bond drives were in full swing. In a converted livery stable just off Sunset Boulevard, Bette Davis and John Garfield (with money from MCA's Jules Stein) opened up the Hollywood Canteen that catered to the thousands of servicemen passing through Los Angeles. The studios retooled their assembly lines to crank out war-themed films that balanced out the period escapism of horror, adventure and comedy productions.

A retrospectively depressing casting challenge dating from Pearl Harbor was locating enough Asian actors in Hollywood to play stereotypical Japanese soldiers and assorted heavies in war movies. After President Roosevelt signed Executive Order 9066 in February 1942, some 110,000 Japanese in the United States— a majority of whom were U.S. citizens— were shamelessly shipped off to internment camps. The vast tracts of Southern California property owned by the Nisei were either sold by the interned owners for a fraction of their worth or simply appropriated by the Office of Alien Property (OAP) and later sold to real estate syndicates rife with cronyism. The considerable Japanese community in Los Angeles simply ceased to exist. The actors who ended up portraying formulaic Japanese baddies during World War II were American citizens of Chinese or Korean descent.

There is no evidence that any of the anti–Japanese fervor during the 1940s spilled over or was aimed personally towards the McGraws because of Freda's Chinese ancestry and Asian appearance. While it is seems incredible to contemplate in the racially diverse California of today, the McGraws' 1938 marriage might have been technically illegal in California. The 1931 California state code on miscegenation prohibited marriage between persons of the Caucasian and Asian races; however, the prohibition was without a legal penalty. Three years after the war, state politicians apparently took a moment to remember why World War II was fought and won by America. The nakedly racist California miscegenation statutes were repealed in 1948.

Still working under the stage name of Crisp, Charlie's film debut wasn't reflective of either the ongoing war effort or derivative of his previous stage roles. He had already missed out on the screen version of *Golden Boy* that was produced in 1939. Charlie's screen bow turned out be in a Bryan Foy–produced horror movie, *The Undying Monster* (1942) made by 20th Century–Fox. Fox was where many Group Theatre alums had ended up and there were certainly lesser places in Hollywood to start out from.

Dubbed "The Keeper of the B's" during his career at Warner Brothers, Bryan "Brynie" Foy

ran the secondary film production unit at WB with great
efficiency until his relationship soured with production
chief Jack L. Warner (a fate
that eventually befell nearly
every competent executive
who worked at the Burbank
studio). J.L.'s voluble exterior
of corny jokes and phony
bonhomie was a cloaking
device for an insecure,
immensely delicate ego.
Warner, who had his name
and favorite job description
"In Charge of Production"

Charles McGraw on December 8, 1941 (courtesy Mildred Black).

emblazoned in raised letters under the Warner Brothers trademark crest on every opening film
credit, had a low tolerance for producers who deigned to think of themselves as autonomous
executives instead of subservient employees. He had essentially forced out Darryl F. Zanuck as
production chief back in 1933 and would soon repeat the process with Hal B. Wallis after a bitter estrangement between the two men was capped by their public fight over which of the two
would retain the Best Picture Oscar for *Casablanca* in 1943. As Jack L. occasionally reminded
miscreant employees ranging from movie stars to grips, there was space available on the studio's famous water tower only for the solitary Warner surname.

Foy moved on to 20th Century–Fox where Darryl F. Zanuck allowed him to do what he did
best: efficiently grind out medium- to low-budget productions that generated entertaining second bill fodder for the Fox Theatre chain while providing a farm system for talent on the way up.
Foy's effectiveness with secondary film production enabled Zanuck to focus his dervish energy on
micromanagement of the top-of-the-marquee Fox projects. *The Undying Monster* was a cut above
the routine horror programmer. A period melodrama story about an ancient family curse in Scot-
land, the picture was artfully directed by John Brahm. Brahm, who would go on to have a successful (if unspectacular) career in film and television, added a dark visual cast to the pedestrian
story. Although the picture was quickly forgotten, Charles Crisp made a distinctive debut playing a Scottish groomsman — his accent was surprisingly good — and bigger things were hoped for.

McGraw's first screen appearance would also be the last time that he would be billed as
Charles Crisp. After an erroneous story in *The Hollywood Reporter*, later retracted, that the
young Group Theatre alum was related to veteran character actor Donald Crisp, Charlie decided
on the surname McGraw as his professional sobriquet. According to daughter Jill, her father
was an admirer of the late, legendarily hard-boiled manager of the New York (baseball) Giants,
John J. McGraw. Charlie also disliked the fact that his current last name was already in use by
Donald Crisp, who had recently won the Academy Award for Best Supporting Actor for his work
in *How Green Was My Valley*. McGraw was an Irish-based appellation that suited the actor neatly.
While he didn't always have the traditional luck, the young actor certainly possessed the Gaelic
gift of gab, particularly when imbibing strong drink. Curiously, Charlie took his time in making the adoption of his surname permanent; he didn't legally change his name from Butters to
McGraw until 1955. He wore the mythical shamrock lineage convincingly. Some of his personal
effects included casual references to his appropriated Irish heritage, including a get-well card

from actor and barroom buddy Scott Brady, who appended "The Irish Never Quit!" while wishing McGraw a speedy recovery.

On the strength of his initial performance and aided by his former Group Theatre connections, McGraw was inked for his second feature *Secret Mission*, which was released as *The Moon is Down* in March 1943. A legitimate "A" production, this soulfully cerebral film (based on John Steinbeck's book) about a Norwegian town being slowly crushed while heroically resisting Nazi occupation was written for the screen by Nunnally Johnson and directed by Irving Pichel. A *Hollywood Reporter* snippet mentioned that with McGraw's appearance in this film, every member of the Group Theatre was now employed in Hollywood. McGraw played a cheerful Norwegian militiaman named Ole who uttered a few lines before he and his compatriot, played by Jeff Corey, were machine-gunned to death by the invading Germans several minutes into the film. Charlie was reunited on this picture with both Lee J. Cobb and Robert Lewis, a Group Theatre founding pillar who served as dialogue director. McGraw had similar roles in subsequent Fox war dramas. In *Tonight We Raid Calais* (1943) he appeared again with Cobb and Group Theatre alum Howard Da Silva; then he acted opposite George Sanders in the absurdly jingoistic *They Came to Blow Up America* (1943). Charlie was obtaining work, but they were all freelance bit parts. The young actor wasn't an established screen commodity and as a newcomer, he could not anticipate steady work.

Charlie sought that Holy Grail of Security for Hollywood actors: the seven-year contract. His Group Theatre colleague, Harry Morgan, had landed a contract deal from Fox (with help from friends Frances Farmer and Henry Fonda) but no such offer was forthcoming for Charlie. After a bit appearance in 1943's *Destroyer* (a well received Columbia picture starring a twenty-seven-year-old Glenn Ford who looked all of fifteen), McGraw appeared in a trio of Universal war films, *Two Tickets to London*, *Corvette K-225,* and *The Imposter*. Charlie's acting ability on the stage was proving to be not only transferable to the screen, but became arguably enhanced. The New York actor was beginning to build a résumé of noticeable bit and smaller parts albeit without achieving screen credit.

In order to accurately assess McGraw's nascent screen career at this point, it is germane to recollect how challenging it was for *anyone* in the film industry, particularly a new actor, to rapidly achieve screen credit in the Hollywood of the 1940s. Unless an actor hit it big immediately, already had a prestigious name or possessed some sort of "hook" with an industry big shot (for select neophyte actresses, this was where the infamous casting couch came in), screen credit was a tough hurdle, regardless of talent. Long before the introduction of the ponderous "crawl" of credits at the end of modern films (bestowing name recognition on every possible functionary including food caterers, carpenters and drivers), it could take a veritable eon for a performer to earn regular screen credit.

The career of Dennis O'Keefe, the solid leading man of the '40s and '50s, is a prime example of the persistence often necessary to build a movie acting career and achieve credit. During a 34-year career in pictures beginning in 1930, O'Keefe appeared in over 200 feature films. O'Keefe's first 144 screen appearances were all uncredited roles until he caught on as a supporting player in B Westerns and comedies in the late 1930s.

McGraw's movie roles to date were several financial rungs above the Central Casting calls for extras, stuntmen and stand-ins that paid $10 for a day's work and a box lunch when shooting off the lot (downtown or in the wide-open expanses of the San Fernando Valley). It was the inconsistency of the paydays and concerns about the future that was stressful. Both Freda and Charlie were from an era where wives, especially those with young children, didn't work. McGraw was traditional when it came to his patriarchal responsibility to put bread on the table.

With George Sanders in *They Came to Blow Up America* (1943).

In order to make ends meet between acting gigs, Charlie worked nights as a pin setter at Sunset Lanes and also tended bar.

Shortly after McGraw was billed as Detective Garrity and teamed up with fellow cop Milburn Stone to chase mad scientist George Zucco across Universal's soundstages in *The Mad Ghoul* (1943), the clarion call to arms finally resonated. As a 27-year-old with a wife and a new baby when Japanese bombs rained on Pearl Harbor, McGraw was exempt from the initial bow wave of draftees. By December 1943, the entire country was completely mobilized with the war entering its second full year. It was Charlie's time to step up for Uncle Sam.

4

What Did You Do in the War, Charlie?

Charles McGraw's World War II service became clouded in deceptive bonhomie over the years. Most of the inaccuracies about his military service are directly attributable to his disassembling to studio press agents who parroted his tales in a succession of publicity releases associated with the release of his films.

Several studio biographies cited World War II combat service by McGraw in General Patton's 3rd Army in Europe at the same time he was actually appearing in his initial films in Hollywood. As late as 1966, a press bio for Charlie in support of the actor's appearance in *The BusyBody* (1967) stated, "Early in 1942, McGraw enlisted in the army. He served in the field artillery for 31 months, much of it in the European theatre of war."[22]

McGraw's blarney about his war service extended to intimates. Millie Black distinctly remembers Charlie sitting on the couch in her North Hollywood living room rubbing his knee and mentioning how his discomfort was caused when he was hit by enemy shrapnel during the European campaign with Patton. She laughed: "I think he told so many war stories that he actually came to believe some of them. The closest Charlie ever got to a battlefield was Fort Sill, Oklahoma."[23]

U.S. Army records obtained under the Freedom of Information Act (FOIA) delineate that "Charles Butters, U.S. Army Serial Number 39724969 enlisted in Los Angeles on 21 January 1944."[24] He was discharged on December 7, 1944, as a private at Camp Beale, California, at the height of the war, serving slightly less than eleven months on active duty. One of McGraw's obituaries noted that he served as a radio operator during the war. In a February 4, 1955, *Cincinnati Post* interview, McGraw remarked that the Army made him a rapid repairman during the war because of his stage and rapid work experience. Another record is McGraw's FBI file which includes a reference to a letter that Freda wrote her husband in 1944 while he was stationed at Fort Sill. The available documentation appears to be incomplete. Due to a 1973 fire in the National Military Personnel Records Center in St. Louis that destroyed a major portion of Army personnel records for the period 1912 through 1959, and the limited information that is deemed releasable by the Department of Defense, there is a minimal amount of material available on his military service.

McGraw's daughter stated emphatically that her father was discharged from the Army for "flat feet and asthma."[25] He was stationed at Fort Sill and was discharged at Camp Beale, California. Camp Beale, now Beale Air Force Base, was established in Northern California near Marysville as a training base for the 13th Armored Division and the 81st and 96th Infantry divisions. The station was home for 60,000 military personnel during World War II and included a 1000-bed military hospital. While the precise details of McGraw's military service remain unknown, it is certain that his abbreviated Army service (slightly less than a year of a five-year

McGraw during his 1944 U.S. Army stint with daughter Jill (courtesy, Mildred Black).

hitch and discharge at the height of the war) was caused by a specific reason; the medical issues cited by his daughter are probably accurate. There is no doubt that Charles McGraw never left the country during his eleven months in uniform, never served in combat and was not wounded in the knee or any place else. During the time his press bios stated he was serving in Europe with Patton, Charlie made bit appearances in a slew of war movies including an Army Signal Corps short made at Warner Brothers, *Mechanized Patrolling*, where he was billed as "Corporal McGraw"!

However he might have felt the need later on to embroider his wartime service, Charles McGraw willingly served his country and as far as it can be ascertained, he did so honorably. The actor doubtless would have been shocked to find out what was transpiring in secret while he was in uniform in Oklahoma with Freda and Jill staying with his parents at 326 Cleveland Street in Akron. In 1943, the actor had been named as a Communist to the FBI by someone euphemistically referred to as "a reliable informant." McGraw's FBI file, obtained under the Freedom of Information Act, is a sobering 17-page document that details the low-level but persistent bureaucratic notion that the actor was a member of the Communist Party of America under an assumed name and, as such, was a potential security risk. The released file, declassified in 1991, is heavily redacted with the names of confidential informants and FBI agents removed.

Federal Bureau of Investigation Case File 100–22316 opens with a September 4, 1944, memorandum delineating the revelation of an informant who advised agents that McGraw, under the name of "Vance Adkins," was a member of the Los Angeles Communist Party living at 2218 Crest Way. The FBI investigated and discovered that Charles Crisp Butters *nee* McGraw lived at *2228* Crest Way. A "friend" of Charlie's compliantly handed over a letter to the FBI from Freda to Charlie, mailed from Akron, which noted that McGraw was in the United States Army stationed at Fort Sill, Oklahoma. After checking with the U.S. Army Induction Station and discovering that McGraw didn't use any names other than those professionally indicated, the matter was stamped "closed." Unfortunately for any American citizen of that era who had a specious dime dropped on them that carried a figurative portrait of Lenin, "closed" actually meant "on hold."

On October 28, 1949, the FBI again investigated McGraw in an attempt to link him to the provided pseudonym Vance Adkins. The phantom-like Adkins, whose connection to McGraw is bizarrely reminiscent of Cary Grant being mistaken for "George Kaplan" in *North by Northwest* (1959), was now reported by yet another informant as transferred to "special leave" from the Los Angeles Communist Party as of 1947 with current whereabouts unknown. The FBI thoroughly investigated McGraw even to the point of making a phony telephone call to the actor's residence and eliciting from Freda that Charlie was busy at Universal Studios working on *Double Crossbones*. After checking the files of all local law enforcement departments and verifying that there was no evidence of Communist activities on the part of "Charles Crisp Butters McGraw," the matter was closed yet again ... until the next time.

After his discharge from the Army, McGraw had to start anew professionally. In less than a year, his contacts in the movie industry had dried up as the world had moved on. McGraw had dabbled in radio work before the war. He now put his distinctive voice to use and worked with success on programs including *Gangbusters, Big Sister* and *American Cavalcade.*

McGraw's radio appearances would increase significantly during the coming years. While it is impossible to come up with an all-inclusive list of the actor's radio credits, Charlie's work over the airwaves was distinctively plentiful, particularly before television began to claim what had been a captive listening audience. With his gravelly voice a natural for detective fiction, McGraw would appear in many crime shows: *Murder and Mr. Malone* (1947), *Ellery Queen* (1948), *Jeff Regan, Private Investigator* (1948), *This Is Your F.B.I* (1949), *Richard Diamond, Private Detective* (1949), *The Whistler* (1949), *Dragnet* (1949) and several episodes of *Suspense* into the 1950s. McGraw was initially nervous about speaking into a microphone on a national radio hookup, but quickly adjusted and applied his usual polish. His opening oration as Lieutenant Dana for the program *The Man from Homicide* in September 1950 was particularly distinctive with his "rocks in a wheelbarrow" vocal delivery:

> According to a man from homicide, it's a dirty, dangerous job that doesn't end until the killer is found. But, I like it. Maybe I just don't like killers ...

FEDERAL BUREAU OF INVESTIGATION

Form No. 1.
THIS CASE ORIGINATED AT **LOS ANGELES**   FILE NO. 100-22316

REPORT MADE AT	DATE WHEN MADE	PERIOD FOR WHICH MADE	REPORT MADE BY
LOS ANGELES	9/4/44	7/8,10,11,14, 15; 8/6/44	dml

TITLE
CHARLES CRISP BUTTERS, with aliases,
Charles McGraw, Vance Adkins

CHARACTER OF CASE
SECURITY MATTER - C

SYNOPSIS OF FACTS: Subject on 11/16/43 was a member of Branch F, Northwest
Sect. L.A.C.P. _____ Party name VANCE ADKINS.
He was inducted into U.S. Army, Los Angeles, 1/21/44,
Serial No. 39724969.

ALL INFORMATION CONTAINED
HEREIN IS UNCLASSIFIED
DATE 1-10-91 BY SP6 BJA/EN

b2
b6
b7C
b7D

AGENCY _____
REQ. REC'D _____
REP'T FORW. _____
BY _____

AGENCY _____
REQ. REC'D _____
REP'T FORW. _____
BY _____

DETAILS:
AT LOS ANGELES, CALIFORNIA:

_____ on June 1, 1943 advised Special Agents _____
and _____ that VANCE ADKINS, 2228 Crest Way, was a member of the Los
Angeles County Communist Party, _____ This informant
had previously on May 4, 1943, furnished Agents _____

On August 2, 1943, _____ advised Special Agents _____
that VANCE ADKINS, 2228 Crest Way, had been
transferred to Branch F, Northwest Section, Los Angeles Communist Party.

_____ on November 16, 1943, advised Subject was a member of
Branch F, Northwest Section, Los Angeles County Communist Party, _____ CHARLES McGRAW,
Party name VANCE ADKINS, address 2228 Crest Way.

Inquiry at 2218 Crest Way disclosed that a CHARLES BUTTERS had formerly
lived at 2228 Crest Way and had been employed by one of the Studios. It was
stated that _____ had been a friend of this individual
and would undoubtedly know his whereabouts.

_____ advised CHARLES McGRAW was a friend of his and

APPROVED AND
FORWARDED:

SPECIAL AGENT
IN CHARGE

DO NOT WRITE IN THESE SPACES
332966

SE 20
RECORDED & INDEXED

COPIES OF THIS REPORT
5 - Bureau
1 - G-2, Los Angeles   cc G2
3 - Los Angeles   9-26-44
                    JCM/mck
                    COPY IN FILE

332766

EX-44

COPIES DESTROYED

SEP 26 1944

Initial memo in McGraw's FBI file, accusing him of being a Communist Party member under the pseudonym "Vance Adkins."

Despite the work and the checks that came with them, McGraw viewed radio as a supplemental rather than principal element to his career as an actor.

For the immediate present, Charlie realized that his professional future resided in the movies. He knew he possessed the talent and the ability to be successful and was weary of existing on short money and always searching for the next job. He also wanted to get paid what he was worth. McGraw later explained his philosophy after he got his feet underneath himself in Hollywood:

I don't go around telling people I'm a bartender because I'm not — I'm an actor. Besides, no producer is going to pay the salary I'm asking to get a former bartender. He's going to pay it to get an actor.... You know something? I bet I could go to Denver and get a job. And I bet they'd pay me exactly what I'm worth. I might even be a bartender again. But when I'm in Hollywood, Hollywood is going to pay me what I'm worth to Hollywood.[26]

Freda and Jill remained with McGraw's parents in Akron during his Army hitch in 1944. Frank and Beatrice Butters remained close to their only son and would proudly keep track of his burgeoning acting career by clipping articles out of the paper and saving them in a scrapbook. Jill McGraw's memory of childhood visits to her grandparents is one of unalloyed fondness for her grandfather with a diametrically opposed view of her grandmother. According to Jill, Charlie's mother made an acid remark about her son's choice of a wife, stating that Freda's Eurasian heritage contaminated the family line. The derogatory comment about her mother, whether misunderstood or taken out of context, caused the latest generation of the Butters family to distance herself emotionally from her grandmother.

McGraw returned to Hollywood, leaving Freda and young Jill at his parents in Akron. His plan was to send for them when he got something going. The actor signed up with a new agent, Paul Wilkins. Wilkins had a strong track record of success with character actors and second-tier leading men until they outgrew his stewardship. Wilkins had opened studio doors for Robert Mitchum, who had been languishing in Hopalong Cassidy Westerns, with breakout roles in *Thirty Seconds Over Tokyo* and *The Story of G.I. Joe.* With his virile good looks and unique laconic presence, Mitchum leveraged his opportunities, achieved true stardom and then promptly dumped Wilkins as his agent. Of course, it was nothing personal about Paul Wilkins, just another turn of the Tinseltown carousel.

Eternal movie gangster Marc Lawrence, whose capacity for cynicism remained topped off during an amazing seventy-year acting career in pictures, remarked that the process of moving up in Hollywood was contiguous to other relationships: "Changing agents ... was like changing broads to change your luck. They did that often in Hollywood."[27]

Charlie needed to be discovered all over again, and after inking his contract with Paul Wilkins, the anxious actor didn't have to wait too long.

5

Bright Boy Gets a Break

Mark Hellinger is nearly forgotten today but was a giant in his time. Hellinger was the pre-eminent Broadway columnist for the *New York Daily News* during the Roaring Twenties and a contemporary and close friend of that omnipotent chronicler of the Great White Way, Walter Winchell. Hellinger's fame eventually outstripped Winchell's because he was more talented and immensely likable. Hellinger was a creative, sentimental writer whose prose was reminiscent of O. Henry's and whose short stories and columns were much more than the staccato gossip that exemplified Winchell's work. As Broadway dimmed during the Depression, Hellinger wrote a couple of screenplays for pictures based on his intimacy with New York including *Night Court* (1932) and *Broadway Bill* (1934). They didn't catch on so he returned to New York. Hollywood wasn't ready for him. Hellinger wanted to make films that reflected the authenticity of life that placed the depravity alongside the glamour:

"Pictures should be a lot more realistic," he declared. "I don't claim to be a genius.... But I think I know the real from the unreal."[28]

A deal with Warner Brothers was struck and Hellinger returned to Hollywood as a writer. It wasn't easy. He continued his syndicated column as a weekly feature while the movers and shakers in the picture business treated him like an upstart. After falling on his face with an initial Bette Davis screenplay, Hellinger was assigned to the Warners "B" unit under Bryan Foy, who taught him that words are complementary to a visual medium. The nascent screenwriter listened and learned. Hellinger's treatise to his era, *The Roaring Twenties* (1939), starring James Cagney as a blue-collar rumrunner who rises to become a New York gangster before memorably dying on the steps of a church, anointed him as a star screenwriter. More pictures followed that bore his indelible stamp of romantic realism as he moved into production: *They Drive by Night* (1940), *High Sierra* (1941), and *Manpower* (1941). Hellinger found his niche as a producer; more than a writer, he was an idea machine, a mover and shaker who possessed the vision and the ability to influence others who made it happen on screen.

Although successful, Hellinger became increasingly unhappy at Warners under both an authoritarian (and possibly jealous) Hal Wallis and that apprehensive skinflint Jack L. Warner, who checked with the studio gate guard each morning to find out when his producers showed up for work. Mark Hellinger was a larger-than-life force field with the vanity and ego to go with it. To be happy, he required free rein, unstinting praise and unrequited love. Anything less made him miserable. He moved on to Fox and then World War II intervened. Movies were suddenly irrelevant; Hellinger had to get in on the fight. Despite all of his influence, he was repeatedly rejected for service due to his heart condition. One doctor advised Hellinger that he was not in good enough physical shape even to receive the medical vaccinations in order to go overseas! Knowing his life was now on the clock, he finally wrangled a four-month assignment as a war correspondent writing human interest stories about the troops.

In 1946, Hellinger had become an independent producer at the newly merged Universal-

International led by Louis B. Mayer's son-in-law, Bill Goetz. As an independent within the studio system, Hellinger basically hocked himself to the hilt to Bank of America and U-I and hoped like hell he would make a hit movie. The producer was shepherding a cinematic version of Hemingway's short story "The Killers" into fruition as the initial film of a three-picture deal. The flamboyant New Yorker was looking for an emblematic duo of hired killers to open his film. Hellinger's selection of Charlie to play Al, one of the two torpedoes of the title role, gave rise to a McGraw-inspired anecdote that was one of the more colorful in the actor's considerable repertoire.

The press bio story about *The Killers* begins in May 1946. McGraw walked into a neighborhood bar in New York City and a bartender told him that Broadway columnist Leonard Lyons noted in his column "The Lyons Den" that somebody was looking for him. The actor read the column and found out that Hellinger was seeking the actor who played the heavy in *Golden Boy* on Broadway nine years earlier for a central part in his upcoming film version of Hemingway's "The Killers." According to McGraw, he only had $1.65 in his pockets and phoned Hellinger collect from the bar telephone; the producer wired him $500 to come to Hollywood to appear in the picture. This story, with slight revisions, appeared in a succession of screen biographies and news releases concluded with Charlie summarizing: "My wife had gone through the months of uncertainty and insecurity without a complaint.... But when I came home and showed her the $500, I think her first thought was that I'd robbed a bank."[29]

Like other McGraw-inspired press accounts, this fable made for good copy, but the tail was probably wagging the dog. A review of long-time Broadway scribe Leonard Lyons' columns for May and June of 1946 failed to turn up a mention of Hellinger's search for McGraw. Related versions of the story had McGraw tending bar and being "discovered" by Mark Hellinger after pouring him a drink.

A more plausible account appeared in the *Akron Daily Journal*. In this version, Charlie, perhaps mindful that his parents and hometown friends would read the article, stated that Paul Wilkins set him up with an appointment with Hellinger and when McGraw entered the room, the producer greeted him with, "Hello Al."

"I told him my name was not Al," Charlie laughed as he recounted the "big moment." "But he told me that as far as he was concerned, I was Al."[30]

It is entirely possible that Hellinger remembered McGraw from *Golden Boy* and did indeed track him down and send for him. One interesting fact stands out. McGraw's freelance contract with Mark Hellinger and his new representation contract with agent Paul Wilkins were both signed on the same date: June 18, 1946. By whatever set of circumstances, it was a fortuitous stroke of casting that boosted McGraw's lapsed movie career.

The Killers drew rave reviews and catapulted Burt Lancaster and Ava Gardner to stardom. Landing the two lead actors was a near thing. Gardner was sent to Hellinger on loan-out from Metro because the nascent producer's first choice, Audrey Totter, decided to work with Robert Montgomery in *Lady in the Lake*. Hellinger also nearly lost Burt Lancaster before he got started. After Hellinger's wife, Gladys Glad, told her husband that Lancaster had definite sex appeal, the always busy producer made an initial appointment to meet with the then-unknown former acrobat at his U-I offices. Hellinger kept the neophyte thespian waiting for nearly an hour and emerged from his inner sanctum to call back a disgusted Lancaster, who was stalking out, ready to return to New York City. The producer calmed the volatile East Harlem product and closed the deal. There is nothing better than good luck to ensure a smash-hit movie. *The Killers* was nominated for four Academy Awards and it was an even bigger winner financially. Simply tabbing the picture as a financial success doesn't do it justice. Hellinger borrowed $875,000 to produce the film. Eleven months after release, *The Killers* had grossed an incredible $2,796,084.02.[31] Hellinger had hit the proverbial grand slam homer. Miklos Rozsa's memorable musical score with the ominous "dum, da, dum-dum" theme (later appropriated for the *Dragnet* television series) became so ingrained in the public consciousness that the tune morphed in a permanent cultural cliché. *The Killers* endures as a seminal motion picture, the *Citizen Kane* of film noir.

Ernest Hemingway's ten pages of short story comprised the initial 13 minutes of the film. This introduction depicts the murder of a broken-down prizefighter, "The Swede" (Lancaster), who acquiesces to his dispatch by two professional killers in an inexplicable display of suicidal fatalism. The balance of the picture is a superbly crafted suspense story written by Anthony Veiller along with a duo of uncredited heavy-hitters in John Huston and Richard Brooks. Although Huston's degree of participation with the script was muted at the time, he played an important role with Veiller in developing the unique story structure that employed a series of interlocking flashbacks. After spending a week working on the script with Huston at the Weylin Hotel in New York City, Veiller wrote a note to Hellinger:

> Mark, I cannot impress upon you too strongly how enthused both John and I are about the theory we have evolved for telling the story. We're sure you will see the tremendous possibilities for something really off the beaten track that it affords.[32]

The always impatient Hellinger was on tenterhooks and cabled Huston back directly about the script:

> … waiting so anxiously. Please phone if there's anything I can do.[33]

The completed script, finalized on April 3, 1946, was worth waiting for. *The Killers* incorporated a number of fundamental film noir plot attributes: a major crime goes awry amidst a thicket of double-crosses accompanied by a backdrop story of unrequited love and obsession. The intertwined story elements are seamlessly woven through the use of character voice-over narratives within the unique series of flashbacks designed by Veiller and Huston. Film noir's favorite "everyman," Edmond O'Brien, is the dogged insurance investigator who unravels the circumstances of the failed robbery, the denouement of the participants and the ultimate double-cross that necessitated the killing of Lancaster. In addition to the skillfully leavened storyline, the depth of characterization that elevates *The Killers* to a film of ethereal quality is the compelling depiction of the fatalistic descent by Lancaster's character from a cocksure tough guy to an emotional husk who welcomes his violent death. For "The Swede," final acceptance of his fate is the only way he can fold the bad hand that life has dealt him.

The director of *The Killers* had a brilliant, if truncated career in Hollywood. Robert Siodmak remains one of the most overlooked distinctive visual stylists of film noir productions. Born in Lower Saxony, Siodmak was a leading practitioner of German Expressionism at UFA during the 1930s. He immigrated to France and then America, keeping one step ahead of the Nazis. After initially landing at Paramount, he joined his screenwriter brother Curt at Universal in 1943.

After experiencing rapid success with *Christmas Holiday, Phantom Lady* and *The Suspect*— all released in 1944 — Siodmak broke through as a top-flight Hollywood director in 1946 with *The Spiral Staircase* and *The Killers*. Siodmak was nominated for Best Director by the Motion Picture Academy for his work on *The Killers* but lost out to William Wyler, who won for his epochal postwar drama, *The Best Years of Our Lives*. Mark Hellinger, who thought highly of Siodmak and wrote that the director "had been breathing so heavily on Hitchcock's collar, that Alfred was beginning to perspire,"[34] ignored the Oscar results and delightedly bought Siodmak a new car.

After helming several more distinctive noir features including *Cry of the City* (1948), *Criss Cross* (1949) and *The File on Thelma Jordon* (1950), Robert Siodmak left Hollywood in 1952. The director had been roundly abused by the mercurially ferocious Burt Lancaster and his production team during Italian location filming of *The Crimson Pirate* (1952). Lancaster's tempermental nature had grown concurrently with his bank account since almost walking out on his breakthrough role in *The Killers*. His rise as a major star, along with the changes in the film industry, had mutated the actor into the forerunner of what would be an enduring subspecies of the genus *Hollywood*: the egomaniacal actor-producer. Lancaster held sway on his film sets like a reticulated python on a feeding binge, crushing and swallowing non-compliant directors, studio executives and anyone else that got in his way. Siodmak's career as a director of major American films ended as he refused to endure having a former acrobat and his sycophant producer, Harold Hecht, bully him into directing a movie their way. Of Lancaster, whom he formerly enjoyed a collegial working relationship with, Siodmak sadly wrote:

> Burt Lancaster has gone through such a change [*since The Killers*] that I cannot consider him normal anymore. His complete inconsideration of others, his tantrums, his language — so filthy that the English crew wrote him a letter one day.... I think he suffers from megalomania and must be mentally sick....[35]

The director retreated to work in Europe, returning to Hollywood to make a couple of inconsequential films including *Custer of the West* (1967) before dying in 1973. Robert Siodmak's legacy of superb films during the 1940s permanently enshrined him as one of the most consequential film noir directors.

In *The Killers*, Charles McGraw was perfectly complemented by William Conrad as his fellow hitman-in-arms. The two men stepping out of the shadows of the gas station and walking purposefully towards the dimly lit diner is one of the most memorable scenes of cinematic trepidation ever filmed. Charlie's face in profile appeared even longer and more merciless than usual. The low-key lighting used by ace cameraman Woody Bredell to accentuate Siodmak's compositions is extraordinary. The subsequent diner sequence ratchets up the tension as McGraw and Conrad laconically go about their business (to dispatch Lancaster) with perverse sadism that is chilling.

"Better go around, Bright Boy," McGraw growls with deadly intent at a gulping Phil Brown who is the sole, unlucky customer inside the diner taken hostage with the counterman and cook. Charlie is so intimidating that he really doesn't need the revolver that he flashes to herd his captives into the kitchen. After finally tracking down and executing Lancaster in his room, the two assassins make their getaway only to reappear at the end of the film.

McGraw ends up gut-shot during a barroom ambush staged by O'Brien and perpetual movie cop Sam Levene. Even though his appearance in the film was brief, Charlie's performance left an indelible impression of dread that resonated with audiences.

The Killers received a huge photo spread in *Life* magazine when released in August 1946 with Charlie and Bill Conrad's pictorial menace splashed on the center pages. Both actors were also singled out for critical praise:

> Even more to the point was the choice of Charles McGraw and William Conrad as the killers of the title. With time and typecasting, you may be able to view this pair of sinister citizens with the assurance of a customer who paid for his seat and expects to be intimidated in air conditioned comfort. As of the moment, however, the chances are that they will make you feel extremely nervous.[36]

Although Charles McGraw signed a one-picture deal for *The Killers* at $750 per week with a one-week guarantee, he was suddenly viewed in Hollywood as a new acting commodity. Many subsequent press reports would list *The Killers* as his film debut. Charlie was forever grateful

"Use your head, Bright Boy...." A scene from the epochal *Citizen Kane* of film noir, *The Killers* (1946). Charles McGraw with fellow heavy William Conrad and a cowed Harry Hayden.

to Mark Hellinger and, not surprisingly, was personally fond of the dynamic producer whom he admired tremendously.

After Hellinger's untimely death, it was observed how *The Killers* served as the career launching pad for a number of actors: Lancaster, Gardner, Jeff Corey, and McGraw. McGraw responded somberly, "It's an awful thing to consider the picture a charm in view of what happened to one of the nicest men who ever lived. Nevertheless, Hellinger must have passed along all the good luck to the four of us and accepted all the bad luck for himself."[37]

6

The Watershed Year

With *The Killers* under his belt and Paul Wilkins continuing to push his name around the studios, Charlie's career began to gain some needed traction, but cinematic success remained tough sledding. He wrote Freda (who was in Akron with Jill during Christmas 1946) that he was up for a part in *If You Knew Susie* with Eddie Cantor at RKO and that while he went to "Julie Dassin's house and Curt's [Howard Da Silva] ranch …"[38] for Christmas, he missed his wife and daughter terribly. However dispiriting the Christmas holidays were, the following year represented a watershed in Charles McGraw's movie career.

McGraw appeared in eight features in 1947. While most of his parts remained minor in nature, the roles became increasingly distinctive as the actor underwent a seminal career transition from unlisted bit parts to a credited supporting player.

Mark Hellinger again cast Charlie, this time as a convict helping execute a break-out in the prison noir *Brute Force* (1947). The producer's second Universal-International feature was arguably a more powerful film than *The Killers*, but behind the scenes, commercial concessions were forced upon the film's director due to perceived box office realities.

Director Jules Dassin was, and *is*, a charming man of rare talent who typically refused to give ground on principle, whether to the Blacklist (the director left the country to continue his career abroad) or L.B. Mayer, who once fired him after a heated confrontation. Nonetheless, Dassin admitted that one of the main themes of *Brute Force* (i.e., "the women on the outside") was solely inspired by Hellinger and the studio brass. The director acquiesced to the addition of a sequence of flashbacks portraying the prisoners (Burt Lancaster, Howard Duff, John Hoyt, Whit Bissell) as hard-luck cases who ended up behind bars due to a gaggle of beleaguered, crooked, or desperately ill women (Ella Raines, Yvonne De Carlo, Anita Colby, Ann Blyth). The insertion of these sequences was incongruous to the overlying theme of the film about the desperate inhumanity of men in prison.

The frustration that Dassin experienced over this compromise with *Brute Force* still rankled nearly sixty years afterward:

> Truly the film is demeaned by the inclusion of "the women." I had to choose between not making the film and yielding to having the women nonsense. Many years later when I looked at the film…. I do not forgive myself.[39]

The clumsily inserted "love interest" scenes convey an absurd, misogynist message to modern audiences that the U.S. prison population was overrun by otherwise upright good guys who ended up in the clink because they were done wrong by a bunch of conniving dames.

Despite the contrivance, Dassin is being too tough on himself. *Brute Force* remains an emblematic example of uncompromisingly violent post–World War II noir realism. It was also a picture that almost didn't get released. Mark Hellinger became embroiled in a nasty personal fight with Production Code czar Joseph I. Breen over the brutal content of the film.

Hellinger made some initial changes when the MPAA rejected the script outright. Sequences

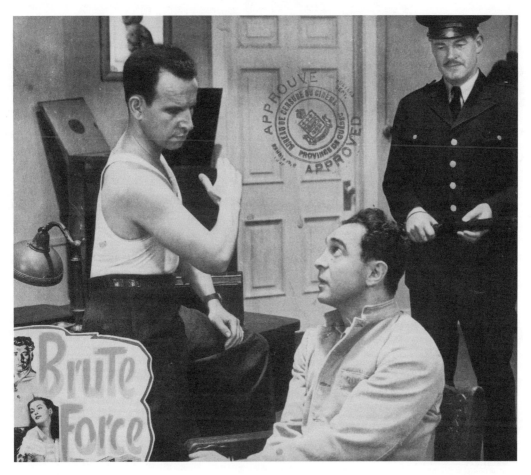

Postwar noir realism as sadism behind bars: Hume Cronyn as Captain Munsey applies the backhand to Sam Levene as Ray Teal looks on in *Brute Force* (1947).

tossed out included Hume Cronyn scolding a prisoner for smoking "weed," a scandal over the sale of marijuana in the prison, Charles Bickford spitting into a convict's face and Cronyn kicking Art Smith in the head after knocking him down. In a further missive, Breen ridiculously demanded deletion of the word "cancer" (relating to Ann Blyth's illness) from the script, because "it upsets the theatre-going public."[40]

Hellinger played the time-honored Hollywood producer's game by removing the more objectionable scenes from the picture while retaining and actually adding other sequences that were not submitted for final Breen review. The strategy backfired when Breen refused to certify the final cut of *Brute Force* for release with the required MPAA seal.

An emotional Hellinger sent a vituperative telegram to Breen over the rejection of his film, concluding:

> I am broken-hearted.... If this is fair play, Joe, then I've been thinking awfully wrong for too many years and I have learned a bitter lesson in the hardest way possible.[41]

Breen, furious, fired back saying that his judgment on the picture was fully in accordance with the Code:

> I am sorry that you have such a low estimate of me and my integrity.... I get some renewed courage

Burt Lancaster in prison garb and McGraw in mufti from the set of *Brute Force* (1947) (courtesy Mildred Black).

that your charge, that I am dishonest, is utterly false. Our major concern had to do with the *excessive and unnecessary brutality and gruesomeness of* your picture.[42]

The prelate censor specifically objected to the climactic scene of Lancaster throwing Hume Cronyn alive from the guard tower down to the prison yard to be torn to pieces by a mob of rioting convicts. Breen closed by adding he would not discuss the matter any further. Hellinger realized that he had gone too far and sent Breen a conciliatory message stating that his intentions in the initial diatribe had been misunderstood. The two men finally patched things up and *Brute Force* was approved for release with a bit more trimming, with the Cronyn body pitch at the finale remaining more or less intact.

Despite the censorship battles, the released film was stark, nihilistic and even vicious, building to a prison breakout that was unlike anything seen on screen before the war. Although selected contemporary observers have conjured up academia-based fantasies that *Brute Force* was making a statement about fascism, or the Blacklist, etc., Hellinger was simply trying to make a realistic prison drama. The best acting sequence in the picture belonged to Hume Cronyn, on loan from Metro, and former Group Theatre eminence Art Smith. Cronyn was memorable as a soft-spoken, conniving sadist of a prison guard, Captain Munsey, who beats prisoners in his office with a rubber hose to the accompanying strains of Wagner; he has a superb confrontation with the drunken prison sawbones-with-a-conscience who is beautifully played by Smith. *Brute Force* turned out to be less than the spectacular success of *The Killers* but was a resounding box office hit for Hellinger, whose producing star continued to rise. McGraw's role as a convict in the prison auto garage, secreting guns and Molotov cocktails for the epic prison break, was a perfect fit. For a much smaller part on screen than in *The Killers*, McGraw got less base salary—$600 per week—but obtained a nice three-week guarantee.

Despite being a nationally known figure for his newspaper column and now a hit movie producer, Mark Hellinger was a genuinely likable fellow to his movie crews and the actors he stocked his movies with. Few producers other than Hellinger would take the time to write an effusive letter to a respected but minor actor like Frank Puglia, who had a brief scene in *Brute Force* as Yvonne De Carlo's father, thanking him for his efforts. Fewer yet received unsolicited letters of thanks from struggling actors like Jack Overman, who won a key part in the film that boosted his career. Hellinger unfortunately didn't live long enough to enjoy and build upon his considerable success. In addition to his bad heart and incipient diabetes, the producer drank copious amounts of Hennessy brandy every night while smoking an endless chain of cigarettes. While observing a sequence staged near the Williamsburg Bridge during the production of his cinematic valentine to New York City, *The Naked City* (1948), Hellinger suffered a major heart attack and was removed to an oxygen tent in his hotel room. He never fully recovered and died of a subsequent seizure on December 21, 1947. The man who boasted of 15 million readers of his newspaper column lost the opportunity to savor the accolades for his final film or to see his recently purchased literary properties come to fruition. *Criss Cross,* a novel by Don Tracy, was intended by Hellinger to be a bookend Los Angeles crime story that would emulate what *The Naked City* did for New York City. The resultant film, directed by Robert Siodmak and released in 1949, proved to be memorable nonetheless. So was *Act of Violence*, sold to Metro by Hellinger's widow, Gladys Glad. One wonders what both of these fine pictures would have been like with the indelible Hellinger imprint.

Despite the tragic demise of a powerful friend and mentor, Charlie's good fortune continued in Hollywood as he played an array of increasingly tougher heavies in a variety of pictures.

One of McGraw's film appearances from 1947 that remains fixedly obscure is *The Big Fix*, directed by veteran James Flood. One of the final films released by PRC before being absorbed by Eagle-Lion studios, the picture stars James Brown, Sheila Ryan and Regis Toomey in a story about a crooked gambling ring's attempt to fix college basketball games. Described as "above-average,"[43] the film has McGraw seventh-billed as Armiston. Since *The Big Fix* has not surfaced cinematically or on television, the 62-minute programmer remains a blank notation on McGraw's career ledger.

The Gangster (1947) initially appeared to be another routine "B" crime drama with stock sets and a recycled plot about the fall of a petty criminal played by Barry Sullivan. Made under the auspices of Allied Artists, a studio birthed by the corporate marriage of a perpetual Poverty Row resident, Monogram Studios, and the Independent Motion Picture Producing Association (IMPPA) as a releasing entity, the film was produced by the King Brothers, a legendary trio of Hollywood fast-buck artists. Frank, Maurice and Herman Kosinski were entrepreneurial hucksters who parlayed their proletarian background in pinball machines and bathtub gin into the motion picture business. The brothers happily embellished their off-color past into a Tinseltown myth of gangsters-as-filmmakers as they cranked out 18 mostly crime-laden films over three decades beginning in 1941. Although they would later keep blacklisted writers like Dalton Trumbo employed under pseudonyms, working with the Kings on a picture could be tiresome. Director John Berry thought they were "vulgar shits"[44] although he was inclined to be partial to Frank King, who was the "brains" of the trio—perhaps analogous to the leadership acumen of Moe Howard in a Three Stooges short.

The Gangster possesses several layers of virtue due to the thoughtful screenplay penned by Daniel Fuchs who adapted from his 1937 novel *Low Company*. Fuchs, who would win the 1956 Academy Award for his screenplay of *Love Me or Leave Me,* recalled his youth around Coney Island in describing Brooklyn's "Neptune Beach" as a backdrop for his tale about first genera- tion Jewish life in the urban jungle:

> A man never knows what he wants, what's good for him, what he should do. Fate hurries him like a witch into mistakes and heartaches. Nobody does what's good for them. Take the Jews. When they were slaves in Egypt, Moses came to them and begged to take them out but they didn't want to go. Ah, it's the same in every line.[45]

The New Yorker wove a dark and fatalistic tale of a self-loathing, insecure small-timer named Shubunka. Shubunka's lustful obsession with a blond ice-queen (played by skater- turned-actress Belita) infects him with a terminal case of protagonist stupidity that resided only in the world of a 1940s "B" film noir. The hook becomes set for the classic femme fatale dou- ble cross. Sullivan's misplaced fixation of the heart causes his junior league shakedown racket to fatally implode. Although the complexity of the dialogue perplexed contemporary critics, it is precisely the ambiguity in Fuchs' prose that makes *The Gangster* a notable film,

Sullivan's performance became the prototype template of the small-time noir loser until overtaken three years later with more memorable panache by Richard Widmark playing Harry Fabian in Jules Dassin's classic, *Night and the City* (1950).

McGraw, as a thuggish henchman, is paired with that ultimate cinematic schmiel, Elisha Cook Jr. Charlie was also reunited with his old *Golden Boy* volleyball partner, Harry Morgan, alongside other accomplished character worthies; Akim Tamiroff, Sheldon Leonard, John Ire- land and Leif Erickson.

McGraw's seminal 1947 film appearance was a memorable role that cemented his reputa- tion as a film noir heavy to be reckoned with.

Director Anthony Mann and cinematographer John Alton were making a name for them- selves at Eagle-Lion Studios during the late 1940s. Eagle-Lion, located at the former PRC lot on Santa Monica Boulevard, had an interesting internationalist history.

The studio was formed in 1946 by the absorption of the ultra-cheap PRC studio by Amer- ican railroad tycoon, Robert R. Young, into a joint releasing organization with English film producer-distributor Arthur Rank. Young, who previously bought PRC as kind of a lark in 1943, was relatively clueless about the movie business. Rank was a powerhouse who controlled 500 theatres in the U.K. and desired access to American cinemas to distribute his product. The initial deal specified that Eagle-Lion and Rank would distribute ten pictures globally per year with each partner producing five each.

After spending $1 million to upgrade the PRC facilities, Young made a couple of astute personnel moves by hiring Brynie Foy away from Fox to run film production and appointing Arthur Krim as president of the joint business operation headquartered in New York. While Eagle-Lion lacked the theatre chains and access to stars to vault into the ranks of the majors, they produced six "high-budget" films in 1946–47. One of these "nervous A" pictures was an interesting film noir, *Repeat Performance* starring former WB contract ingénue Joan Leslie, who left the Burbank studio after getting fed up with the pernicious cheapness of Jack L. Warner. *Repeat Performance* and the other five films all lost money. Eagle-Lion got caught in the 1947 box office swoon that would accelerate over the next decade. The studio quickly retrenched by shuttering PRC for good, driving a stake through a brand trademark that had been dubbed by wags as "Pretty Rotten Crap." Foy quit as head of production with Krim assuming his respon- sibilities. Eagle-Lion then hired Foy, Edward Small and Walter Wanger as independent producers who would use the studio's facilities, some of their contracted players and a percentage of upfront cash. Small was a proven moneymaker as a producer and Wanger had a spectacular reputation that had only recently begun to tarnish. During their second year, Eagle-Lion began to garner profits by churning out economical, fast-paced crime films that played well with the public.

T-Men (1947) was envisioned as a second-tier "docudrama" of a noir subgenre that originated at Fox by Louis De Rochemont with *The House on 92nd Street* (1945). The plot was straightforward: Two undercover Treasury agents (Dennis O'Keefe and Alfred Ryder) penetrate a gang of counterfeiters based in Los Angeles and triumph over the bad guys after the predictable mayhem. In an uplifting example of talent and creativity trumping formulaic design, *T-Men* turned out to be a considerable film.

The opening sequence with the implacable McGraw mug looming out a doorway where he lay in wait like a feral beast, established the ominous visual mood of the picture. After getting past the obligatory Reed Hadley voice-over narration reverently intoning hackneyed hosannas about the greater glory of the Treasury Department, the balance of the film is a tense drama of undercover agents pitted against the ruthless counterfeiters. John Alton's uniquely shaded camerawork proved a tribute to both the cinematographer's vision of the piece and his trusting partnership with director Anthony Mann. The director of photography's adoption of a naturalistic visual style in *T-Men* was not without some trepidation according to Alton:

> The studio and Anthony Mann ... said they had confidence in me and that I was to photograph the story exactly how I saw fit. So we shot scenes just as they came along. We shot under all conditions. Some of our night shots were made without any lights at all. I know some people thought the scenes wouldn't match and it would turn out to be a horrible mess. Fortunately, it turned out as I was sure it would.[46]

Alton was absolutely correct. The picture was as authentic-looking as it was dramatic. None of the actors wore make-up and the street scenes were shot with masked cameras so that the passersby didn't realize that they were in the middle of a movie scene. The flawless Alton visuals were perfectly complemented by the terse, literate script of John C. Higgins and the rugged performances of O'Keefe, Ryder, the ubiquitous Wallace Ford, McGraw and others in the cast. Max E. Youngstein, Edward Small's right-hand man in New York and later a power at United Artists, realized they had a hit from day one and sent Small the following telegram after the premiere:

> The reaction of last night's screening *T-Men* ... was the most enthusiastic reaction that I have ever seen. This is no line of bull. This is a fact.[47]

There certainly wasn't any B.S. either when it came to the ultimate profitability of *T-Men*. The picture was made for around $424,000 and became a major hit. According to the film's nominal producer, Aubrey Schenck, *T-Men* ended up grossing $3,000,000, an extraordinary amount of money for a "B" film in the late '40s.

No doubt some of the realism of *T-Men* and the other Eagle-Lion crime films was due to the guiding hand of Bryan "Brynie" Foy, whose off-screen pals included such shady luminaries as con-man Jake "The Barber" Factor, Jersey City mayor and Hudson County political boss Frank "I am the Law" Hague and the notoriously corrupt Chicago machine boss, Ed Kelly. Foy outdid himself by hiring his close friend, West Coast mobster Johnny Roselli, first as an "artistic consultant" and then a producer under the Eagle-Lion banner.

At the time of his debut as a movie producer, Roselli had been hooked up in Hollywood as a West Coast representative for the Chicago mob for nearly twenty years. Known amongst his brethren as "the Hollywood Kid," Roselli worked with Tony Cornero, managing illegal gambling during late '20s into the 1930s when Los Angeles was the stereotypical "wide open" town under the corrupt mayoralty of Frank Shaw. After arranging to have the house of a reform city official firebombed by a cadre of corrupt police, Shaw's distinctive legacy became that of being the first mayor of a major American city to be recalled via a special election in 1938.

At the time of his fortuitous career opportunity at Eagle-Lion, Johnny Roselli was on parole for his role in the International Alliance of Theatrical Stage Employees (IATSE) payola scandal. The powerful union was an abject tool of organized crime that first sold out the membership with sweetheart deals and then extorted labor peace from the movie studios. The disreputable machinations behind the inexplicable early release of Roselli and other mob chieftains (they served three years of a ten-year sentence) came from the highest levels of the U.S. government. President Harry Truman, whose résumé included a long-term stench from the corrupt Pendergast political machine in Kansas City, had plenty to answer for about these engineered paroles but never had to. In 1945, Truman would pardon Nick Schenck of Loews International, who was caught trying to bribe Federal investigators just he did with the gangsters earlier. Truman's Department of Justice refused to cooperate with a Congressional investigation of a public scandal that quickly disappeared from the headlines.

The history of labor relations in Hollywood would be fascinating grist for a docudrama, but this subject, then and now, is too close to the bone for anyone to dare touch. Although the annals of many entertainment unions including the Screen Actors Guild and other artist guilds are honorably clean, a major portion of Hollywood's labor relations over the years was governed by a shady alliance of pliable union leaders, studio moguls and organized crime. A casting call for the players in this drama would include Joseph Kennedy and his sons, Jules Stein and Lew Wasserman at MCA, numerous movie stars, many of the famed moguls and authentic gangsters like Roselli, Frank Nitti, Tony "Joe Batters" Accardo, and Murray "Curly" Humphries, with their longtime Hollywood fixer, Sidney Korshak, pulling the strings for the "boys in the backroom" in the Windy City.

While it is unclear what Johnny Roselli's specific production responsibilities were at Eagle-Lion, future court records would stipulate that he served as an associate producer for *T-Men*, *Canon City* and *He Walked by Night* and was down for a 10 percent interest in each film. Bryan Foy and Eagle-Lion might have achieved a dubious Hollywood first by having an actual gangster directly involved in the production of their popular crime films.

Actual Hollywood mobsters aside, the studio had a celluloid gangster in Charles McGraw, who was the cinematic equivalent of dry ice. As Moxie, the ruthless torpedo of the counterfeiting gang, McGraw's work in *T-Men* was well described as having "raised movie cruelty to a new level ..."[48]

McGraw alternately tortures Dennis O'Keefe by breaking his fingers, cold-bloodedly executes an unarmed Alfred Ryder, and memorably parboils hapless Wallace Ford by locking him in a Turkish steam bath. While Charlie predictably perished in the finale as dictated by the Production Code, his demise was a fitting finale to a gem of a pitiless performance.

McGraw's performance in *T-Men* caused a minor stir in both in casting offices and selected Studio City watering holes. McGraw even had his relentless profile from *T-Men* displayed in a *Life* magazine full page photo spread on the film. The actor's daughter noted that some of her father's boon companions took to calling him Moxie. According to Jill McGraw, this nickname (along with the evolving sequence of similar roles that her father played in these films) began to subtly alter his behavior. She claimed that her father began to assume his screen mantle of the heavy by emphasizing his gravelly voice and projecting a tongue-in-cheek "tough guy" per-

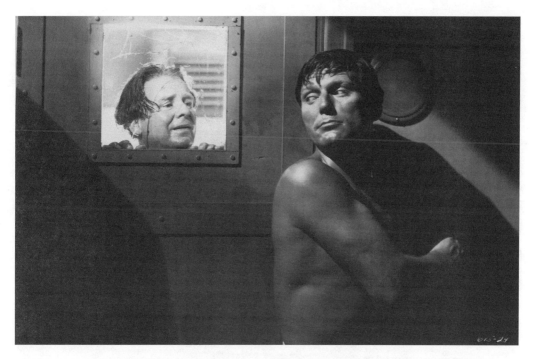

McGraw as Moxie parboils Wallace Ford in a steam bath in *T-Men* (1947).

sonality to his intimates, the press and around the house. While this role played fine on the set or with cronies during happy hour, it was not welcomed by his young daughter.

Actor Mickey Knox came to Hollywood after the war and met McGraw through a mutual friend, actor Curt Conway, who had a small part in *T-Men*. Knox recalled Charlie with affection: "Charlie was a terrific guy and a wonderful character. We met at some joint in Hollywood where all the younger actors hung out. He was a little grim, but funny and good to be with."[49]

One of Knox's singular memories of Charlie was McGraw's macho self-promotion of his virility: "He bragged to me that he made love to Freda every day."[50]

Despite the recent surge of work, McGraw remained anxious about the future. His absences for location shoots (leaving Freda and Jill in a small Hollywood apartment) were wearing on both the actor and his family. McGraw leased an apartment on 6424 Yucca Street on August 18, 1947 at $40.82 per week. Charlie helped defray some of his living costs by acting as the apartment manager.

McGraw would conclude the year by appearing in several pictures that weren't released until early to mid–1948. In *The Hunted* (1948), co-starring Preston Foster and ice skater–actress Belita, McGraw had an uncredited bit part as a wrought-iron police detective near the end of the film. Produced for Allied Artists Production Company at Monogram, the film's principal virtue was the gritty screenplay penned by ace scripter Steve Fisher. Belita attempts to hide out as an incognito hash slinger after reputedly double-crossing the trusting Foster by murdering the D.A. who previously sent her up to Tehachapi for a jewel robbery. Since Foster is the cop who also sent Belita to the slammer and allowed his ardor to trump his professional instincts by letting her stay at his apartment after her release, he gets the bit in his teeth to track her down. The film becomes a fairly interesting matter of discerning who is actually getting double-crossed and framed. Director Jack Bernhard, who previously caught dark lightning in a bottle with Jean Gillie in an underrated picture penned by Stanley Rubin, *Decoy* (1946), went

"The Man in Black"— McGraw with Roy Rogers in a publicity shot from *On the Old Spanish Trail* (1947) (courtesy Mildred Black).

through the motions on this one. Although an Allied Artists picture was an ostensible rung upward on the Poverty Row ladder, *The Hunted* possesses the production values equivalent of dinner for two at Pink's Hot Dog Stand on La Brea Blvd.

Much better was *Berlin Express*, a full-scale "A" production by RKO.

Berlin Express is frequently mislabeled as a film noir. Despite the voice-over narration and dark shading, the picture is a mystery-thriller based on a Curt Siodmak story about postwar intrigue involving an assassination plot onboard a non-stop train from Paris to Germany. The picture had a blending of Hitchcockian suspense elements borrowed from *The Lady Vanishes* (1938) and *Foreign Correspondent* (1940) and some post–World War II multi-lateralism by having all of the principals in the story represent an Allied nationality. *Berlin Express* didn't have all of the quality attributes of a Hitchcock film, but it was a well-crafted and entertaining picture.

A German doctor is killed when a bomb goes off in his train compartment. The murder is witnessed by an American, a Frenchwoman, a Russian soldier and a British man who are all questioned. It is revealed that the murdered German was actually a stand-in for the actual doctor, a heroic figure attempting to unite postwar Germany. The international quorum of witnesses from the train quickly band together to find the real doctor in the bombed-out streets of Germany. Naturally, not everyone is who they appear to be.

RKO Studios certainly pulled out all the stops on this picture. Personally supervised by RKO production chief Dore Schary and directed by one of their top contract directors, Jacques Tourneur, *Berlin Express* starred Merle Oberon, Robert Ryan and Paul Lukas. Although Oberon was starting on the downside of a glamorous career, she was still a genuine "A-list" star who earned $125,000 for her work in the film. Oberon looked

McGraw's movie career began to gain traction in 1947. Charlie and Freda during a well-earned night out at the Biltmore Hotel on July 24, 1947 (courtesy Mildred Black).

gorgeous in the film and no wonder: She was married to the film's cinematographer, Lucien Ballard. Ballard created the unique lighting that showcased Oberon's beauty while obscuring facial scans from a 1937 automobile accident. Conversely, Robert Ryan, an RKO contract property coming off of his Best Supporting Actor–nominated performance in *Crossfire*, was paid a mere $17,400, less than two other actors under the title.

Despite the compensation vagaries of the studio system, with a total budget of over $1,740,000, *Berlin Express* was the production equivalent of *Titanic* (1997) for RKO in late 1947. The picture was filmed over 16 weeks with a full week of location exteriors in bombed-out Frankfurt and Berlin. McGraw played a neatly barbered USFET (U.S. Forces European Theatre) Colonel Johns in an uncredited role that required his presence on the RKO soundstages from October 3–8, 1947. *Berlin Express* was more than another payday for McGraw. It was an opportunity for the actor to prove that he could play straight parts with the same skill with which he routinely essayed menacing heavies. As McGraw remarked afterwards, "I guess they thought I could only act with a gun in my hand."[51]

As 1948 began, Charlie landed another small role, this time in a Paramount comedy titled

Hazard. Directed by comedy veteran George Marshall and starring Paulette Goddard and a mis-cast Macdonald Carey, it featured Charlie as a henchman for professional gambler Fred Clark. Goddard is a beautiful chanteuse who loses a bet to Clark and has to pay it off by marrying him. Goddard hightails it out of town with Carey, as Clark's collection agent, in hot pursuit. Natu-rally, Carey and Goddard fall for each other in spite of myriad obstacles. The picture was sad-dled with both a weak script and an uncomfortable Macdonald Carey, who seemingly recognized that he was out of his depth playing opposite the beautifully confident Paulette Goddard. McGraw and Fred Clark got on well and the two actors would become friendly while appearing in *Joe Butterfly* together at Universal nine years later.

Things were starting to get better career-wise, but the actor's professional life still remained touch and go. A stage actor by training, McGraw continued to tread the boards while on the West Coast. In May 1948 he played in a Los Angeles production of *The Survivors*, written by Irwin Shaw and Peter Viertel for a "princely" $40 per week. He became a mainstay at the Pasadena Playhouse and other little theatres in the greater Los Angeles area. McGraw received perhaps the greatest critical acclaim of his career for a September 1954 revival of *Street Scene* at the Pasadena Playhouse where he played opposite Angela Greene and Coleen Gray. The *L.A. Examiner* called him "… the dominating figure of the evening" with the *Los Angeles Times* stat-ing that McGraw, "… turned in one of the outstanding performances as Frank Maurrant." While Charlie clearly respected his thespian roots, it was now about making a living, and in the imme-diate postwar period, things remained a struggle to keep afloat. In a heartfelt letter written while in rugged Kern County filming the Roy Rogers oater, *On the Old Spanish Trail* (1947), McGraw complained to Freda about the horrible location and how much he missed his wife and daughter. More significantly, the actor advised that he "had spoken to Paul and the Gold-wyn job is almost set so we are going to buy us a home where you can be completely carefree."[52]

7

The Lion Goes Black

The "Goldwyn job" referred to by McGraw was a major supporting role in a film production at that most sylvan of Hollywood studios, Metro-Goldwyn-Mayer. The picture that Charlie signed on for, *Border Incident*, was emblematic of the convulsive changes that were rippling through the Culver City studio monolith.

"As Metro went, so did the film industry" was a cliché that became a microcosm of the tumultuous fortunes that would roil Hollywood in the early 1950s. After a glorious reign of a quarter of a century, Louis B. Mayer's dance card as the head of MGM was nearly filled up, but hardly anyone in Tinseltown saw it coming.

Although Mayer was the absolute monarch of Culver City and viewed as the senior prelate of Hollywood studio barons, the legendary mogul was never an owner, merely a spectacularly well-compensated employee. Mayer was beholden to the studio's New York holding company of Loews, Inc. Nick Schenck, Loews grey eminence in New York, viewed the slippage of Metro's postwar box office receipts with concern. Although Schenck and Mayer had long been bound together by a shared interest in continued profits, their working relationship was as convivial as two cats stuffed in a pillowcase being dragged behind a pickup truck. Under the combined pressures of the government anti-trust consent degree that forced the studios to divest themselves of their theatre chains, the nascent emergence of television, and the changing tastes of postwar audiences, L.B. Mayer was compelled to hire Dore Schary, former production chief at RKO, as MGM production head in July 1948. While all of the Hollywood studios were experiencing a marked decline in their postwar box office receipts, the Metro situation was keener and more personal. Mayer was becoming desperate to fade the heat coming from Schenck in New York.

L.B. Mayer was banking that Schary, a former Metro writer, would prove to be a success doppelganger to the legendary MGM wunderkind production chief, Irving Thalberg. For his part, Schary was eager to resume his career in film production after gagging on a brief taste of life under Howard Hughes at RKO.

Schary and Mayer quickly clashed over management style. Mayer could erupt in legendary tirades, but delegated sweeping authority to creative production heads like Arthur Freed. Schary was cerebral, low-key and gentlemanly, but proved to be an incessant micromanager who took many decisions personally. Although a lot of the so-called "message films" that Schary subsequently produced at MGM were often in search of an audience, these financial foul balls were masked by the initial successes of his tenure. The robust financial bonanzas included *Adam's Rib*, *On the Town* and, most notably, the Battle of the Bulge drama *Battleground* (1949). This particular film had been terminated by Howard Hughes at RKO—a major reason why Schary quickly bailed after Hughes bought the studio. Revived by Schary at Metro, *Battleground* was nominated for four Oscars, winning two for Best Story and Best Cinematography. Nick Schenck believed Schary might indeed be the second coming of Thal-

The frustrated stuntman: Charlie clowns with an unknown friend at Republic Studios during filming of *The Old Spanish Trail* (1947) (photograph courtesy Mildred Black).

berg and the heir apparent to Mayer, who by now was openly chafing over Schary's selection of pictures.

Mayer hated the Schary-inspired crime noirs like *Tension, Scene of the Crime, Caught, Mystery Street, Side Street* and *Dial 1119*. Even the classic *The Asphalt Jungle* (1950) became a target of executive invective. According to the fulminating mogul, John Huston's picture was "full of nasty ugly people doing nasty, ugly things."[53] In addition to being flummoxed by the anti-trust debacle and the gnawing encroachment of television, Mayer remained fixated in a *Classics Illustrated* comic book worldview accentuated by his extreme Homily Americana yearning for family-based entertainment that had prevailed so profitably at his studio during the preceding two decades. Unfortunately for L.B., the country's preferences for cinematic entertainment had moved on after V-J Day while the mogul's own tastes remained *status quo*. Postwar filmgoers were no longer satisfied by the level of dramatic tension generated by Mickey Rooney mustering up the courage to ask his "Dad," actor Lewis Stone, for a ten spot in order to settle a restaurant bill in an Andy Hardy picture. The charming Nick and Nora Charles *Thin Man* series had also run its course and was similarly retired. Mayer had lost touch with the movie-going public.

The Schary-Mayer relationship initially soured over Schary's production selections and then curdled into open warfare when Mayer belatedly realized that his influence with New York had precipitously ebbed as Schary's had risen. The showdown occurred in April 1951 when Mayer delivered a profane diatribe to Schary, threw him out of his office and sent a fulminating ultimatum to New York. Nick Schenck sided with the younger production chief and Mayer tendered his resignation. The contest between both men ultimately had less to do with production decisions and more with the twin, interlocking gravitational fields, money and power, that kept Hollywood spinning on its axis. The aging studio system was creaking, but still reflected the essence of contemporary geopolitics; there was only room for a single dictator to run a movie studio.

Never was a film produced at MGM during the Mayer era that was more at odds with the mogul's wholesome entertainment values than *Border Incident* (1949). It must have physically pained L.B. to see the studio's Golden Jubilee banner adorn this strikingly dark picture that was packed with "nasty ugly people." Dore Schary had already scooped up Anthony Mann from Eagle-Lion in November 1948 for $100,000 as a pro-active package deal that included an ongoing story treatment concerning the exploitation of illegal immigrants propping up in American agriculture. Eagle-Lion could not finance the estimated $650,000 cost of the picture. The working title of *Wetback* was quickly deemed too provocative even by 1949 standards and was replaced by the more palatable and marketable designation of *Border Patrol* which morphed into the final release title of *Border Incident*.

Although a writer named George Zuckerman received partial screen credit for the original story of *Border Incident,* his treatment included completely different characters than the final script and outlined a divergent plot that included a series of water-borne alien smuggling sequences. John C. Higgins, one of Hollywood's most dependable crime scenarists and screenwriter of the previous Anthony Mann noirs *T-Men, Railroaded,* and *Raw Deal,* composed the original story and screenplay that ended up being filmed. Higgins' final draft screenplay included a fascinating opening sequence with a sweeping vista of the Aztec pyramids and a stirring narrative paean to Mexican culture and the "civilizing" influence of Christianity by terror:

> ... then, over four hundred years ago, Cortes and his conquistadores struck the Indian nations. Temples were raised to the new god ...[54]

Not surprisingly, this thought-provoking prologue that touched on some of the root causes of the immigration debacle did not pass muster with the Metro production brass. By April of 1949, the previously approved prologue and epilogue in the script were scrapped and Higgins was compelled to compose new versions that were personally approved by producer Nicholas Nayfack. These revisions emphasized the greater glory of the United States government working in harmony with our neighbor to the south. Aerial stock footage of the All-American Canal in California's Imperial Valley, and actors playing U.S. and Mexican officials in a conference room awash with flags, replaced the previously envisioned scenes. The voiceover narration for these sequences was sonorously intoned by radio announcer Knox Manning in lieu of Hollywood's preeminent "voice of docunoir," actor-narrator Reed Hadley, who was off appearing in a Western for Robert L. Lippert.

Fortunately, the clichéd rewrites of the film's edges did not soften the hard-edged message of the finished product. The exposure and break-up of an Imperial Valley alien smuggling ring by a multinational team of immigration agents remains a visually stunning picture under Alton's moonlit visages of desperate men and assorted mayhem filmed on location near Mexicali, Mexico.

Using the successful thematic template from *T-Men* resulted in both pictures having plots that were veritable mirror images. However, *Border Incident* was a legitimate attempt to address a serious subject that remains highly topical to the present day. While the finale includes the simplistically mandated, "we've got it all solved now" flag-waving histrionics, the balance of the picture is a stark, uncompromising drama which forced audiences to reflect that the kitchen tables of the "land of plenty" are supported by some pretty miserable underpinnings.

Ricardo Montalban ably portrays an undercover Mexican policeman who attempts to pen-

McGraw as Jeff Amboy gets the drop on undercover agent Ricardo Montalban as Howard Da Silva recognizes his own liability as Charlie's crooked employer too late in *Border Incident* (1949).

etrate the illegal operations of a corrupt and venal rancher (Charlie's old Group Theatre buddy, Howard Da Silva). Da Silva ruthlessly exploits the migrant workers who work on his land, pays them next to nothing and then discards them as chattel. Worse yet, a motley crew of cinematic blunt instruments including McGraw, Arthur Hunnicutt, Jack Lambert, Arnold Moss and Alfonso Bedoya collaborate on a gruesome sideline of hunting down the migrant workers like game when they attempt to return to Mexico. In a shocking opening sequence, the ruthless gang is shown in the desert twilight, murdering the helpless workers, stealing their money and dumping the corpses in a bog.

Anthony Mann possessed formidable regard for Charlie as an actor and was especially enamored of the existential outlines conveyed by the distinctively chiseled McGraw mug shot under the low-key lighting of John Alton. A close-up of McGraw's craggy profile filling up the entire screen, illuminated by a flashlight in the Imperial Valley night, conjures up the notion of a film noir version of Mount Rushmore. One envisions McGraw's face in bas relief profile alongside Lawrence Tierney's scowl, Robert Ryan's sneer, and Robert Mitchum's bemused cool, complete with lifted eyebrow, blasted into a South Dakota mountainside.

Charlie portrays ranch foreman Jeff Amboy with ruthless élan, adding a guttural rasp of racism towards the Mexican workers to what was becoming a typical portrait of avarice and cruelty. His contentious relationship with the smuggling kingpin, the suavely corrupt but cowardly Da Silva, culminates in a memorable double cross that proved nearly anti-climactic compared to a preceding and more memorable rubout. In what was the most darkly innovative cinematic elimination of a leading man during the 1940s, Charlie literally sowed screen infamy by running over Montalban's American undercover counterpart (played by hoofer George Murphy — one of the oddest casting choices in movie history) with a furrow cultivator during a startlingly brutal scene that one somehow expects to end before Murphy's death, but that doesn't. *Border Incident* remains a violent and disturbing film that is replete with chilling sequences. The mayhem ends with McGraw being gut-shot during a wild finale of a firefight, toppling off a craggy mountain peak, shrieking, into a dark ravine.

Even on a barren location shoot in the Imperial Valley, McGraw and a few others in the cast managed to have some laughs. This particular escapade was emblematic of the practical jokester lifestyle of many of the Hollywood stuntmen, extras and bit players that Charlie was so fond of. McGraw and others in the company were staying at a flyspecked El Centro hotel that included a decidedly blue-collar bar heavily populated by Mexican agricultural workers. Stuntman-actor Frank McGrath came up with a novel method to dispel boredom. Resembling Charlie in stature and profile, McGrath stood up near the bar exit and announced loudly, "My name is Charles McGraw and I can whip any fucking Mexican in this stinking bar."[55] McGrath immediately ran upstairs to his own room and listened with amusement to the subsequent pounding on McGraw's hotel room door down the hallway by several outraged patrons who wanted to take the actor up on his "challenge." Charlie, who had been sleeping off his own drunk, had to put on an impromptu Oscar-caliber performance of aggrieved innocence in order to avoid mortal injury. The next morning, McGraw and company became briefly convulsed while reliving the episode. Charlie had reason to feel good. He was embarking on the busiest year of his screen acting career.

8

In Demand

While *Border Incident* was a major film credit for Charles McGraw, it was the first of nine feature films that the actor appeared in during 1949. Finally Charlie was in demand as a movie actor. Several of the pictures he worked on during 1949 were not released until well into the following year. A Universal publicity release noted that,

> Charles McGraw has been so active in leading roles that at the moment, six movies in which he is featured—*Convict Molly X, Terror* (working title of *The Threat*), *Side Street, Ma and Pa Kettle Go to Town, Border Incident* and *Double Crossbones* are still unreleased.[56]

Adding to the parade of hard-cases that began with *The Killers,* McGraw continued to appear in crime dramas, but was also cast in several comedies that allowed him to stretch his acting expertise and demonstrate that there was more to his professional repertoire than playing a menacing heavy.

Once More My Darling (1949), a Universal-International production, was a lighthearted screwball comedy about a movie star (Robert Montgomery) being recalled to active duty by the Army's Criminal Investigative Division to sweep a debutante (Ann Blyth) off her feet and find out what became of some stolen jewelry. Of course, Montgomery ends up becoming smitten with Blyth amid much comedic mayhem co-starring regal stage legend Jane Cowl as Montgomery's attorney mother, along with Taylor Holmes, Roland Winters and Steven Geray.

In one of those strokes of good fortune that are essential to a successful career in Hollywood, the director of *Once More My Darling* was Michael Gordon, the former Group Theatre manager who summoned McGraw to the audition of *Golden Boy* in New York for his initial big break back in 1937. In casting McGraw, Gordon knew exactly what he was getting. Charlie was letter-perfect as Ann Blyth's overly protective chauffeur and ex-pug Herman Schmelz, who proudly informs Montgomery that he is "seven times a middleweight contender."[57] Charlie shows a deft comedic touch in several amusing sequences including complimenting Montgomery on his behavior, then immediately warning him that he will beat his brains out if the movie star becomes caddish with young Blyth.

Michael Gordon, whose directorial credits in Hollywood would range from *The Web* (1947) to *Pillow Talk* (1959), ran into professional misfortune with *Once More My Darling.* A week into production, a terse press release advised that Gordon had been replaced as director by Robert Montgomery, the picture's star and producer. The replacement didn't come as a surprise to those familiar with the dynamic leading man.

Montgomery was one of Hollywood's elite. After success on the Broadway stage, he came to town in 1929 and became a bankable leading man with MGM over the next 16 years. The dapper actor was president of the Screen Actors Guild (twice), served with distinction in the Navy during World War II and stepped into directing on *They Were Expendable* (1945) when John Ford became ill. Montgomery established his directorial acumen with his previous two pictures—both noir films. He starred in and directed the gimmicky *Lady in the Lake* (1946), based on Raymond Chandler's novel, and filled those same jobs on the interesting *Ride the Pink Horse* (1947) where he was paired with producer Joan Harrison, a talented Hitchcock acolyte. *Once More My Darling* would be the first feature of Montgomery's new Neptune productions headquartered at Universal-International and would again match him with Harrison.

Montgomery, who faced down an actual threat of real-life IATSE gangsters who attempted to muscle in on the SAG, was a man of action. When Michael Gordon began by averaging seven set-ups a day, and kept cast and crew on the set till nearly 7:00 p.m. every day with a high waste rate of exposed film, the star didn't hesitate. He quickly replaced Gordon behind the camera and increased the efficiency of the production. Montgomery would invariably end each working day by rehearsing the first scene to be shot the next morning and still sent everyone home before 6:00 p.m. The dual grind of acting while directing in Hollywood was an onerous chore that had been mastered by a select few: Orson Welles, Charlie Chaplin, Gregory Ratoff, Otto Preminger. In fairness to Michael Gordon, he probably would have been replaced by Robert Montgomery no matter what he did. The star-director was a well-organized manager. He worked with an acting stand-in who would recite the star-director's dialogue during rehearsals, then donned both acting and directing hats when filming began. Montgomery explained:

> The assistant director gave the go signal with the word, "action," but I called "cut" when the scene ended. If I was satisfied with the scene, I checked cameraman, script girl, dialogue director, sound technician, and wardrobe man, as well as the assistant director for errors. If they detected none, I marked the scene for printing.[58]

Even with all the care and talent, *Once More My Darling* received mostly middling reviews and didn't do well at the box office. Though at least one critic got carried away "delightfully light and frothy as the head on a cold glass of beer"[59]), the picture simply didn't work. Montgomery becoming romantically involved with the diminutively youthful Blyth strained credulity and taste: Montgomery was forty-five while Blyth was twenty and resembled a teenager. Montgomery's directorial efforts in feature films invariably proved to be more interesting than successful. His move to embryonic television in the early 1950s with the anthology program *Robert Montgomery Presents* proved to be a much more lucrative venture for him. The actor ended up being the first media advisor in history hired by an American president, Dwight D. Eisenhower. For Charlie McGraw, whose freelance salary was now up to $1000 per week, *Once More My Darling* was a significant credit in a year of exceptional good fortune.

Anthony Mann tapped Charlie again, this time for *Side Street* (1950) over at MGM. Extensively shot on location in New York City, the picture is a classic "blind alley" film noir with Farley Granger and Cathy O'Donnell reprising their innocent lovers-as-victims roles from the seminal *They Live by Night* (1947). Mann quickly discovered one of the benefits of working at MGM instead of Eagle-Lion: Metro had the resources to obtain the actors he wanted even if they were under contract to other studios. Granger was borrowed from Samuel Goldwyn (the young actor was rapidly becoming disenchanted with the film business under the mercurial producer) with O'Donnell being obtained from that king of independent producers, David O. Selznick, who habitually rented out his contract players to pay off his incessant gambling losses.

Side Street opens with Granger as a broke letter carrier, married to O'Donnell and with a kid on the way. When he succumbs to temptation and steals 30 grand of payoff money from a crooked lawyer's (Edmon Ryan) office, he sets off a tidal wave of unforeseen consequences.

It turns out that the lawyer is running an extortion racket using sultry Adele Jergens as a honey pot snare to bed and then blackmail married businessmen. After a profitable tryst with a Wall Street executive, an increasingly greedy Adele ends up facedown in the East River, courtesy of the lawyer's strong-arm partner James Craig. New York's finest, led by Paul Kelly (who also provides the voice-over narration) and McGraw, start investigating. In the interim, the panicky Granger lies to his wife about a new job and forks over just enough cash so she can avoid delivering their baby in a charity ward. As the ironies pile up, Granger becomes a second-story prowler in order to visit O'Donnell and his new son in the hospital that he paid for with stolen money. He confesses his sin as the couple experiences the habitual spasm of conscience while in a family way. Granger decides to return the money to attorney Ryan, but naturally it is too late. After multiple plot contortions, Granger enters a shadowy Greenwich Village underbelly of clip joints and shabby apartments to track down the vicious Craig and get back the money ahead of the closing police. Along the way, he is waylaid by the underrated Jean Hagen, brilliantly playing a shopworn "B" girl. Snookered, badly beaten, Granger is being taken for the proverbial ride after the suddenly inconvenient Hagen is strangled by her erstwhile boyfriend (Craig) who is racking up an impressive body count. After a wild chase in a taxi cab that careens through lower Manhattan, it ends up with the hack overturned on Wall Street and Craig tattooed with police bullets. Granger manages to survive, more or less intact, as a much wiser man who will be reunited with his family ... perhaps.

Side Street is an emblematic Anthony Mann film noir: fatalistic, suspenseful and superbly crafted. The screenwriter, Sydney Boehm, was a former newspaperman who wrote with an obsessive sense of the noir crime policier. Starting with *The High Wall* in 1947, Boehm's busy typewriter reeled off nothing but crime melodramas: *Mystery Street, The Atomic City, The Big Heat, Second Chance, Rogue Cop, Black Tuesday, Hell on Frisco Bay, Violent Saturday, Six Bridges to Cross, The Bottom of the Bottle* and *Seven Thieves*. Boehm's story in *Side Street* plays on the classic noir premise of the innate weakness of the human condition causing a head-long rush into perdition. Kelly's narration drones on about Granger's character, "... he's only human ..."[60] implying that one only has to give in to temptation just once in order for the hounds of hell to be let off their leads. When Farley jimmies the lawyer's filing cabinet and takes the money, the die is irretrievably cast and his character has lost control of his fate.

Anthony Mann went with veteran MGM lenser Joseph Ruttenberg this time out. John Alton would have captured a darker version of New York; however Mann strove for a documentary look and narrative style that emphasized the micro human saga within the macro view of the huge metropolis. This perspective had been hugely popularized by Mark Hellinger in *The Naked City* (1948). Mann was not content with mere cribbing and added a clever visual variance. The opening credits show a dizzying aerial sequence over the Empire State Building that moves into lower Manhattan. Ruttenberg was put aloft in a dirigible above Manhattan for three hours. A plank was put in the open door of the airship and, "to get his shots, Ruttenberg sat on the edge of the plank with his camera (and himself) tied to the plank."[61] The balance of the film uses numerous location scenes from all over the city: Central Park, Battery Park, the Bellevue Hospital morgue, Greenwich Village and the Fulton Fish Market. The overturning-car finale at Wall Street had to be filmed repeatedly, much to the chagrin of Anthony Mann, when the taxi cab would not flip over per the script when it hit the curb.

Granger and O'Donnell didn't rekindle their "wild at heart" proletarian passion that made *They Live by Night* such a compelling picture, but the pair certainly was the epitome of star-crossed noir lovers. As with all of Mann's noir films, it was the supporting cast, peopled with distinctive actors including McGraw, Adele Jergens, Harry Bellaver, Whit Bissell, Sid Tomack and Ed Max, that gave *Side Street* an authentic human feel that proved such an apt match for the urban backdrop.

McGraw was tersely brusque as Paul Kelly's right hand man, Detective Stan Simon. At Jergens' apartment, he unsentimentally scans the recently departed address book and blithely

On the set of *Side Street* (1950) are McGraw, Paul Kelly, John Gallaudet and a visiting Keenan Wynn (courtesy Mildred Black).

remarks that she apparently "knew everyone in New York."[62] He next offends the housekeeper by calling her a cleaning woman. Even though his part was secondary, Charlie made himself noticeable with nice bits of business, slipping a proffered cigar in his pocket for later enjoyment while questioning a well-to-do businessman and leaning against a squad room door with an evil grin to bar a suspect from exiting. *Side Street* was another quality film credit on McGraw's résumé, and the year was still young.

Over at Universal-International, McGraw appeared in four films at the reconstituted studio in 1949. *The Story of Molly X* (1949) starred June Havoc as a gang leader who ends up in the State Prison in Tehachapi. Charlie's appearance in this picture as a tough police captain appeared to be an afterthought by screenwriter-director Crane Wilbur.

Wilbur began as an actor on the Broadway stage in 1903 and had an unusually long and prolific career. Crane Wilbur was a true motion picture pioneer. He began as a film actor in 1910, and appeared opposite Pearl White in *The Perils of Pauline* (1914). When Wilbur's movie career faltered, he returned to New York as a playwright during the Roaring Twenties. Wilbur wrote, staged or acted in eighteen different Broadway productions between 1920 and 1934. Returning to Hollywood when opportunities dimmed along the Great White Way, he began composing original stories and screenplays for mostly "B" films. When Wilbur commenced second unit production work on *The Story of Molly X* in January 1949, he had a screenwriting résumé of forty feature films, also directing about half that total, during the preceding fifteen years and had logged over 45 years in show business.

With the working title of *Tehachapi—The Story of Molly X*, Wilbur continued exploring

In *Side Street* (1950), homicide copper McGraw stares down Paul Harvey. Note the photo of Adele Jergens in the grasp of Harvey.

what was becoming his favorite cinematic obsession: the reality of life in prison. Behind the scenes, the casting for *Molly X* resembled a frenetic game of Hollywood musical chairs. Ginger Rogers was originally signed for the leading role but backed out due to cold feet. (Ginger's debut as a tough broad behind bars would be delayed until Phil Karlson's *Tight Spot* in 1955.) Shelley Winters, Jeff Chandler, Tony Curtis, Helena Carter and Hugh Reilly were all at one time cast members of the nascent production, but left or were replaced for one reason or another.

After Wilbur began location shooting at the Women's Prison at Tehachapi, California on July 12, 1949 with June Havoc in the title role, Scott Brady and Charles Drake, the two male leads, were suddenly replaced by John Russell and Elliott Lewis on August 1. Russell was a former combat Marine with striking good looks who looked like a comer. Lewis was an acting lightweight from radio who would go on to be a highly successful television producer. What was evident by these eleventh hour replacements was that Wilbur reduced the film's budget by another $8000. It appeared there was considerable pressure by U-I on Wilbur to keep the total costs of *Molly X* under a half million dollars.

The once sizable role of Captain Breen (interesting surname selection of the Production Code censor) that was originally intended for Jeff Chandler was reduced to a smaller part that McGraw stepped in for from August 2–8, 1949. Charlie was in truculent, tight-lipped form as a take-no-prisoners copper who implied that, for a hardened criminal like Havoc, doing time in the mountain prison was more than a tad too lenient. (Prison life in *Molly X* resembled an evangelical women's boot camp with softball games, choir practice and empathetic counseling.)

The film is dominated with a bravura performance by the little-used June Havoc as Molly X. Casting the kid sister of stripper Gypsy Rose Lee as a revenge-obsessed female gangster who goes to prison could have turned the picture into high camp. It worked out fine as Miss Havoc, an underrated actress, played it with extreme professionalism. She was appropriately hard-nosed while leading a gang of crooks on robbery capers and was not above using her sex in order to exact lethal revenge on the yegg who murdered her husband.

After Havoc arrives in Tehachapi, she becomes a model prisoner until her doppelganger in crime, Dolores Hart, whose husband was rubbed out by Havoc, arrives and matters quickly begin escalating. Although the finale requires a quantum leap of credibility, a notable thematic subtext had Havoc's character, while imprisoned, relate that her life of criminality was attributable to being sexually abused as a child by a degenerate stepfather. Crane Wilbur deserves credit for including this dash of realism that was just short of miraculous to observe in a Hollywood movie produced during the late 1940s.

Adding additional heft were the location sequences at the women's state prison in Tehachapi (Universal-International donated a new Hammond organ for use by the inmates in appreciation of the prison's cooperation with the filming) and the San Francisco locations during the beginning of the picture. The San Francisco sequences included the skyline view from the famous Top of the Mark Restaurant (cleverly used blown-up plates taken by Wilbur's second unit crew). The restaurant shown in the film with the actors was actually a set on a Universal soundstage. One wishes that Shelley Winters could have played the Dolores Hart role — she would have been a much better match for Havoc — and that McGraw's part wasn't whittled down to a routine supporting role. *The Story of Molly X* remains a forgotten period film noir that is one of the more distinctive entries from Crane Wilbur's prodigious cinematic résumé.

Ma and Pa Kettle Go to Town (1950) allowed Charlie to burnish his comedy acting chops. As Shotgun Mike Munger, he takes it on the lam with 100 grand, hiding out at the new Kettle home that the rustics won during their previous feature film adventure. Only after McGraw has Ma and Pa Kettle bring his "empty" bag to his "brother" in the Big Apple, does the fun really start. While the gangsters are chasing the elder Kettles all over Gotham to grab the loot, Charlie is gradually being anesthetized by the Kettle clan of sixteen freckled-faced progeny who are running roughshod all over him. With pros like Ray Collins, Ellen Corby, Jim Backus, and Bert Freed in the mix along with Charlie, there were bound to be plenty of laughs in this picture. *Ma and Pa Kettle Go to Town* was a popular entry in a film series that evolved into one of Universal-International's few dependable revenue streams during the 1950s. Inspired by Percy Kilbride and Marjorie Main's supporting performances in *The Egg and I* (1947), the Kettles would provide inspirational fodder for generations of rural television comedies including *The Real McCoys, The Beverly Hillbillies* and *Green Acres.* The Ma and Pa Kettle series endured for six additional features before concluding in 1957.

Percy Kilbride's premature departure before the final two Kettle films wasn't a mortal wound. The slatternly appearing Marjorie Main was the heart and soul of the Kettle series even if her habit of occasionally gazing skyward and conversing with her deceased husband while on the set struck some of her co-stars as a trifle odd.

McGraw finished his week's work with the Kettle family on September 7, 1949 and stayed on the Universal lot for *Double Crossbones* (1951). Although McGraw worked on this picture for a month, from September 13 to October 12, 1949 with production ending before Halloween, the film wasn't released until April of 1951. It's not difficult to understand why this picture went through extensive cutting after multiple, unenthusiastic previews. The film was a peculiar musical starring Donald O'Connor as an accidental pirate who sings, dances and farces his way through adventure and danger to win the hand of comely Helena Carter. Despite a $700,000 production budget and a skilled comedic director in Charles Barton, the film falls flat because the script simply can't bridge the untenable theme of a swashbuckler comedy laden with musical numbers that is not a children's picture. The critics judged the picture "uninspired"[63] and "not up to standards."[64] Starting with a working title of *Half Pint Buccaneer*, Universal also failed in their attempt to leverage the multiple talents of their long-term contract star, Donald O'Connor.

O'Connor would finally emerge from the shadows of Deanna Durbin and Abbott & Costello at Universal, hitting his stride as a bankable star with the improbably successful Francis, the Talking Mule pictures. He would also score big in *Singin' in the Rain* over at Metro where they understood how to make musicals.

Double Crossbones paired O'Connor with Will Geer and a host of other character players in pirate mufti, most notably the gargantuan actress Hope Emerson as Maiden Ann Bonney. The multi-talented Emerson, who would be nominated for a Best Supporting Actress Oscar as a memorably sadistic prison matron in *Caged* (1950), could act, sing, dance and play the piano with consummate skill. She was also over six feet tall and weighed in at 240 pounds. During one scene when she had to be amorous with a timorously reluctant O'Connor, Emerson temporarily halted production when she inadvertently lurched into her diminutive leading man, pinning him against the ship's rail. The pratfall wasn't in the script and "neither was a cracked rib for O'Connor which had to be taped at the studio hospital before he could continue with the picture."[65]

Charlie was cast as Captain Ben Wickett, who confronts O'Connor in the opening scene of the film while flourishing a cutlass and remains front and center until taking a flying header over the Jolly Roger rail into the ocean. Makeup artist Bud Westmore certainly had McGraw look the part of a pirate. A Universal publicity release for the picture stated:

> In addition to livid scars and a scurvy beard, the character actor has been blessed with scar tissue pulling his right eye in a half-closed slit.[66]

Charlie so resembled a fearsome buccaneer that no one would reportedly sit with him in the studio commissary. Characteristically, the actor came up with a wry comment concerning his alleged alienation from the company: "[S]o, I am bringing my lunch in a paper sack ... and I think I am developing an inferiority complex."[67]

While it is doubtful that McGraw was socially constrained by pirate makeup or anything else, *Double Crossbones* garnered a genuine sense of inadequacy for Universal-International at the box office. After being released, the picture quickly faded from theatre marquees to reemerge as a late-night oddity on television during the 1960s. The picture has recently reappeared on DVD as part of a pirate movie collection released by Universal. Certainly a film with Charles McGraw and Hope Emerson in pirate garb toasting their collective health, merits rediscovery and enjoyment by a new generation.

McGraw made a final appearance over at Eagle-Lion in one of the most visually striking pictures associated with that short-lived Hollywood studio. This time around, director Anthony Mann cast McGraw as a fearsome "citizen soldier" under the command of the dreaded Robespierre in the period historical French adventure drama, *Reign of Terror* (1949). Continuing their sublime partnership, Mann's latest film was lensed by that virtuoso of noir photography, John Alton. If the combination of Mann and Alton weren't enough, *Reign of Terror* was nominally produced by the great William Cameron Menzies, of *Gone with the Wind* and *The Thief of Baghdad* production design fame. Menzies was probably the most accomplished set designer and storyboard sketcher who ever worked in Hollywood. *Reign of Terror,* alternately titled *The Black Book,* resembled a sumptuous historical lithograph. Mann claimed that he got the cost of the sets down to a mere $40,000 due in large part to Menzies:

> I got William C. Menzies to do them after interesting him in something new — that is, finding out for how little not how much the entire job could be done. Costume films usually have mammoth sets, but we built completely with flats…. Ceilings were used and the lighting was arranged from the floor, skirting the need to use rigging… "Imagination" was used to save costs in shooting the guillotine scene by placing the camera directly above the execution platform! We eliminated the necessity of shooting the back of the platform and most of both sides. By doing so, the mob scene was kept down to 90 people but gave the impression of many more.[68]

Unfortunately for those associated with the picture, the appreciation of their efforts was not reflected by a large audience turnout. The executive producer was the esteemed Walter Wanger, whose career was in freefall after the disastrous flop of *Joan of Arc* (1948), a poorly received spectacle starring Ingrid Bergman. The expensive failure ate up all Wanger's money, including the television rights he owned for David O. Selznick's films which were used as financing collateral. Eagle-Lion was able to sign Wanger to an independent production deal largely because he was desperate. *Reign of Terror* did little for Wanger's cash flow problems. Formerly one of Hollywood's most successful independent producers, Wanger would soon endure the triple whammy of declaring bankruptcy, shooting his wife's lover (the spouse, actress Joan Bennett, was having an affair with agent Jennings Lang) in the testicles, and then briefly going to prison.

Reign of Terror possesses a classic noir plot historically transplanted into the chaos of post-revolutionary France after the 1789 uprising. Robert Cummings plays a mythical Charles D'Aubigny, who impersonates an executioner named Laval in order to get close to the evil Maximillian Robespierre (Richard Basehart). Cummings is trying to get his hands on a book ("the McGuffin," as Alfred Hitchcock called it) which is the wannabe dictator's list of anticipated victims. Obtaining the Black Book will permit the democratic opposition to denounce and depose the power-mad Robespierre who is on the cusp of dictatorship. A voluptuous Arlene Dahl provides the romantic diversion for Cummings with an added plus of a terrific performance by Arnold Moss as a cynical, double-dealing leader of the secret police. Moss was a classically trained actor who spent most of his career on stage and had a Ph.D. in theatre studies. His rich bass voice, used to great effect on radio and in the theatre, contained nary a trace of his native Brooklyn. He also gets to wrap up the picture with an amusing bit of business about Napoleon Bonaparte.

As the sergeant in charge of torture and mayhem for Robespierre, McGraw had sparse dialogue but his face seemed to be in the frame of every other camera shot. Charlie was playing Moxie again, only this time with a bearded, greasy face, and wearing a period military uniform adorned with bent plumes and topped off with an outrageous fur hat. While in pursuit of Cummings and Dahl, McGraw deigns to threaten that queen of movie matrons, Beulah Bondi, and a group of peasant children (including a young Russ Tamblyn) with a brandished sword. Charlie later tortures Arlene Dahl behind a bakery while intermittently growling, slurping wine and stuffing food into his mouth.

Reign of Terror had a bifurcated production and release schedule. The picture was filmed at Eagle-Lion Studios and the Sherwood Forest area of Northridge, California from mid–August to early October 1948. The world premiere, held on June 16, 1949, in New Orleans was so underwhelming that Walter Wanger pulled the film back and had it extensively reedited. The picture was renamed with its original working title of *The Black Book* and released again, this time in

New York on October 15, 1949. The results of the retooling escaped critical notice as the film was regarded as an interesting, if standard, "B" programmer.

Would you trust this man? A wardrobe still of McGraw as the brutal sergeant from *Reign of Terror* (1949) (courtesy Mildred Black).

The last of McGraw's quartet of Universal films in 1949 was the least satisfying. *I Was a Shoplifter* (1950) was a potboiler programmer concerned with shoplifting-as-racketeering. Charlie is buried in the credits as "Man"—a bit part. Ditto for Rock Hudson as a store detective and Peggie Castle as a telephone operator. The leads are played by stolid Scott Brady—Lawrence Tierney's younger brother was a journeyman actor—and the colorless Mona Freeman. The audience is left only with lethal Andrea King as the shoplifting majordomo who has 24-year-old Tony Curtis in tow playing a hit man named Pepe. It wasn't enough to rescue this one. Devoid of suspense or humor, *I Was a Shoplifter* wasn't released until the end of April 1950.

Despite the indifferent ending to the year, Charlie's best role of 1949 was a memorable starring performance that hoisted his career up to the next level towards legitimate stardom. It was produced by the studio where McGraw would make some of his best-remembered films, RKO Radio Pictures.

9

The Capital of Noir

All of the pictures now called "film noir," produced by Hollywood during the classic period of 1940–1960, were variously pegged at their inception as crime dramas, mysteries, suspense films or melodramas. Few, if any people in the American movie business had ever heard the term film noir when these pictures were made. Film noir is strikingly different from other identifiable cinematic genres like comedies, musicals and westerns. There is no other classification of films with elasticity of meaning and elusiveness of definition that gushes forth a continuing, explanatory deluge of books, articles and scholarly treatises.

Film noir was initially coined as a genre term by a French critic named Nino Frank in a 1946 film journal piece to describe a series of Hollywood films screened in postwar Paris including *The Maltese Falcon*, *Double Indemnity*, *Laura*, *The Woman in the Window* and *Murder My Sweet*. These somber movies were perceived as fundamentally different from pre–1941 Hollywood fare. Frank's critique tugged at the common dark thread of criminality by describing the modern "social fantastic"[69] that coursed through this unique series of films.

Here was a new, culturally based reality that departed from the conventional Hollywood virtue of the stainless-steel hero, the reprehensible bad guy and the stereotypical happy ending. Conventional characters morphed into ambiguous, conflicted protagonists as the once-clear line between cinematic angels and helots became kaleidoscopically blurred. The traditional roles of women and men on screen became warped. Fate, temptation and compulsion became intertwined with violence … and it could demonstrably happen to anybody.

The French initially defined film noir as a uniquely American genre in the detached manner of the informed intellectual. Noir was described through the existential prism of culture, changing social convention and aesthetic tastes rather than mere cinematic formula, appearance or theme. Film noir defined truly lives in the shadows, resisting cultural and cinematic exactitude. The challenge to delineate film noir is reminiscent of the utterance of a Supreme Court jurist who, while struggling to quantify obscenity in a concurring judicial opinion, finally gave up and simply stated, "I know it when I see it."[70] Elusive in terms of explanation, film noir remains an immediately recognizable style.

It is appropriate to provide some cultural distinction between the term "film noir" from the word "noir." As film historian Foster Hirsch pointed out, the word "noir" has evolved into a marketing cachet for "a literary genre, a pop album and a perfume."[71] Noir as applied to film is a retrospective phenomenon that strikes a resonant, soulful vibe within film fans, historians, nostalgia buffs and lovers of American popular culture. The audience lives vicariously through the connection with darkly cast, fate-driven films with stories about adults who wore fedoras and nylons instead of backwards baseball caps and blue jeans designed with holes. While nostalgia buffs and senior citizens appreciate film noir as representative of a familiar, simpler time, younger people tend to visualize a part of their soul in the dark mosaic of the story and become willfully cognizant that the unfolding narrative could happen to them. The distinctive style of many RKO productions released during the classic film noir period of the late 1940s through the early 1950s garners the studio the retrospective sobriquet of "The Capital of Noir." Hardly anyone who worked at the Gower and Melrose Street complex in Hollywood during those years could have conceived of such a historical retrospective. Less than the results of any auteur, the characteristics of many RKO films were rooted in both the evolution of the studio and the artistic contributions of their long-term craft employees.

Radio-Keith-Orpheum Studios came to fruition as the progeny of Joseph Kennedy's Film Booking Office (FBO) organization and David Sarnoff's RCA Corporation in 1929. When Kennedy acquired control of the Keith-Albee-Opheum chain of vaudeville theatres to exhibit the product and absorbed the old Pathe Studio in Culver City, the new RKO was on its way. By the early 1940s, RKO had undergone through so many different corporate and ownership transitions and teetered on the edge of bankruptcy so frequently that the sole sustaining constants were a declining number of artfully financed "A" productions, a peerless technical department and, most critically, a solid theatrical chain to distribute product. Under the well-intentioned but fiscally obtuse management of George J. Schaefer, RKO lost millions in ill-fated deals with Orson Welles and Samuel Goldwyn. Film historians typically find it difficult to fault Schaefer's stewardship of RKO though. If it wasn't for Schaefer, *Citizen Kane* wouldn't ever have gotten made.

Although the enduring influence of *Citizen Kane* on the visual technique of film is unquestionable, it would be erroneous to attribute RKO's pedigree as a "film noir studio" solely to the pioneering use of deep focus, expressionistic photography in *Kane*. What would become a timeless film classic was based on the singular skills of director of photography Gregg Toland and Welles, who viewed RKO as a mere contracted entity and employed as many of his own Mercury Theatre resources as he could. Virtually overlooked in the decades of praise for the *Citizen Kane* production were the crafts and technical departments of RKO. Besides the later directorial fame of film editor Robert Wise, there was the costumer Edward Stevenson, set director Darrell Silvera along with the art and makeup departments who comprised a legion of forgotten contributors. Ever the iconoclast auteur, Orson Welles again went outside RKO for a director of photography when he hired Stanley Cortez to shoot his second film, *The Magnificent Ambersons* (1942).

Another overstated notion is that of RKO Studios serving as a "graduate academy" of editors-to-directors (Robert Wise, Mark Robson, Edward Dmytryk) who consciously selected and made their films to a personal style. Wise had it right when he remarked about RKO populist predilection for the film noir style:

> Really, the studio wanted to make pictures that worked at the box office. The stories chosen were flowing out of the popular tastes of the time.[72]

More than just the studio's catering to contemporary tastes, the shaded RKO film noir style was rooted in the technique of the contract cameramen who put their expressive stamp on films made at the studio over an entire generation.

Nicholas Musuraca, Harry J. Wild and, to a lesser extent, George Diskant worked with a plethora of producers and directors during their careers at RKO. As directors of photography, the work of these men is most responsible for the distinctive camera visuals that would come to be associated with the shaded noir ambient look. Musuraca, whose career at RKO dated back to the old FBO regime in 1927, remained a fixture at the studio until 1954 and lensed over 160 features. The veteran director of photography was the cameraman of choice for dark-shaded melodramas and crime films. Robert Wise remarked:

There were (RKO) cameramen who had that moody style, like Nick Musuraca who shot *Blood on the Moon*. If you used one of them, you'd get that sort of look....[73]

Musuraca photographed what might be the first "true" film noir, *Stranger on the Third Floor* (1940), and mastered a dark, reflective technique that was favored by many renowned directors. The roster of filmmakers that Musuraca shot film for is a veritable Who's Who of film noir: Robert Siodmak, Robert Wise, John Brahm, Mark Robson, Jacques Tourneur, John Farrow, Nicholas Ray, Fritz Lang and Ida Lupino. While these estimable directors ordered their own set-ups, frequently picked the particular lens and virtually always chose the scenes and close-ups, there is no question that Musuraca and his contemporaries unconsciously established the lighting and the look that epitomized the RKO dark noir visuals.

Another major element of RKO's film noir heritage was the studio's singular efficiency in making "B" films. RKO became superbly accomplished in the production of formulaic, cheap features during the war years under studio chief Charles Koerner, who succeeded the hapless Schaefer. People went to the movies continuously during World War II. Nearly ever material item was rationed, money was tight and there wasn't too much to do except go to the local theatre and try to forget about loved ones in harm's way. During the summer, a movie theatre was often the solitary location to bask in rarified air conditioning within what was still largely a country of small towns. The studios churned out movies faster than Henry Kaiser constructed World War II *Liberty* ships as "B" pictures filled the bottoms of continual double bills.

Budgets on most of the RKO programmers were usually in the $100,000–$200,000 range. This financial threshold assured a certain percentage of profits with the pictures being distributed to the studio's national movie theatre network. Talent was spotted and signed and everyone worked in a collegial environment that was demanding, but fraternal. Barbara Hale, who was signed by Charles Koerner in 1942, fondly remembered a wartime RKO that was "like a big college."[74] Many of the characters used in the "B" features were either contracted acting talent or artists such as Kay Kyser and Harold Peary borrowed from RKO's radio arm at RCA/NBC. Inexpensive, popular second-bill series such as the Great Gildersleeve, the Saint, the Falcon and Mexican Spitfire flourished at RKO. Add to it a high quality "B" unit developed by Val Lewton that turned out literate horror-fantasy films along with the previously cited craft and technical departments. RKO Studios possessed a dedicated cadre of employees with diverse skill sets who knew how to make pictures fast, cheap and frequently good.

Several of these second-tier pictures were spectacularly successful. Val Lewton's *Cat People* (1942)—Lewton's films were invariably saddled with clichéd titles foisted on him by Koerner—grossed an unbelievable $4,000,000 in the U.S. on a capital investment of less than $200,000. *Cat People* is frequently credited with saving an RKO organization that was once again verging on bankruptcy. As Lewton's artful films became successes and earned larger budgets, they became special exceptions to the majority of the typical second-features ground out by the nominal RKO "B" unit. The "B" unit films were cannon fodder for the RKO theatre chain to put something up on the screen after patrons were already settled in the seats for the first feature. Imbuing care and quality into "B" films became much more challenging at RKO following World War II. Lewton left the studio for what was believed to be greener pastures and bigger budgets. The heralded producer subsequently became miserable after producing flops at three successive studios and would die of a heart attack in 1951. Box office receipts precipitously declined after 1946. More notably, Howard Hughes bought RKO in 1948, which resulted in *everything* at the studio being turned upside down.

Besides the "B" movies specifically, the production of films in Hollywood during the studio system era was a structured, industrial process. Each major studio had large craft departments, time clocks, overhead, fixed assets, and real estate that were the trappings of a factory environment The industrial perspective of Hollywood filmmaking supports a valid, if contrarian viewpoint to the more unctuous dissemination about the auteur theory of filmmaking. The director-as-auteur theorem invariably casts the film director as an omnipotent, individual stylist responsible for most every nuance within an entire motion picture. The director was frequently less of a creative influence than the producer or the studio itself.

Under the traditional studio system, a film's producer, representing the studio, assembled the key elements (story, screenplay, actors, director) and was frequently the creative orchestrator of a given film. A singular example of this hierarchy was the career of legendary producer Hal Wallis at Warner Brothers. As accomplished a director as Michael Curtiz, whose 30+ pictures under Wallis included *The Sea Wolf, Casablanca, The Adventures of Robin Hood,* and *Yankee Doodle Dandy,* was never allowed to select actors, scripts, technicians or much of anything else. Curtiz was there to direct the shooting of the picture and that was all. Wallis micromanaged matters down to the minutiae level such as his personal selection of a live cockatoo to sit in Sydney Greenstreet's bar in *Casablanca.*

Despite this tiered arrangement, individual directorial stylists were not wholly canceled out, just uniquely challenged. An elite group of high-powered directors earned authority to run their own projects based on consistent quality results and profits. With repetitive box office successes came greater leeway, money and trust. Bankable directorial legends such as Hawks, Wyler, Stevens and Capra operated almost autonomously within a given studio or project with Capra, Wyler and Stevens forming their own production company after the war. These elite filmmakers were the cream of the crop, that many others keened to join.

Within the strictures of the system's time, budget and formulaic constraints, ambitious contract film directors exerted themselves to put a distinctive stamp of quality and style on their work. Nearly every young "B" film director wanted to move up to bigger budgets and more autonomy. Joseph H. Lewis was dubbed "Wagon Wheel Joe" due to his propensity for using different camera shots through varied sagebrush motifs in the numerous oaters he directed. Despite his directorial heavy lifting and obvious talent, Lewis never made it to the rarified air to helm front-line feature films. Edward Dmytryk, a former editor who labored in the trenches of "B" films before being anointed as a top flight director at RKO, put it frankly,

> You tried to get the studio brass' attention with something creative that would be noticed in the dallies ... this was how one tried to move up and out of "B" films.[75]

What Dmytryk remarked on correlates directly to what filmmaker-historian Martin Scorsese would later term "directing by smuggling"[76]: how directors tried to get their point or vision across to the audience while complying with studio dictates and remaining in step with prevailing moral and censorship standards as exemplified by the Breen Office. The long struggle between artistic expression and commercial realities for filmmakers had the studio brass perched firmly in the catbird's seat during the 1940s.

Each of the major studios evolved their own distinctive style that was more demonstrative than any group of individual film directors. MGM was the gold standard of sweeping romance, historical dramas, musicals and wholesome family entertainment. Fox went for mature, compelling drama, documentary-style films and took risks. Warners cranked out populist films peopled by working class stiffs, gangsters and gum-popping hash slingers with the proverbial heart of gold. During the so-called "golden age of Hollywood," MGM, Warner Brothers, Fox and RKO became analogous to Cadillac, Ford, Chevrolet and Oldsmobile. Hollywood was an industrial principality that was sustained by different factories all making the same product. It was the brands that were different.

The vast majority of the second feature productions at RKO and other studios, with lean-to-the bone budgets and short schedules, were completed as quickly as possible using inexpensive talent, sets and technical staff that were readily available and under contract. The objective was always to get the product to the theatre as quickly and cheaply as possible in order to maximize the profit potential. Rough-hewn studio executive Sid Rogell's management of second unit production at RKO was an emblematic case-in-point. As succinctly described by director Richard Fleischer, the evaluation process for RKO second features was somewhat less than artistic:

> Not many of the B pictures churned out by the Rogell unit were ever previewed. They were manufactured and dumped in the theatres owned by RKO. It didn't make any difference how good or how bad they were, they had their home on the lower half of a double bill. The only screening they got before release was in a projection room at the studio for Rogell and a few other people. I attended these screenings sitting next to him. About halfway through, he'd fall asleep. Either lights coming on or the obligatory noisy chase and shoot-out at the end of the film would wake him. Sid would stand, say two words—"Ship it"—and leave.[77]

Despite (and because of) this sausage-grinding methodology, the second features that slipped under the radar screen and remain appreciated as viable entertainment were a tribute to skilled and economical filmmaking that triumphed over multiple obstacles. Any artistic quotient was a result of interpersonal collaboration by people who took pride in their craft rather than any inspirational leadership from the revolving door RKO executive suite. Innovative producers and directors along with talented actors and a skilled, dedicated technical crew who cared enough to perform quality work despite the constant pressure from the studio brass to hurry up and get it done.

Charles McGraw returned to an RKO that was radically different from the studio where he had previously appeared in *Blood on the Moon* (1948) barely more than a year earlier. That memorable top-flight picture was completed under the Schary regime before Hughes bought the studio. If there is such thing as the "noir Western," this exquisitely crafted film, helmed by Robert Wise, is certainly the template.

Filmed in Sedona, Arizona and the town of Castaic, north of Los Angeles, screenwriter Lillie Hayward's *Blood on the Moon* is a beautifully crafted tale of unstable alliances and duplicity. Iterant cow puncher Robert Mitchum blunders into a range war instigated by his erstwhile buddy, Robert Preston. Preston is playing a deceitful triple game by romancing cattle rancher Tom Tully's lustful, gullible daughter (Phyllis Thaxter) while selling her rancher pop down the river with the homesteaders led by Walter Brennan and conniving with a corrupt Indian agent (Frank Faylen).

Mitchum was never better as the tough but mellow cowpoke. His "live and let live" loner code becomes gradually reversed by the realization that his erstwhile pal Preston is a rabid scoundrel who needs to be put down for the greater good.

Robert Wise selected Nicholas Musuraca as his DOP precisely to obtain the desired shaded look of dimly lit frontier streets, box canyons and darkened hotel rooms above a shabby saloon. A main event fight scene between Mitchum and Preston staged in a shadowy adobe bar is a worthy comparison to the best visuals that John Alton and Tony Mann ever offered up in one of their shared Eagle-Lion film noirs.

McGraw was distinctive as one of the leading homesteader agitators with the memorable moniker of Milo Sweet. Replete with beard, belted six-gun and a stogie clamped in his jutting jaw, he was memorably decked out in a furry buffalo robe that was worthy garb for a Winnipeg traffic cop in the dead of a frozen Canadian winter. Edward Stevenson's costume and wardrobe work in *Blood on the Moon* was truly authentic. From Mitchum and McGraw to Tully, Preston, Walter Brennan and everyone else in the cast, the picture was a visual primer on how cowboys should *look* as well as act.

McGraw goes West as Milo Sweet in the classic ***Blood on the Moon*** (1948).

Charlie and Robert Mitchum had initially met at Universal back in 1943 when they both had bit roles as sailors in *Corvette K-225*. Mitchum was now a star and McGraw was a supporting player who was looking for bigger things too. During the filming of *Blood on the Moon*, the pair truly hit it off and became friendly during the twenty-two days that McGraw spent on the picture. Mitchum loved true characters—he was one himself—and he immediately pegged Charlie as a fellow desperado who could match him drink for drink and story for story.

McGraw's return to RKO in 1949 placed him a completely different situation as an actor. Although his latest picture *The Threat* would entail less than a fifth of the budget than that of *Blood on the Moon*, this time Charles McGraw would be the unquestioned star.

The Threat (1949), with a working title of *Terror*, was envisioned as a typical second feature by the Rogell "B" unit. Felix E. Feist, son of an MGM executive, was an independent writer and director who cut his teeth working in the shorts department at Metro during the 1930s. Feist knew how to imbue quality into a shoestring Rogell assignment, having previously directed the perversely entertaining *The Devil Thumbs a Ride* (1947) starring Lawrence Tierney. Feist shot his latest picture on RKO soundstages with exteriors around the San Fernando Valley and out in the desert by Santa Susana at the Iverson Ranch. He would bring the film in slightly under budget at $221,235.

Charlie was hired at $1000 per week for a two-and-a-half week shoot and played a vengeful killer, "Red" Kluger, who breaks out of Folsom Prison to take vengeance on the D.A. (Frank Conroy) and police detective (Michael O'Shea) who sent him up. McGraw's erstwhile moll, willowy Virginia Grey, is brought along for a wild ride which includes smuggling the kidnap victims through the Inland Empire backroads of California in a moving van. The film becomes a highlight reel of McGraw-inspired mayhem including torture of the unfortunate Conroy with a pair of pliers and the cold-blooded murder of a policeman. The exciting escape denouement is climaxed by McGraw terrorizing everyone in a sweatbox of a shack hideout until the tables are finally turned.

McGraw's work in *The Threat* was akin to a virtuoso performance by a spitting cobra. Charlie spewed forth a hail of venomous insults, coercion and actual bullets in a portrayal of unabashed ruthlessness that startled audiences with its intense ferocity. McGraw's indelible performance reinforced his typecasting as a heavy, but he didn't worry too much about it if the picture was realistic and he was getting paid. "Oh, I don't mind playing the bum and tough guy

Charlie as maniacal Red Kluger staring down Frank Conroy and Michael O'Shea in *The Threat* (1949).

in pictures if it's real," Charlie explained. "But some of those long-haired writers kick it in the head because they seldom go outside a studio or college library. I really blow my top when they try to foist on me some foreign-born writer's idea of the New York or Chicago gangster world."[78]

The Threat garnered enthusiastic reviews in the trade papers and was widely received as a minor league *White Heat* (a film that had premiered with great fanfare a couple of months previously). More specifically, Charlie's performance became a minor sensation that invited comparisons to Richard Widmark's ruthless turn in *Kiss of Death* (1947). McGraw became a sensation and received the greatest public acclaim of his entire acting career:

> The honors of the show, however, are nabbed by Charles McGraw, whose distinctive voice, polished acting style and commanding presence help him dominate in the part of the gangster.[79]
> [F]ilm is particularly notable for star appearance of Charles McGraw. His interpretation of a ruthless and cold-blooded killer … is one of the year's best and it sweeps yarn along to stirring recital.[80]
> McGraw was an admirable exponent … of the hatchet-faced, rasp-voiced character with which the screen hoodlum has made us familiar.[81]
> Charlie McGraw's cold killer performance is a humdinger etched in uncompromising cruelty that helps keep the menace in high factor.[82]
> The title role is played by new-comer Charles McGraw and he does an outstanding job. His performance is so natural that he doesn't seem to be acting at all.[83]

Virginia Grey, McGraw's co-star, even went out of her way to compare Charlie to Burt Lancaster and Kirk Douglas.

Charlie's agent Paul Wilkins, moving quickly to capitalize on the bow wave of rave reviews, arranged for a full-page image of McGraw on the rear of both *Daily Variety* and *The Hollywood*

Charlie has a grasp of matters with Virginia Grey in *The Threat* (1949) (courtesy Mildred Black).

Reporter on Friday, November 4, 1949, lauding the star for his performance in *The Threat*. McGraw's positive notices and the plethora of fan mail addressed to him that was received by RKO following release of the picture convinced Howard Hughes that he needed to move quickly to lock up the suddenly marketable actor to a long-term deal. In an interesting recollection, Jill McGraw remembered her father at home, writing some of his own fan mail to RKO during this period in what was no doubt an inspired effort to impress the studio to offer him a long-term contract, better roles or both. How many of the so-called "fan letters" were actually written by McGraw remains a mystery. What was undeniable was that the positive publicity associated with McGraw's performance in *The Threat* made him a hot prospect. After viewing the first rushes on his next film, RKO offered Charlie a seven-year contract starting at $750 per week. McGraw inked the deal on January 14, 1950.

The McGraw–RKO agreement was indicative of the contractual half-nelson that the major studios continued to exert on their contracted artists. Even though Olivia de Havilland won her suit against Warner Brothers in 1944 that ended the pernicious custom of the studios adding suspension time to the term of a contract (this practice was found to violate California law against indenturment), the majors still retained a lot of contractual leverage. Although there were annual per week raises to a ceiling of $3000 per week in year seven scheduled for Charlie in the contract, the studio could terminate the agreement at any time. RKO also did not pay McGraw at any time for 12 weeks per year, including the possibility of suspension without pay for a veritable laundry list of possible sins, and could terminate the deal if McGraw got sick or was incapacitated for three consecutive weeks. The actor could perform no entertainment work whatsoever in films, radio, stage, or anywhere else without RKO's express permission.

Although the studio system was in the latter stage of its Cretaceous Period and the moguls continued to stomp around like the plutocratic dinosaurs of old, the tectonic plates under Hollywood in 1950 had begun to shift under the dual stresses of nascent television and especially the removal of studio theatre chains due to the anti-trust settlement with the government. Renowned action filmmaker Phil Karlson, who began as an assistant director back in the 1930s, believed the effect of the government consent decree was what fatally doomed the old movie industry. He recalled years later:

> People say television is what killed our industry. This didn't kill our industry. What killed our industry was divorcement. Studios and theatres, that's what killed us. When they came in with the idea that this was a complete monopoly — the guy that's making the picture that owns the theatre it's playing in and whatnot — that's when we got in trouble.[84]

The new pressures exerted more strain on the studio bosses. To cut costs, a plethora of writers and secondary artists were let go when the movie theatres were gradually separated from the studios; the consent decree took several years to take actual effect. Increasingly, the balance of power in Hollywood shifted away from the studios to the artists and their agents along with the unions and guilds. As exemplified by L.B. Mayer's professional demise, the studio moguls who were once the forerunners of cinematic innovation became startlingly ossified in their inability to face business realities and strategically manage what was a dynamically changing postwar movie market.

Television was initially dismissed or ignored as a no-account upstart instead of a direct competitor. Moguls like Jack Warner and Howard Hughes myopically treated their contracted talent as *property* (this term aptly summarized Hughes' view about loaning out his contracted artists to other studios) rather than collaborative employees. The initial policy of holding a pat hand in a climate of rapidly falling box office revenues quickly resulted in financial desperation that forced unprecedented compromises by the studios with their premier talent. Lew Wasserman at MCA obtained a revolutionary deal from cash-poor Universal-International for Jimmy Stewart that earned the great star fully half of the profits from *Winchester '73* (1950). Stewart ended up grossing $600,000 for a single film in an era when the top male star, Clark Gable, made only half that amount in salary during an entire year. The handwriting was on the wall of every major Hollywood studio: Power, once ceded, is seldom reacquired. The oligarch dictatorship of the studios that had ruled Hollywood since the days of silent movies was beginning to crumble. Fewer films would be made and the studios would pay dearly or be forced to become partners with their top talent.

Despite the strictures, Charlie was initially delighted with the RKO contract. For the first time, he obtained a measure of long-term financial security for himself and his family. His days of tending bar and setting up bowling pins to make ends meet were over. McGraw was excited by his good career fortune, but he was distracted by other diversions. With the largess from his plethora of work in 1949, Charlie was finally able to purchase the dream house that he had promised Freda.

10

The Other Side of the Hill

The slumbering San Fernando Valley was gradually awakening to the postwar suburban expansion by the end of the 1940s. The World War II population of 176,000 in the Valley had doubled by 1950 and would do so again by the end of the decade. Farmland was starting to quickly disappear due to a relentless real estate boom that was laying down tract houses faster than the infrastructure of sewers and paved roads could keep up. The land in the Valley seemed endless and the prices were cheap.

In 1949, McGraw purchased a hillside property at 3751 Reklaw Drive in Studio City. The house was a dogleg to the left off of Sunrise Terrace, just up the hill from Laurel Canyon Boulevard and less than a mile from the main drag of Ventura Boulevard. The house was originally built in 1936. It was eventually expanded it to 3200 sq. ft. with three bedrooms and three bathrooms including a downstairs room by 1950. The large backyard was a perfect setting for that emerging symbol of Southern California leisure and affluence, the swimming pool. McGraw quickly had an Olympic-size pool installed. Photos of the McGraw backyard while the pool was being installed display a hillside vista in Studio City with wide stretches of open land intermittently dotted with houses. Studio City, just over the hill from Hollywood, wasn't even close to being filled up in 1949.

Jill McGraw remembered that as a child, the seemingly vast expanses of the Valley just beyond Sepulveda Boulevard in Sherman Oaks were perceived as "all country."[85] The San Fernando Valley had been the exterior soundstage of Hollywood ever since D.W. Griffith filmed the Civil War battle scenes for *The Birth of a Nation* on a sloping rise that later became Forest Lawn Cemetery. At the crest of the Cahuenga Pass, Universal Studios' huge lot loomed over the entire valley like a gatekeeper. RKO had their ranch studio facility on 110 Encino acres (just east of Burbank Boulevard) that included a railroad station and a large town set where *The Hunchback of Notre Dame* (1939) and *It's a Wonderful Life* (1946) were filmed. Farther out in Calabasas, the Warner Ranch comprised nearly 3000 acres of rolling hills that was the backdrop for *National Velvet* and where Harry Warner had his estate and raised a stable of prized racehorses. The Valley was also used by the industry elite as a utilitarian playground. Beginning in the 1930s, Hollywood royalty including Clark Gable, W.C. Fields, Al Jolson and Francis Lederer among others had weekend country estates complete with orange groves out in Encino and Canoga Park. This practice would continue into the 1950s with James Cagney, Lucille Ball, Barbara Stanwyck and other cinematic notables owning large ranches in the still country environs of Chatsworth and Reseda.

The Valley also became home to a number of odd amusements. Foremost among these attractions was Monkey Island, located on three acres at 3300 Cahuenga Boulevard. A large troupe of monkeys ran amuck on a 100-foot plastic "island" complete with trapezes, waterfalls and palm trees. Inclined rustics could buy peanuts and throw them to the simians. Cargo netting was strung up to keep the primates secured, but escapes into the surrounding country

Charlie and Freda McGraw on holiday in the early 1950s (courtesy Mildred Black).

Keith's Café, Ventura Blvd, November 1950 (courtesy Mildred Black).

became routine. Period advertising touted, "No bars, No cages, No danger" and "1000 monkeys running loose."[86]

As suburbia encroached after the war, the perception of the Valley by Hollywood's elite became increasingly snooty as the working class moved in and tract homes replaced the orange groves and vistas of ranchland. From his long-time estate at Toluca Lake, Bob Hope sniped that the San Fernando Valley was becoming "like Cleveland with palm trees."[87] Robert Redford complained that his childhood was negatively impacted: "When we moved to the Valley, I felt like I was being tossed into quicksand."[88] Novelist Peter Israel neatly summed up the perception of greater Hollywood about the Valley in his 1974 novel *Hush Money*: "L.A. is surrounded by valleys, but there is only one valley and to everybody who lives on the other side of the hill from it, it's a standing joke." Israel's perceptive barb about the Valley is well-founded. Comedian Dick Martin, who used to tend bar at Herbert's Drive-In on the corner of Ventura and Laurel Canyon Boulevard, remarked that when he hit it big with Dan Rowan and moved to Hollywood, he would jokingly ask his buddies like Chuck Connors and Tim Conway (who lived in the Valley) if "they had their passports renewed to travel over the hill" to visit him.

None of this badinage about the Valley gave McGraw the slightest pause about the location of his domicile. Aside from going to locations for film shoots during the mid- to late 1950s, Charlie's Studio City residence was virtually next door to where he would be working for many years. Although best remembered for his RKO films, over a quarter of McGraw's total output of movies were produced at nearby Universal Studios. Also, Charlie may have landed a fat movie contract at RKO — his salary was the contemporary equivalent of over $5400 per week — but the actor remained working class in outlook and professed zero tolerance of the phony B.S. that

Charlie, Jill and Freda on the set of *Roadblock* (1951).

was so much a part of Hollywood and the film business. Of course, Charlie's tolerance for bull-shit was markedly enhanced when he was the one slinging the bull.

Studio City was home to the stuntmen, doubles, cowboys, electricians, best boys and mostly supporting actors— the proletariat of the film and the nascent television business. Right down the hill from Charlie's house was Republic Studios, a low-budget assembly-line where more Westerns and serials were foaled than from any other Hollywood studio. Ventura Boulevard was also a fun place to be during the evening hours. Drinking was a time-honored custom throughout much of the film colony. As director Raoul Walsh put it, "[T]here was a lot of laughing water around in those days."[90] The pubs of Studio City (O'Brien's, Keith's, The Blarney Stone, Herbert's Drive-In, and the Laurel Room) remained crowded with stuntmen and actors from Republic along with the usual assortment of local characters. Bobby Hoy, who first met McGraw in a Studio City bar in the early '50s, loved the ambience:

Studio City was great. Like a small little town. Everyone knew everybody. I had a good friend who worked at the 76 station. Everyone drank together: Actors, stuntmen, cops and crooks. We used to drink with Jack Whalen, the bookie who got killed in Rondelli's one night.[91]

The camaraderie between the actors, stuntmen, bar employees, and the other locals who hung out in the joints of Studio City became insular and unique. A movie star like Gene Autry was just another one of the boys buying a round. Millie Black, who worked in Studio City for years, remembered, "We all stuck together and had so much fun."[92] In an era before breatha-

The Butters Family enjoys an evening at the Biltmore in 1950 shortly after moving into the Reklew Drive house. Left to right: Frank Butters, Beatrice, Freda, Charlie and Jill (photograph courtesy Mildred Black).

lyzer tests and review boards, the L.A.P.D. would frequently cut slack for simple rowdiness or perhaps give a drunken actor a ride home. Millie recalled the Van Sickel father-and-son stunt team "trying to jump across Ventura Boulevard over the tops of the car and that was when three cars in a row was traffic!"[93]

McGraw quickly became known to everyone on the Boulevard. The new house on the hill was used for entertaining friends on weekends by the pool while the actor settled in at RKO for some of the most notable work of his career.

11

"Not Enough (Blood) to Suit Me"

On the strength of *The Threat*, McGraw was immediately cast in the cops-and-robber programmer *Code 3* by RKO. It was noted that McGraw's role as a policeman in *Code 3* "put him on the right side of the law rather than against it when he did brutal murderers in *The Killers* and *The Threat*."[94]

RKO Studios took ample opportunity to trumpet McGraw's new contract:

Charles McGraw Gets Contract: With only one film and the "rushes" of a second to his credit at RKO Radio, Charles McGraw has been signed to a seven-year starring contract by this studio. McGraw, a young Broadway stage actor is a discovery of the late Mark Hellinger who introduced him to films as one of the two killers in *The Killers*. He made his bow at RKO with a stellar role in *The Threat* and then was signed for *Code 3* which is now in production.[95]

Code 3 evolved from a number of different writers. The Earl Felton story treatment was based in part on a non-fiction article (*Gravesend Bay* by Richard Carroll and Charles Peet) concerning the 1934 armored car heist at the Rubel Ice Company in Brooklyn. Another script was written by Gerald Drayson Adams with Robert Angus and Robert Leeds receiving credit as well. While both Adams and Felton received screenwriting credit, the final shooting script for *Code 3* reflects the definitive style of Earl Felton, one of Hollywood's most pithy and incorrigible hard-boiled screenwriters. He started out at Warners in 1936, wrote the original story and screenplay for *The Beautiful Blonde from Bashful Bend* at Fox, and really hit his stride at RKO starting in the late 1940s. Felton, who got around on crutches due to childhood polio, was perfectly matched with director Richard Fleischer on *Code 3*. The noir programmer would be the second of an eventual seven cinematic collaborations. The duo proved to be a superb writer-director team.

Dick Fleischer was the son of the famous animator Max Fleischer, creator of Popeye the Sailor and Betty Boop. The younger Fleischer was clearly a prodigy. His acumen as a stage director while at Yale impressed an RKO talent scout and Fleischer was quickly signed by the studio as a director. After paying his dues making *March of Time* documentaries and the remarkably innovative *Flashback Flicker* shorts, Fleischer was subsequently assigned to Sid Rogell's "B" picture unit in 1947. *Code 3* would be Dick Fleischer's sixth feature at RKO. Not surprisingly, the 34-year-old director was ambitious and was looking for a path out of second-tier film direction.

Fleischer completed the picture that would be released with the memorably cogent title of *Armored Car Robbery* in an economical 16 days of filming. The efficient production time was impressive based on the number of locations that were used: Wrigley Field in South Central L.A., the oil fields near Torrance at 233rd Street, out in the Valley by Ventura Blvd and Vineland Street, and the Metropolitan Airport tarmac.

As Lieutenant Cordell of L.A.P.D. Robbery-Homicide, Charles McGraw was John Law personified. His partner on the crime beat was Hollywood's prototype Irish cop, James Flavin.

Men at work: Director Richard Fleischer reviews matters with McGraw during the filming of *Armored Car Robbery* (1950) (courtesy of Mildred Black).

Jimmy Flavin was a West Point graduate who ditched a military career for acting. From being the second mate on the ship that captured *King Kong* (1933) to bludgeoning Henry Fonda with an axe handle in *The Grapes of Wrath* (1940), Flavin worked constantly during a 44-year career in Hollywood with over 450 film appearances, most of them as cops. McGraw and Flavin proved to be a taciturn pair of bookend L.A. robbery-homicide detectives who communicated between pauses. They are matched against arch criminal Dave Purvis (William Talman) who masterminds a daring armored car robbery at L.A.'s now-forgotten Wrigley Field baseball park. During the robbery and subsequent gunfight, Flavin is fatally wounded and Purvis escapes. McGraw seethes. He has lost his alter-ego and didn't foil the robbery. After uttering the bluntest expression of bereavement in film history ("Tough break, Marsha") to Flavin's widow in the hospital waiting room, McGraw's pursuit of Talman and the robbery gang immediately gathers momentum.

   William Talman was a worthy screen adversary for Charlie. A Dartmouth graduate, Talman came to Hollywood as an Actor's Equity rep in the late 1940s with his then wife, actress Lynne Carter, and signed a contract with RKO. From his debut as a merciless killer in *The Woman on Pier 13* (1949), Talman's baleful acting skills cemented his reputation as a purveyor of malevolent menace in *The Hitchhiker* (1953), *City that Never Sleeps* (1953), *Big House U.S.A.*

"Tough break, Marsha": McGraw offers the bluntest expression of bereavement in film history to Anne Nagel in *Armored Car Robbery* (1950).

(1955) and *Crashout* (1955). Talman's ominous persona, accentuated by his protruding eyes, high forehead and wavy hair, gave him the visual cast of a malevolent space alien who happened to wander into a film noir. Certainly no one at the time believed that the actor would later earn national recognition as that relentlessly inept district attorney Hamilton Burger, matched against an even more ominous film noir heavy turned good guy, Raymond Burr, in television's *Perry Mason*.

In *Armored Car Robbery*, Talman beds burlesque queen Adele Jergens while double-cross-

A break in the action during the filming of *Armored Car Robbery* (1950): L to R: Charles McGraw, Steve Brodie and Don McGuire (courtesy Mildred Black).

ing and then finishing off her low-life husband (Douglas Fowley) who impeded the gang's escape after being inconveniently gut-shot by McGraw during the robbery. Jergens and Talman celebrate Fowley's death and sole possession of the robbery loot during passionate clinch inside a room at a San Fernando Valley motor court; it is apparent that there is no chance for redemption for this noir-crossed pair.

McGraw, decked out in classic Robbery-Homicide mufti of belted raincoat and pulled-down fedora, is relentless in pursuit of the holdup gang who killed his partner. No punches are pulled as he closes ground on the elusive Talman while inhaling reheated squad room java and snapping off terse Earl Felton dialogue:

> Lab technician (extending bloody painter coveralls for examination): "Whoever wore these got plugged. Note the hole."
> McGraw (looks down): "I see it. I put it there."
> Cop (inspecting abandoned getaway car): "There's a lot of blood in the backseat, lieutenant."
> McGraw (glances in the car): "Not enough to suit me."[96]

In an exciting finale, Talman ends up decapitated on the Metropolitan Airport tarmac courtesy of an arriving airplane, amid a blizzard of purloined greenbacks. His work complete, McGraw finally relaxes long enough to share a laugh with his new partner (Don McClure), recuperating in the hospital after being clipped by a Talman bullet. *Armored Car Robbery* is a fast-paced, entertaining 67-minute caper film that will likely hold up forever. Adding heft is the superb location filming that provides an insightful look at the Los Angeles of over a half century ago.

McGraw confronts one of the most striking femme fatales in noir, the sultry Adele Jergens in *Armored Car Robbery* (1950).

An interesting historical perspective about censorship provided in some of the correspondence about armored car robbery between RKO and the Production Code Administration. The Code office was run by the resolute Joseph I. Breen. Breen's office had Motion Picture Association of America (MPAA) approval authority over all movies released for public exhibition. The studio moguls cemented this system into place after the hue and cry by the Catholic Church and similar public moral guardians who threatened a boycott of Hollywood's product, hereafter dubbed "pre–Code" films, during the early 1930s. The studios believed that they needed an independent overseer to rein in the prurient impulses of filmmakers to protect their golden goose from … themselves. Although Breen was a pompous moralist, the actual censorship road-block was a narrowly written, rigid code that the studios chained themselves to. The Code system became an administrative limbo bar which producers and directors had to navigate under or around in order to get their pictures approved for release. The initially submitted script for *Armored Car Robbery* raised some of the moralistic hackles at the Breen office which were retrospectively typical. Breen urged RKO to ensure that Adele Jergens' breasts remained appropriately hidden during the burlesque numbers in the film. Any hint that Jergens' character was a loose woman (i.e., stripper) must be either "eliminated or downplayed."[97] Breen was also appalled that the audience might conclude that the Jergens character, Yvonne Le Doux, was actually having extramarital sex with Bill Talman's amoral gangster in a motel room. Breen demanded that some of the minimally suggestive dialogue between the two actors during the hotel room sequences be revised to reflect a more exculpatory relationship. Earl Fenton made some cosmetic changes to the script to allay Breen's fears before filming began and the finished product was stamped with the MPAA seal and released.

Armored Car Robbery opened in Hollywood at the Pantages Theatre as the second billed feature under *The Good Humor Man* on June 8, 1950. The RKO programmer garnered mostly positive reviews with McGraw's lockjaw performance being noted as especially praiseworthy. Charlie would be subsequently considered for several major RKO projects that didn't come off: *The Johnny Broderick Story*, about a legendary Broadway copper, and *The Golden Gloves Story*, slated to be helmed by Felix Feist. It was beginning to become increasingly clear that shelved, canceled and delayed movies at RKO Studios were now the normal mode of operation.

In order to put the balance of McGraw's film work at RKO along with his relatively quick departure from his contract in perspective, the studio's decline under the certifiable management of Howard Hughes merits an appropriate measure of detail.

12

The Certifiable Howard Hughes

While the profusion of books, articles, movies and television programs about Howard Hughes are biblical in scope, his ownership of RKO Studios has often been little more than a footnote compared to some of his more notable exploits. One of the most bizarre personalities ever to control a major film studio, Hughes' disastrous stewardship at RKO arguably hastened the decline of the entire studio system in Hollywood.

In addition to his notable aerospace and business accomplishments, Hughes previously produced several memorable films: *The Racket* (1928), *Hell's Angels* (1930) and *Scarface* (1932). While Hughes could drive complex engineering projects and hired capable people to run his other businesses, the balanced temperament and specialized skill sets required to run a delicately complex operation like a movie studio were noticeably absent from his personal repertoire. Hughes frankly didn't care too much about the business of making movies to turn a profit. He was a man governed by his personal obsessions and foremost among them was sex. Owning a studio gave Hughes unfettered access to beautiful women. His long-time director of Hughes Tool Company and majordomo Noah Dietrich explained:

> Howard's involvement with RKO had other motivations than the pursuit of profit and furtherance of the art of the cinema. It also aided the exercise of his libido. I was never certain throughout Howard's long association with the motion picture industry whether his amours were an offshoot of that activity or film production was a screen for his romantic adventures.[98]

Since his near-fatal airplane crash in Beverly Hills while piloting his prototype XF-11 aircraft on July 7, 1946, Hughes' oddball personal behavior quirks (including constantly washing his hands to avoid germs and secluding himself from public view) became increasingly pronounced. These obsessive traits eventually morphed into genuine neurosis as Howard Hughes became the world's richest reclusive psychotic. He would eventually exist in penthouse hotel suites secluded by a phalanx of aides, hair uncut, nails overgrown, lying naked on filthy sheets, watching endless movies in between enemas, pills and self-administered narcotic injections. By the time of his death in 1976, Hughes was a pitiable wreck who weighed less than 100 pounds, was covered with bedsores and had broken hypodermic needles imbedded in his pipe-cleaner thin arms.

While Hughes' tragic excesses would earn him posthumous notoriety, at the time he assumed control of RKO Studios he was viewed as a unique, if mercurial source of money and influence in Hollywood. From the first moment Hughes purchased RKO on May 11, 1948, for the bargain price of $8.8 million, the new mogul's famed eccentricity was on display. After touring the RKO main complex on Gower and Melrose Streets, Hughes' response to being queried about what he thought of the entire property (including sound stages, buildings and thousands of employees) was tersely clipped off to an underling: "Paint it!"[99]

As studio owner, Hughes permitted minimal freedom of ideas and decision-making by experienced RKO executives and immediately began meddling in film production details. The incumbent RKO production chief, Dore Schary, believed his initial concerns about Hughes were alleviated after during a reassuring meeting with the laconic Texan. Hughes then directed Schary to halt production on three features, including *Battleground* and *The Set-Up*, and demanded that his production chief fire Barbara Bel Geddes due to her lack of sex appeal. Schary resigned from RKO on July 1, 1948.

The next falling shoe was the layoff of three-quarters of the studio's employees several weeks after they were reassured that their jobs were safe. Production was cut to the bone as the studio survived on a backlog of films already in the hopper from the Schary era. Film executives struggling to revive the studio were either fired or quit in despair after attempting to work for Hughes.

The core business of RKO making films for a profit became secondary to Hughes' varied obsessions including accentuation of Jane Russell's breasts, purging real and imagined Communists from the studio payroll and stashing starlets like concubines all over town to await his late night phone calls and infrequent personal appearances. Howard became especially fixated with remaking the endings of films. As director Richard Fleischer put it, this particular Hughes mania earned him the reputation of an "anal erotic."[100] Since Howard Hughes' attention span was akin to a rotating 360-degree lighthouse beam that momentarily paused on an individual picture then quickly moved on, the incomplete films at RKO piled up and release dates kept getting pushed backward.

Howard Hughes around the time he bought RKO Studios.

Perhaps the principal example of how Hughes' irrationality was ruining RKO was McGraw's next feature, *His Kind of Woman* (1951). Originally titled *Smiler with a Gun*, the picture was a full-blown "A" production about a gambler forced to involuntarily impersonate an international syndicate chief who is involved in criminal intrigue down in Mexico. The project was intended to showcase the studio's two biggest contract stars, Robert Mitchum and Jane Russell. Fifth-billed Charlie had a secondary role as a gangster henchman; he also narrated the film's introduction.

Robert Mitchum was the biggest male star on the RKO lot and would stick loyally by Howard Hughes throughout his seven-year contract that he inked in 1947. The laid-back actor owed Hughes big-time after Mitchum's notorious 1948 pot bust in a Laurel Canyon bungalow. Hughes, making a decision of personal loyalty that was also good business for RKO, stood firmly behind Mitchum with a guaranteed loan and a retainer for famed Hollywood trial lawyer Jerry Geisler to negotiate the charge down to a misdemeanor beef. Hollywood gossip also had it that

Hughes additionally faced down his fellow studio moguls at a high stakes poker game and warned them to lay off of blackballing Mitchum. With a neat plea bargain arranged by Geisler and his finances covered, Mitchum breezily termed his brief incarceration in the L.A. county prison farm at Castaic " … like Palm Springs without the riffraff."[101] The star returned to RKO with his popularity greatly enhanced.

Jane Russell successfully dodged Hughes' romantic blandishments but remained one of Howard's principal fixations dating back to the Croesus's earlier obsessive vision in *The Outlaw* (1943). The unpretentious Russell became an increasingly popular Hollywood star. She shared a unique screen chemistry and a warm, platonic friendship with the equally unaffected Mitchum, who nicknamed her "Hard John."

McGraw and Mitchum picked up their joint propensity for bullshitting hours away in saloons right where it left off during their assignment in *Blood on the Moon* (1948). Mitchum's younger brother, John, later to become a noted character actor in his own right, asserted that Charles McGraw was cast in *His Kind of Woman* as a possible counterbalance to the recalcitrant Mitchum, who was allegedly having trouble with the RKO hierarchy. While there is no evidence to support this assertion, the younger Mitchum would later strike up an enduring friendship with McGraw, of whom he averred, "[He] kept going 20 hours per day and drank two cases of beer during the same period."[102]

Production filming on *His Kind of Woman* began on March 27, 1950, with the veteran John Farrow at the helm. Farrow was an accomplished director whose professional résumé included a string of impressive noir films: *The Big Clock* (1948), *Alias Nick Beal* (1949), *Night Has a Thousand Eyes* (1949) and *Where Danger Lives* (1950). A hard-drinking philanderer (the director was married to actress Maureen O'Sullivan), Farrow was universally disliked for his rude, often abusive treatment of actors and crews.

Shortly after shooting began on *His Kind of Woman*, the director's cantankerous disposition triggered a memorable incident that was vividly recalled by Bobby Hoy. McGraw and Mitchum walked onto the soundstage one midday and were sharing a laugh when Farrow, a good distance away and not able to see the pair clearly, whirled to a production assistant and yelled to get those two loudmouths off the set. Charlie and Mitchum looked at each other, shrugged and repaired to Lucy's El Adobe Café, a favorite lunch joint across the street where the tacos were delicious and the beer was on ice. After a few cold pops, Mitchum mentioned to Charlie how much fun New Orleans was, particularly during Mardi Gras. McGraw replied that he had never been to the Crescent City. The inebriated pair wound up in New Orleans on Bourbon Street the next day, having a fine time, while RKO was attempting to figure out what happened to their two leading actors who seemingly vanished into thin air. Bobby Hoy finished the story:

> They [RKO executives] go to Lucy's and they hear the cashier say that that Charlie and Mitchum were talking about Louisiana and New Orleans or whatever. So Hughes and his people find them down there and they have a man down there who works for Hughes or whatever. They find them at the hotel and say, "Here are two tickets. Get them on the plane and get them back here." So [McGraw and Mitchum] get the tickets and cash them in! They take the Super Chief, the train, and they get into New Mexico. They see a sign for cold beer and cochina dolls. So they get off. The next thing you know, they see the back of the train heading for the horizon! So, people put two and two together or whatever, and they fly an airplane in to take them back to Hollywood. You know, Hughes loved those guys....[103]

Hughes did admire the sporting life style of his AWOL actors and got them back in the fold in time to have Farrow wrap up shooting on May 23, 1950. Charlie performed smoothly in his henchman role, being killed in a climactic gun battle with Vincent Price, and moved on to other work. However, the production of *His Kind of Woman* took on a life of its own. Hughes screened the film but, as was his habit, didn't like the ending. The film languished for months in post-production while Howard dithered with other issues. After some additional process shots by Robert Stevenson in October 1950, Hughes summoned Richard Fleischer in December of 1950. Fleischer was currently on suspension for refusing to direct a hackneyed "B" programmer. He desired either immediate ascension to top-tier productions or, more pointedly, a release from his RKO contract. Moreover, he desperately wanted his most recent film, *The Narrow Margin,* released intact by RKO. At the recommendation of Sid Rogell, the frustrated director wrote an impassioned plea to Hughes that resulted in a perfect *quid pro quo* for both men. Howard wanted the ending of *His Kind of Woman* to be more dramatic and exciting. Fine. Fleischer would reshoot the ending according to the studio head's detailed instructions, provided that *The Narrow Margin* was released intact and he was released from his contract when the ending was reshot. Hughes agreed.

Earl Felton rewrote the additional scenes and Fleischer went about having a yacht set built on Stage 22 at the RKO Culver City lot. During the late-night story meetings that Fleischer and Felton would have with Hughes—a lot of back and forth yelling by the director and writer was necessary to communicate with Hughes since he was stone deaf and didn't care to acknowledge it—the ending of the film got longer and longer as the yacht set began to expand to *Spruce Goose*–like proportions. Another yacht had to be located by Fleischer in San Pedro with the appropriate engine room interior to please Hughes. The entire production of *His Kind of Woman* became like a kid's science project for Howard to tinker with. Whatever Hughes wanted got built, bought or otherwise added to the picture as the budget and schedule went over the transom.

Shooting on the revised ending for *His Kind of Woman* began on January 10, 1951. After the added scenes were completed and privately screened, Hughes pronounced himself satisfied, except for the actor who played the lead gangster character, Ferraro. Hughes said the actor in Farrow's original footage, annoyed him. No problem. Fleischer went through the grueling process of locating and testing dozen of actors until Hughes agreed with the selection of the ominous Robert J. Wilke to play the heavy. The well-regarded Wilke, fondly remembered by Hollywood old-timers for his superb portrayals of Western heavies and a great golf game, stepped in and the subsequent Ferraro sequences, nearly every scene that Fleischer had already completed, were begun again. After the new scenes with Wilke were almost done, actor Raymond Burr appeared at Fleischer's elbow on the set one day explaining that he had been contracted by Hughes to play Ferraro. Stunned, the director phoned Hughes' office and they confirmed the change. All of the Wilke footage was scrapped. Fleischer started over again.

By May of 1951, after more than a year of working on *His Kind of Woman,* Robert Mitchum's disposition reached critical mass. For the frustrated actor, the film had become akin to an indeterminate sentence back at the Castaic honor camp. The endless shooting, including dozens of screen tests with different Ferraro actors and the debilitating fight scenes in the steam-filled engine room and the ornate yacht set with Hughes requiring retake after retake, had all taken their toll. Mitchum's already robust intake of off-hours alcohol increased to stupendous levels. The star had reportedly taken to stashing booze around the set and was taking nips while working. RKO production records of these final weeks provide an apt account of Mitchum's deterioration and subsequent meltdown:

5/26/51: Waited for Mr. Mitchum from 3:30 p.m. to 4:25 p.m., get made up and dressed. Unable to photograph him due to his eyes, rehearsed only.
5/28/51: Company waited from 1325 till 1350 for Mr. Mitchum.

5/31/51: [O]ne hour spent shooting two versions of several scenes.

6/01/51: Finished shooting 1650. Crew cleared set. Dismissed 1700. Mr. Fleischer rehearsed with Mitchum and Burr until 1800.

6/2/51: [C]ompany waited from 2:30 to 3:40 for Mitchum. Changed setup. Made shot with Burr and Caruso when we learned Mitchum would not be back.

6/8/51: Dismissed Mitchum at 1545, Burr at 1610/ Production Closed.

6/7/51: "From 0900–0925, Director and Mitchum having conference.[104]

According to Dick Fleischer, what happened behind the scenes was that Mitchum's temper finally blew during the iterative shooting of the final fight scenes on the yacht set. Flying into a drunken rage, the star got into a physical altercation with some of the stuntmen and subsequently destroyed the entire set. With Job-like patience, the director sent the company home and had the set rebuilt overnight. Fleischer confronted his hung-over star the next morning and obtained a humiliated pledge of further cooperation. The filming resumed. Shooting was mercifully wrapped on June 12, 1951. There was a single day of retakes with Burr that would be used to open the film and some continuity shots of Russell and Mitchum on August 3, 1951.

His Kind of Woman debuted on August 29, 1951, to mixed reviews. The film was notable for Mitchum and Russell's screen kinetics as well as Vincent Price's joyously hammy performance as a conceited Hollywood actor. The film's legacy is something less than film noir, but more of a "movie-movie" with a galaxy of unique screen personalities clipping off pithy, funny lines which transcend a farfetched story that nobody cared about anyway.

For RKO, the film was another step down the road to financial perdition. From an original budget of $1,109,538, the extravagant new sets, months of added scenes and countless retakes added another $850,000 to the final tally—almost precisely what the picture lost at the box office. For Charlie McGraw, his fame and fortune ended up on a marked upswing as his most definitive screen role had arrived.

13

The Sleeper That Almost Wasn't

The "golden age" of Hollywood was not a screenwriter's utopia. Once one got past a short list of elite scribes, most writers were treated as secondary contract employees who were often forced to silently watch their work be either butchered or appropriated by others amid low-ball studio paydays. For every Ben Hecht, there were many more writers who had to take what they got, which often wasn't very much.

Stanley Rubin was determined to start producing films after a decade of churning out screenplays and original stories at Universal. Despite (or because of) serving on the first negotiating committee of the Writers Guild with the studios in 1942 (Rubin recalled that he hadn't received a single raise that bumped him past $65 per week during his first four years at Universal), the former editor of the *UCLA Bruin* knew that producers had financial and creative control over projects and made the money. Rubin also felt that there were other writers who were better at the craft than he was. A modest man, he believed that his talent as a writer would be better served in the capacity of producer who selected the screenwriter. In addition to his considerable abilities and native Bronx moxie, Rubin's ace in the hole was his agent, Ray Stark. Stark, nicknamed "The Rabbit" by his mother-in-law, vaudeville legend Fannie Brice, possessed a shrewdness that belied his short stature and buckteeth. He would later become one of Hollywood's most consistent and powerful money-making producers. He negotiated a deal for Stanley Rubin to sell an original story and screenplay to RKO and produce the subsequent film. The studio quickly agreed to Stark's terms. Rubin had recently won the nascent Television Academy's first Emmy award for his production of de Maupassant's *The Necklace* and looked to be a comer.

RKO quickly reneged on their agreement to have the thirty-three-year-old Rubin produce *Macao* starring Robert Mitchum and Jane Russell. Howard Hughes refused to entrust an "A" film budget and his two biggest stars to a rookie producer on his first solo project. Ray Stark worked out an acceptable compromise. RKO would allow Rubin to produce a "B" film of his own selection — story, director, writer and cast — in order to prove himself for future top-tier projects. Stanley initially didn't care for the studio breaking their commitment, but quickly acquiesced to the middle ground. It would turn out to be a fortuitous set of circumstances for the new producer. *Macao* (1952) ended up as a Hughes-inspired muddle that employed eight different writers and two directors before it was mercifully wrapped. The consolation prize became something much better.

Rubin became enamored of an original story entitled *Target* written by Martin Goldsmith and Jack Leonard that he bought for $5000. *Target* was a tense yarn about an L.A.P.D. detective escorting a crime boss's wife back to L.A. via train to testify about a "payoff list" with a team of mob torpedoes is in hot pursuit. Rubin correctly believed the tale combined the tough-toned elements of a hard-boiled crime drama with the suspense of a true mystery. After reuniting Earl Felton and Richard Fleischer to write and direct the picture, Rubin supervised a synergistic team of actors and technicians of significant ability and synchronized teamwork: "I never worked with a more relaxed, harmonious group—cast, director, writer, photographer, you name it."[105] Charlie was cast in the lead role as the detective-sergeant alongside Marie Windsor and Jacqueline White.

McGraw is pitted against the mob while transferring material witness and tough-as-nails gangster's widow Mrs. Neil (Windsor) out to L.A. via train from Chicago to testify before the special rackets grand jury. The trip turns deadly before it starts when thugs whack out his aging partner (Don Beddoe) shortly after they arrive in Chicago to transport Windsor under guard to Union Station. The balance of the film has the mob pursuing McGraw and Windsor in an effort to bump her off and prevent her testimony in Los Angeles with considerable twists and turns along the way.

The crooks first try to bribe McGraw and begin getting rough when he proves to be incorruptible. The story nimbly segues into a subplot with a lady on the train (Jacqueline White) and her hyperactive kid (a talented juvenile, Gordon Gebert) who become entangled with McGraw during the trip. McGraw displays a deft touch with comedy when he has to periodically disengage from the child while building a mutual attraction for the perplexed White (who turns out to be the *actual* Mrs. Neil). All of this byplay occurs while Charlie strives to keep his mission confidential amid the non-stop action within the claustrophobic environment of the moving train. In the end of the original cut of the film, Windsor is killed by the mob and revealed to be a policewoman as the bewildered McGraw discovers that his deceased partner was on the payoff list as a corrupt cop and that he (McGraw) was also under suspicion. Charlie recovers his élan in time to foil the bad guys and rescue the comely White, whom he squires away down the Union Station ramp towards the Los Angeles County Courthouse to testify.

McGraw was astoundingly effective in *The Narrow Margin*. Richard Fleischer iteratively reminded Charlie that he was always "under pressure,"[106] directorial guidance that positively influenced McGraw's performance. The actor took center stage, displaying the full range of emotions of a multi-faceted characterization: tough with the crooks, sarcastically disdainful with Marie Windsor, bereaved and guilty over his dead partner, and charming and romantic with Jacqueline White. Stanley Rubin recalled, "Dick and I really believed in Charlie and he did a terrific job."[107] McGraw's truculent terseness was on display from the film's opening sequence. When partner Don Beddoe idly queries Charlie during a cab ride about what kind of a dish "Mrs. Neil" (Windsor) will turn out to be, McGraw quickly retorts: "The sixty cent special. Cheap. Flashy. Strictly poison under the gravy."[108]

Marie Windsor was the perfect foil as the vitriol-spitting gangster's wife, reluctantly protected by McGraw on the train trip west and ultimately revealed as an undercover cop. Windsor, the ultimate film noir bad girl, possessed luxurious bedroom eyes that accentuated a delectable 5'9" figure of jaw-dropping sexuality. Her visual charms were just one part of the package. Marie was a superb actress who worked hard at her craft and possessed a burning ambition to become a legitimate movie star.

Putting McGraw and Windsor together proved to be a master stroke of casting. Earl Felton's screenplay is highlighted by some of the most dyspeptic, bare-knuckled billingsgate ever. Here is one of the memorable exchanges between the star-crossed pair:

> McGraw: Sister, I've met some hard cases in my time, but you make 'em all look like putty. You're not talking about a bag of gumdrops that'll get smashed—you're talking about a dame's life. You may think it's a funny idea for a woman with a kid to stop a bullet for you, only I'm not laughing.
> Windsor: Where do you get off being so superior? Why shouldn't I take advantage of her? I want

to live. If you had to step on someone to get something you wanted real bad, would you think twice about it?

McGraw: Shut up.

Windsor: In a pig's eye, you would. You're no different than me.

McGraw: Shut up!

Windsor: Not till I tell you something, you cheap badge pusher! When you started this safari you made it plenty clear I was just a job with no joy in it. Remember?

McGraw: Yeah, and it still goes, double.

Windsor: Okay, keep it that way. I don't care whether you dreamed up the gag or not; you're going right along with it, so don't go soft on me. And once you handed out a line about poor Forbes getting killed 'cause it was his duty. Well, it's your duty too. Even if this dame gets murdered.

McGraw: You make me sick to my stomach.

Windsor: Well, use your own sink! And let me know when the target practice starts.[109]

Jacqueline White was cast as the other female lead by pure chance. A contract player who came across as apple pie natural on screen, White had notched appearances in "A" productions such as *Thirty Seconds Over Tokyo* (1944) and *Crossfire* (1947) along with lead roles in RKO 'B" features. The Beverly Hills native had married late in 1948 and left California with her husband to start up an oil business in the frontier environs of Wyoming. She vividly recalled the serendipitous nature of her casting opposite McGraw:

> After I came back to Los Angeles and had my first baby, I went to the RKO commissary to visit friends with my new child. Richard Fleischer saw me in the commissary and asked me if I was interested in the picture. Of course I was thrilled and immediately agreed.[110]

The suddenly *un*-retired actress also indicated that her husband, intent on building a business career and what would turn out to be a family of five children, was somewhat less thrilled with his wife's acceptance of what would be her final screen role., but good-heartedly toughed it out.

The hemmed-in atmosphere of a train was captured perfectly by Fleischer, who used a hand-held camera in several sequences, a major innovation over a half-century ago, to accentuate the train motion and close-in action. The "train" was a set and the motion of movement was created by the moving camera and the design of the set itself. Gordon Gebert, the nine-year-old actor who played Jacqueline White's son in the film, was fascinated with the technical aspects of filmmaking. Now an architect, Gebert recalled watching the train set being built at RKO with "breakaway pieces to accommodate the huge cameras and the ability to have the set jiggle."[111] The sequences using actual trains were confined to exteriors at Union Station, Chatsworth and the RKO Ranch. Fleischer's shooting script reflects the impressive acumen of an innovative and creative film director. In a process reminiscent of Alfred Hitchcock's technique, many of the key sequences on the train set were storyboarded on detailed charcoal sketches that were included in Fleischer's script.

One sketch shows the exterior of McGraw's train window in the frame as Charlie pulls the shade down and the camera being held as the reflection of David Clarke is cast in the window and then panning left to right as he walks along the platform. Similarly deft are the skillful scene transitions such as Marie Windsor filing her nails and shifting to a close-up to the churning wheels of the roaring locomotive. These technical flourishes accentuated the already rapid pace of a film designed to keep audiences on the edge of their seats. A striking departure from contemporary productions was the absence of a musical soundtrack. The only accompaniment to the action was the whistle and roar of the moving train. Lacking the bucks to finance a masterly soundtrack from a Miklos Rozsa or Max Steiner, Rubin and Fleischer opted to eschew musical accompaniment, enhancing the suspenseful tension of the picture. The brief action sequences were similarly polished. Stuntman Johnny Daheim helped stage a terrific fight scene

Film noir's most wonderfully dyspeptic couple: McGraw and Marie Windsor in *The Narrow Margin* (1952).

between Charlie and David Clarke in the train lavatory. Daheim and Charlie recognized each other as kindred souls and began a personal friendship that would last through several more films and numerous "last calls" in Studio City.

Jacqueline White remembered Charlie with affection:

What you saw with Charlie was what you got in person. He was a wonderful actor to work with.[112]

She recalled the actor as delightful to be around and a consummate performer, always on time and knowing his lines cold. White never noticed a hint of the renowned McGraw affectation for alcohol during the filming of the picture. Marie Windsor recalled McGraw as the antithesis of a tough guy and brushed off the actor's fondness for the grape:

[McGraw] was a sweetheart. He had an alcohol problem, but he didn't drink on the set on our pictures that I recall. He was a sweet man, he had a lovely Chinese wife and a gorgeous daughter....[113]

Marie Windsor became socially friendly with Charlie and Freda for a time. She visited the McGraws at their holiday cottage at Malibu where the couple would rent a vacation house for several weeks during the summer in the early 1950s.

The picture initially came in right on budget at $230,000 with most of the scenes being shot at RKO with the exteriors at Union Station, the RKO Ranch out in Encino and the train line running through the then-remote city of Chatsworth in the eastern San Fernando Valley. Under the title *Target*, filming began on May 27, 1950 and wrapped on June 13 — a total of 13 shooting days. Despite the efficiency, the retitled picture of *The Narrow Margin* was not

McGraw and Jacqueline White in the publicity photo used for the one-sheet poster of *The Narrow Margin* (1952).

released until May 2, 1952, nearly two years later. Not surprisingly, the reason for the inordinate delay was Howard Hughes.

Howard was initially delighted when he screened the picture, but had a question for the producer. He sent a note to Stanley Rubin asking if there could be retakes with Robert Mitchum and Jane Russell that could subsequently be edited into the completed footage so that the two stars could replace Charlie McGraw and Marie Windsor! After taking a day or so to digest this

Freda, Jill and Marie Windsor at Malibu Beach in the early 1950s (courtesy Mildred Black).

absurd request and frame an appropriately politically correct response for the boss, Rubin advised Hughes that *Target* would have to be scrapped and shot over from the beginning in order to replace the two lead characters. Succumbing to reality or becoming otherwise distracted, Hughes backed off of his initial request to recast the picture and the film languished on the shelf for several more months.

Hughes's next gambit was more traditional. The studio head decided that Jacqueline White was not credible as a gangster's widow and he also did not cotton to the idea that McGraw's partner was a corrupt cop. Additionally—not a surprise to anyone who presently worked at RKO for longer than two weeks—Howard believed that the conclusion of the film was insufficiently exciting.

One of the lighter moments from *The Narrow Margin* (1952): McGraw, Jacqueline White, Gordon Gebert, with rotund Paul Maxey lurking in the background.

In a startling thirteen-page memo to Jim Wilkinson, head of the RKO editing department, Hughes offered a plethora of recommendations on how to not only edit the film, but how to fundamentally "improve it":

> Jacqueline White remains an innocent bystander (just a divorcee with a little boy so that we don't have two widows) who happens to be traveling on the train. She has no connection with any of the other characters. She turns out to be the target merely because McGraw is seen talking to her, and the heavies naturally think she is the girl ...
>
> Marie Windsor remains a tart to the end and McGraw winds up handing her over to the authorities in Los Angeles—mission accomplished.[114]

Hughes rambles on, shotgunning scenario after scenario for the slam-bang ending. Several of his suggestions for an appropriately exciting conclusion included:

> I can see a situation where there is a hell of a chase though the train and ... the fat man gets jammed in a tight aisleway and there is a hell of a pileup like a football game.... Maybe the heavies at this point are trying to act nonchalant and are trying to walk through the car without attracting attention. This ought to be a Club Car packed with people, including a lot of drunks.... [T]he little boy finally pulls one of the gunmen's coats aside, disclosing the revolver, at which point maybe the drunken passenger reaches for it.... The heavies would then climb up on top of the train and start chasing McGraw rearward and we would have the chase on top of the train during which we could work in the approaching tunnel.... Incidentally, it wouldn't hurt a bit to have McGraw stumble and fall a couple of times on top of the train during this chase rearward.... [H]e starts to fall over the

side and perhaps grabs onto a piece of the air conditioning equipment just in time to keep from falling off the train…. The top of these streamlined trains is not only round but very slippery and running on it will be plenty dangerous and exciting.[115]

Perhaps out of breath at this point, Hughes finally arrives at the bottom line:

I want to eliminate completely the scene between Jacqueline White and McGraw in which it develops that she is the gangster's widow, that the D.A. told her to come to Los Angeles by herself, that McGraw took $1500 from his buddy and suspected that it was bribe money. It is the above scene in which the whole story falls apart. I do not believe for one moment that Jacqueline White is the gangster's wife. I do not believe the D. A. told her to come to Los Angeles unprotected…. In other words, in the reconstruction of the picture, I want to be sure it is clear that Jacqueline White is not the gangster's wife, McGraw is not on the payoff list and McGraw did not borrow $1500 from his partner.[116]

Aside from his usual desire to ratchet up the conclusion of the film to the level of a Mack Sennett two-reeler, Hughes' recommendations are ill-considered. For one thing, McGraw's character was never on the payoff list as Hughes indicated, so there was no change required. Additionally, the suspense generated by the identity switch of Mrs. Neil from Marie Windsor to Jacqueline White was one of the unique plot twists of the picture that made it so startlingly entertaining. Unfortunately, no one at the studio had the horsepower or cunning to completely nullify Hughes' zeal to change the film. The picture sat for over a year in the projection room while Howard was preoccupied with other matters.

Thirteen months after Hughes' memo about cutting the film, replacement scenes for *The Narrow Margin* were shot on December 18–21, 1951. Production designer and now-director William Cameron Menzies, who was on the lot helming *The Whip Hand* (1951), was assigned to direct the retakes. A total of 19 scenes and 12 3/4 pages of dialogue were filmed in four days to replace selected scenes already in the can. Jacqueline White was flown in from Wyoming to participate. All of the scenes that addressed the Forbes character (Don Beddoe) as a corrupt cop were removed from the previously shot film.

The excised footage included the torpedo played by David Clarke telling McGraw after their washroom fistfight to take the money as his revered and lately departed partner, Forbes (Don Beddoe), did. Clarke tells a stunned Charlie,

"Your pal Forbes didn't feel that way. We always found him easy to do business with."[117]

Clarke then drives the point home by waving a newspaper in McGraw's face with a bold type headline: REVEAL SLAIN L.A. OFFICER ON SYNDICATE PAYROLL—FORBES TOOK $10,000 BRIBE. This unexpected development was elaborated on during a further excised scene between Jacqueline White and Charlie when she tells him that she kept her identity as "Mrs. Neil" secret from him because she saw Forbes' name on the payoff list and also knew that Forbes lent some $1500 to Brown (McGraw). The crooks were testing Brown to see if he was as pliable as his partner. Brown confesses that while he didn't know anything definitive about his partner, he didn't ask Forbes where he got the money to lend him because he was afraid what his partner might tell him. White responds with a left hook to the gut: "Before I married Frank Neil, I never got around to asking how he made his money either."[118]

McGraw jarringly realizes that his many assumptions about his partner, Forbes, Marie Windsor who was a policewoman and Jackie White, not the type of "dame" who would marry a gangster, were stunningly wrong.

Both of these well-designed sequences were replaced by new material featuring reptilian character actor Peter Brocco (a carryover from the cast of *The Whip Hand*) as a "brains heavy" who eschewed violence and attempted to stage-manage "Mrs. Neil's" elimination as a "business decision." Brocco, who enjoyed a long Hollywood career playing unsavory creeps, attempts to bribe McGraw while on the train and at a whistle stop in Colorado. There were additional retakes to smooth off the rough edges on some of the Felton dialogue that offended the Breen Office and to ensure that all inferences to the corruption of the Forbes character had been removed.

While some of Hughes' contorted reasoning to change the film is apparent from his editing memo, the principal motivation to water down the compelling police corruption angle remains obscure. Stanley Rubin believes that Hughes might have been personally offended or otherwise uncomfortable with the very notion that a policeman could have been corrupt. There is also a possibility that Howard might have had his eye cocked on his studio and the film industry's long-term relationship with the Los Angeles Police Department.

The self-interest in maintaining goodwill with the L.A. P. D. had always been assiduously cultivated by the major movie studios. Police corruption in Los Angeles was a dicey subject for public discussion in 1950. The legacy of the Los Angeles Police Department was not steeped in virtue. Both the city and the police department were attempting to live down a history of official corruption that was shockingly blatant. In addition to Mayor Frank Shaw being recalled in 1938, a large portion of police department manpower was solely dedicated to the protection of gambling and criminal interests during the 1930s. The Los Angeles County District Attorney from 1928 to 1940 was a corrupt former lieutenant governor named Buron Fitts. Fitts, who ended his life a suicide, was finally eased out in 1940 due to a scandal of personal involvement with a prostitution ring staffed by underage girls. Since the days of silent movies, both the local police departments and district attorney's office in Los Angeles frequently obliged the major studios by suppressing or downplaying potential scandals when celebrities ran into trouble. Municipal assistance usually took the form of giving a studio like MGM first responder rights in order to corral a drunkenly amuck Spencer Tracy or winking at minor offenses involving celebrities, alcohol and automobiles. The *quid pro quo* provided by the studios included generous campaign contributions and positive public relations for the police department. Movies went out of their way to portray the L.A.P.D. as a reverentially efficient and pure law-enforcement firmament. Even a daring, breakthrough film like *The Asphalt Jungle* (1950), featuring burly actor Barry Kelley as a venally corrupt police lieutenant, was pointedly set in a Midwestern U.S. city, not Los Angeles.

Jack Webb would permanently memorialize the L.A.P.D. into contemporary public folklore as the dry-cleaned force of android-like law enforcement archangels when *Dragnet* premiered on television in 1951. It was a sturdy mirage that withstood large-scale scrutiny until Watts blew up in 1965. The truth was that while Los Angeles civic governance had markedly improved by 1950, some holdover rogues remained in the ranks and the force was periodically convulsed with scandals commensurate with the times. It was also axiomatic that those in charge of the internal housecleaning, such as Chief William H. Parker, who pushed through significant reforms and ended the most blatant corruption, were also the same people inclined to cover up transgressions. In short, the L.A.P.D. of 1950 was neither a Jack Webb–laundered script or a nihilistic James Ellroy novel ... so long as you were a Caucasian, kept your head down and didn't stray from the city's segregated racial and geographic boundaries.

Whether provoked by intrinsic or business reasons to alter the story of *The Narrow Margin*, the bottom line was that only Howard Hughes had final cut at RKO during the early 1950s. The added costs of the new scenes with the edits and additional overhead pushed the final cost of *The Narrow Margin* to $263,503. In spite of Hughes' meddling, the picture that was finally released in May 1952 was a joyously entertaining film. The reviews were nothing short of sensational. Rubin and Fleischer's little film was compared to the suspenseful masterpieces of Alfred

Hitchcock with McGraw and Windsor's performances singled out for fulsome praise. In terms of return on investment, the picture was a tremendous bargain. It was held over at the Trans-Lux Theatre New York (where the second week of box office receipts exceeded the first) and also in Los Angeles, where it opened at the Globe Theatre in downtown L.A., the Iris on Hollywood Boulevard, and the El Rey on Wilshire. RKO Studios, treading frantically in a sea of red ink, had an unexpected hit on its hands. *The Narrow Margin* was nominated for Best Motion Picture Story at the 25th Academy Awards in 1952, a distinction unheard of for a "B" picture with a modest budget.

The unexpected success launched Richard Fleischer and Stanley Rubin up to the rarefied Hollywood stratosphere of gilded "A" productions with remunerative paydays. Rubin had to suffer through one more Hughes-inspired mutilation of his work first, though. His screenplay and production of *The Man He Found*, about Hitler surviving World War II, was remade at Hughes' edict into a ridiculous anti–Red screed called *The Whip Hand*. Rubin took his name off the picture and left the studio by the end of 1952. He went to 20th Century–Fox, producing "A" tier features including *Destination Gobi* (1953) and *River of No Return* (1954). Television became Rubin's métier as he developed and produced a plethora of successful series including *G.E. Theatre*, *Bracken's World*, and *The Ghost and Mrs. Muir* and made-for TV movies such as the Emmy-winning *Babe* and *Dummy*.

Extremely adroit in all his dealings with Hughes, Richard Fleischer neatly engineered his exit from RKO as part of the bargain for seeing through the *His Kind of Woman* debacle while convincing the studio head to release *The Narrow Margin* without further butchering. After helming the delightful family drama *The Happy Time* for Stanley Kramer at Columbia, Fleischer landed a dream assignment from Walt Disney to direct *20000 Leagues Under the Sea* (1954) (with Earl Felton writing the screenplay) and never looked back. Fleischer enjoyed an ably distinguished filmmaking career that placed him on an accomplished plateau attained by few others in Hollywood. *The Vikings* (1958), *Compulsion* (1959) (his favorite film), *The Boston Strangler* (1968), *Tora, Tora, Tora* (1970) and *10 Rillington Place* (1971) are among his noted credits.

Marie Windsor toiled away in the ranks of "B" movies and television, never achieving the stardom that she strove for so fervently. There were a few other choice parts, notably in Stanley Kubrick's *The Killing* (1956) opposite Elisha Cook Jr. as the prettier half of film noir's least-likely-to-succeed couple. Windsor's career in films and television was ultimately fulfilling, but she had to come to terms with not achieving her dream of being a movie star. When queried about *The Narrow Margin* and Richard Fleischer, a trace of residual regret crept through:

> Well, he [Fleischer] was a darling man. I think that [*The Narrow Margin*] was what got him out of the B pictures. I wished he had remembered me when he jumped to the As, but I never worked for him again. So, we're good friends, we see each other and he's always been very fond of me, but I guess to him I'm still a "B" actress [*pause*].[119]

None of the hullabaloo about *The Narrow Margin* affected Jacqueline White in the slightest. She happily left the film business for good, returned to Wyoming and raised five children while building a highly successful business with her husband. Miss White's recent return to the film festival guest circuit has been welcomed by cinema fans with alacrity.

As for McGraw, his only public comment about *The Narrow Margin* occurred around the time that the picture premiered. Asked about his switch from hoodlum to an honest police detective, Charlie replied: "Now I can face the kids in our neighborhood without feeling that I'm out on parole!"[120]

14

Missing the Brass Ring

Parole would prove to be impossible for McGraw in his final starring vehicle at RKO, *Roadblock* (1951). This programmer was the final picture of Charlie's noir trifecta at RKO. *Roadblock* was the progeny of another collaborative writing collage that included a pair of film noir's most accomplished writers.

Geoffrey Homes, better known under his actual name of Daniel Mainwaring, composed the story synopsis *Walk a Crooked Mile* from a 1948 story he penned with Richard Landau, originally titled *The Grief Shooters*. Mainwaring already earned his noir chops at RKO with the classic *Out of the Past* (1947) and *The Big Steal* (1949). This time out Mainwaring's yarn was based on an actual robbery of a $2 million payroll by an unrepentant postal inspector named Joseph Fahey who got nabbed in 1924 and ended up doing 13 years in Atlanta.

The final screenplay was composed by RKO house writer George Bricker and the always dependable Steve Fisher, whose distinguished noir résumé began with *I Wake Up Screaming* (1941), included *Lady in the Lake* and *Dead Reckoning* (1947), and would continue through the 1950s with *City That Never Sleeps* (1953) and *Hell's Half Acre* (1954). Fisher would make a successful conversion into television, scripting *Barnaby Jones* and *Cannon* among other formulaic series. Other scenarists were not as fortunate with making the transition from movies to the quick turnaround of TV.

As screenwriting opportunities began to evaporate in the 1960s, some of the older writers who tried to move into episodic television struggled with the speed that was required for the small screen. One casualty of this transition was gifted scribe Earl Felton. Felton was a brilliant writer who procrastinated on deadlines while enjoying life. His collaborator and friend at RKO, Dick Fleischer, had to cajole Felton to get anything done during daylight hours. Stanley Rubin specifically recalled that during preproduction on *The Narrow Margin*, Earl's best writing took place in the evening after several belts of Scotch. Felton became so despondent over his lonely struggles with life — many of his friends had gone and Hollywood had changed — and television script deadlines that he tragically put a bullet in his brain in 1972.

With the screenplay completed, *Roadblock* went into production as another RKO quickie. Filming began on October 2, 1950 and concluded on October 17. The director, Harold Daniels, was a former actor whose film career dated back to 1935. He helmed a couple of previous bargain-basement second features including *The Woman from Tangier* (1948) featuring the sultry Adele Jergens. Daniels was looking to establish himself as an efficient director and didn't dally. He brought the picture in at $192,365.17, slightly under the $200,958 budget. Daniels was not as effective in disguising the limited production values in *Roadblock*. Many of the interior scenes are ruthlessly austere, notably the bleak barroom and airport terminal sets that are reminiscent of a barren PRC production instead of a feature made at a major studio. *Roadblock* was by far the cheapest-looking film that McGraw appeared in during his tenure at RKO.

As star-crossed insurance agent Joe Peters, McGraw portrays one of the more conflicted

McGraw gets the drop on Peter Brocco in *Roadblock* (1951).

characters in his repertoire of hard cases. Peters falls hard for a lush "B" girl played by ingénue actress Jean Dixon. A vixen with a sweet tooth for the good life, Jean requires a lot of finery and Charlie just can't swing it on his $87.50 per week pay envelope. The lovesick anguish inflicted on McGraw as he is jerked around by the manipulative Dixon is something to see. Desperate, he subsequently concocts a clever mail robbery scheme with a local crime boss. In a twist of noirish irony, Dixon discovers, too late, that McGraw is the authentic article and she ditches her delusions of grandeur. It is past time for a happy ending, though, as fate is now propelling the couple's disintegrating destiny. When the caper goes awry, the former honest-john Charlie crosses the line into pure criminality, taking it on the lam from the police as the whole scheme unravels. One key sequence has Charlie observing his handiwork after dispatching his erstwhile robbery partner to be barbecued in a burning car at the bottom of a ravine. Visually assessing the inferno elicits a contented expression of the familiar McGraw cruelty that was at odds with the previously fulsome character of the fatally love-struck insurance agent. The Jekyll-Hyde transition of Joe Peters was complete. Charlie reverted to a character type which movie audiences had grown to expect from him.

Naturally, the Breen Office had to be sated with a formulaic finale to this exercise in perverseness. McGraw inevitably buys it, riddled with police bullets, rolling face down in the cement-coated L.A. riverbed. The film concludes with a Nicholas Musuraca camera dissolve from a rear shot of La Dixon, wiggling away from Charlie's bullet-pierced body. One concludes that she is either devastated about McGraw's fate or simply en route to ensnare her next sucker ... or perhaps both.

Joan Dixon was a marginal actress, but a stone-cold looker. She debuted in another lively RKO "B" crime drama, *Bunco Squad* (1950), and concluded her career in 1958 with a résumé of nine feature appearances and a couple of television credits. However truncated her acting career ended up, Dixon's life off the set attracted a certain notoriety in the press and at the studio. The twenty-one-year-old ingénue's three-week marriage to Chicago magnate Theodore Briskin in 1952, with the annulment handled by mob fixer Sidney Korshak, might have influenced the convoluted circumstances concerning the attempted sale of RKO by Hughes during the same year.

The supporting players in *Roadblock* were standard "B" film proletariat: Milburn Stone, Louis Jean Heydt, Lowell Gilmore, Peter Brocco and the veteran Dewey Robinson. Word must have filtered down to director Daniels about Howard Hughes' fixation with slam-bang finales. The final chase sequence filmed at San Fernando Road, Figueroa Street, the Ramp Bridge, and also in the L.A. Riverbed by the Broadway Bridge, was roaringly action-packed.

While there is no available record of Hughes or anyone else at the studio tinkering with

McGraw possessed a rugged romantic look that was seldom used during his contracted time at RKO Studios. With a dreamy-looking Joan Dixon in *Roadblock* (1951).

Roadblock, the film wasn't released until September 17, 1951, one month short of a year after shooting wrapped. RKO's sense of alacrity in delivering their finished product to the public continued to inch forward with all of the precipitous speed of a glacier.

After three starring vehicles, albeit in "B" productions, Charles McGraw appeared to be primed for bigger things, but he would never again have his name at the top of a major studio film credit. With RKO being dismembered by Hughes, and television gaining momentum, the opportunities for stardom were evaporating faster than the morning dew on the Hollywood hills.

Top-tier features released by the major studios were shifted to visual innovations and increasingly expensive location productions in an attempt to pump up declining box office receipts. These overblown "A" productions, many of them sprawling Biblical or period historical epics loaded with stars, began to roll out in wide ratio CinemaScope, Technirama, Vistavision or Superscope. These mega-pictures, beginning with *Quo Vadis* (1951), earned large profits, but they also cost a great deal to make, meaning that fewer films were getting produced by the major studios. Additional gimmicks to lure customers into movie theaters such as 3-D had a brief fling with an increasingly fickle public that increasingly tended to stay at home at night and watch television.

The opportunities for McGraw to grab the cinematic brass ring were disappearing, but his ambition remained confined to that elusive actor's goal of steady employment. Charlie was sim-

Charlie didn't get to play the noir chump until doing a bang-up job opposite Joan Dixon in *Roadblock* (1951).

ply trying to earn a living, not be a star. There were also indications that McGraw was not entirely at ease by simply *being* an actor.

According to actor Mickey Knox, who became friendly with Charlie during the late 1940s, McGraw appeared tense while preparing to act. A long-term dialogue coach and astute observer of actors, Knox believed that however effective in front of the camera, McGraw, "never came to terms with himself as an actor — he was nervous on the set."[121] Knox would not be the only person who would make this observation about McGraw at work. Because Charlie was inwardly nervous, he outwardly cloaked his anxiety with jokes and colorful bravado that fooled many, but not all of his contemporaries. McGraw's nervous tension might also have contributed to his habit of maintaining a certain distance in his personal relationships as well as the increased consumption of alcohol that was now an engrained part of his daily routine. The actor's social distractions certainly clouded up a concentrated focus on his career. Charlie loved to hang out, laugh, drink, and tell stories till the wee hours. His penchant for being the first and last person at the bar was attracting notoriety and a certain reputation. Director Richard Fleischer noted: "Charlie was a damn fine actor, but it took me awhile to notice that he had a problem ... beer."[122]

McGraw's personal firewall between his acting career and penchant for barroom revelry would be tested during the filming of what would be his final RKO contracted feature, *One Minute to Zero* (1952). A contemporary Korean War saga starring Robert Mitchum and Claudette Colbert, the picture was initially assigned to Ted Tetzlaff, the renowned cinematographer of Alfred Hitchcock's *Notorious* and an able director of suspenseful features including *Riffraff* (1947), *Under the Gun* (1951) and *The Window* (1949) — an inspired suspense film worthy of Hitchcock.

Under the working title of *The Korean Story*, there were nine weeks of location shooting in South Korea by a large second unit team from RKO. The location sequences were logistically complex, expensive and became bogged down in bad weather and the red tape associated with attempting to film in a war zone within a foreign country. Many of the aerial sequences in the film were subsequently shot stateside at a Las Vegas airbase.

As with nearly every major RKO production during the early 1950s, this film was plagued with delays, cost overruns and myriad changes in key artists and personnel. The principal difference between *One Minute to Zero* and other RKO pictures of this era were that the majority of the delays were not solely caused by Howard Hughes. The producer, Edmund Grainger, decided that he wanted a bigger name director so Ted Tetzlaff was quickly replaced by the veteran Tay Garnett. Garnett was an engaging Irish pixie with considerable talent. He was also an episodic alcoholic who was prone to go off on benders as circumstances dictated. Filming on Garnett's *The Postman Always Rings Twice* (1946) at MGM was delayed due to the director's headlong swan dive off the wagon. Lana Turner described Garnett's deportment during the filming of *Postman* as "a roaring, mean, furniture smashing drunk."[123] Garnett would eventually swear off drinking and join Alcoholics Anonymous some years later. However, during the location shoot on *One Minute to Zero* in Colorado Springs, Garnett became sick with a reported case of pneumonia that delayed production for a week. The director's impromptu sabbatical was a precursor to further delays. When leading lady Claudette Colbert became seriously ill with pneumonia, the shoot was idled for several weeks and then shut down entirely as Colbert was so sick that she had to withdraw from the picture.

These unforeseen circumstances provided perfect timing for Howard Hughes to step in and make a bad situation worse. While Garnett was back in Hollywood in discussions with Lew Wasserman about obtaining Joan Crawford as a replacement, Hughes telephoned him and told him to return to Colorado Springs. Howard had signed Ann Blyth to replace Colbert. Garnett's reaction to Hughes' decision was: "ANN BLYTH?"[124]

The casting of the diminutive 23-year-old actress instead of the mature, elegant Colbert playing a romantic lead opposite big Bob Mitchum necessitated Andrew Solt being flown to Colorado Springs to rewrite most of the script. Additional production delays were caused by the temperamental Colorado weather. Sets destroyed by rain and snow had to be rebuilt. The mountain temperature swings went from the seventies in the afternoon to the thirties in the evening, making setups and shooting difficult for the crew. The picturesque mountain plateaus where Garnett staged the majority of the battle scenes led to more unanticipated problems. The area was literally infested with rattlesnakes that slithered up from the ground to take in the mid-day sun. The reptiles had to be dodged by a production crew who, when observed from a distance, appeared to be hopping around like fire dancers on white-hot coals. Trees shot in full leaf during the spring-summer had to have fake branches wired to them to match the film shot earlier as fall deepened into winter. As the director put it, "[W]e had the longest shooting schedule in recent years with the possible exception of *Cleopatra*."[125]

In the meantime, a live rattler might have been useful to the RKO accounting department in gaining the attention of Hughes and the production staff who appeared oblivious to the escalating costs. The total expenditures on *One Minute to Zero* ballooned to over $2,260,000. A large portion of the budget overage was due to the Colorado location in what was remote territory in 1952. RKO was compelled to build an entire Anderson camp to house the company because the town of Colorado Springs didn't have enough lodging available. Credit Howard Hughes with ensuring that the company enjoyed first-class location lodgings. The Anderson tents had plywood floors covered with linoleum tile and each unit had its own heater, shower and bathroom facilities. Many of these facilities had to be rebuilt after being damaged by the surly weather.

Mitchum, McGraw and Ann Blyth (seated on left) enjoy a meal in frigid Colorado Springs during the location filming of *One Minute to Zero* (1952) (courtesy Mildred Black).

Charlie McGraw was unaffected by any of these issues. The interminable delays were the nature of the business, particularly at RKO. Besides, wasn't sitting around on location what buddies, beer and a deck of cards were for? What must have been gratifying for Charlie was that he was finally being adequately compensated for his work. McGraw was paid $13,364 for slightly over five weeks' work, a plush level of compensation in 1951. Even though he was earning well and having fun, Charlie sorely missed his wife and daughter when he was working on location.

One of McGraw's most notable paradoxes was his consistent protestations about familial separation when he was working on location. Conversely, when back home, McGraw spent an increasingly greater portion of his off-hours down the hill on Ventura Boulevard in various bars while Freda and Jill remained home alone. McGraw's behavior during the five-week separation of the *One Minute to Zero* location shoot was typical. He flew in Freda and Jill for a brief visit during the shoot — Jill recalled Mitchum's clowning during a raucous dinner party culminating with the star briefly dropping his pants— but spent most of the time in the mountains as a geographical bachelor. Several weeks after his family's return to California, Charlie phoned his pal, Dick Martin, and asked him to take Freda out to a movie to break the monotony of the separation. Martin, who kept McGraw's beer schooner topped off at Herbert's Drive-In on Laurel Canyon and Ventura, relished any opportunity to indulge his comedic impulses. The nascent comic squired Freda out to a movie in a gentlemanly manner and promptly wrote a telegram

to McGraw and Robert Mitchum advising: "Took Freda out as you requested (stop). WOW!!
Love, Dick."[126] After the telegram was received, Charlie and Mitchum telephoned Martin at Herbert's, and the three of them yukked it up over this bit of long-distance burlesque.

The family interludes aside, the remote location and production delays in Colorado Springs
provided the requisite downtime for a pair of barroom buccaneers like McGraw and Mitchum
to get into trouble. The two men were joined by Bob's younger brother John Mitchum, who
landed a bit part as an artillery spotter in the picture, and took to drinking at the Red Fox
Lounge at the Alamo Hotel in Colorado Springs. With the star-struck hoi polloi surging around,
the actors, gassed by alcohol at an altitude of nearly 7,000 feet, would often cut up outrageously.
Charlie inadvertently performed one good deed by inviting some local girls to their table one
night and John Mitchum met his future wife, Nancy Munro. Soon, though, McGraw was in the
middle of a scrape with Robert Mitchum that made the newspapers spill ink all across the country.

Subsequent press accounts varied that Mitchum was either protecting "another member
of the motion picture industry,"[127] i.e. McGraw — not exactly the acme of vulnerability inside a
bar — or quelling a disagreement between several soldiers from nearby Camp Carson who were
ad-hoc drinking companions. The eyeball witnesses weren't agreeable on root causes either.
John Mitchum recalled a bellicose McGraw as the primary instigator but a military policeman
who was at the bar stated that Mitchum interceded in an argument between a lieutenant colonel and a private over military protocol. However the years and alcohol fogged the memories
of those who were present about what started the donnybrook, nobody who was there debated
the outcome.

Army Private Bernard Reynolds, a former prizefighter, squared off against Mitchum in the
Red Fox bar and was subsequently hospitalized with a concussion and a possible skull fracture.
Several of the witnesses present stated that when Mitchum had his man down, he eschewed Marquis of Queensbury rules and kicked the recalcitrant grunt in the head. Reynolds had to be carried out with Mitchum, McGraw et al. subsequently beating a tactical retreat back to camp.
Predictably, the contretemps ended up in the newspapers with Mitchum on the hot seat. It all
turned out to be much ado about not too much. Mitchum would prove as adroit at public disassembling about the results of his alcohol-fueled mayhem as he was reciting dialogue on screen.
The star trotted out some telephonic whimsy to the press about it all just being "a saloon hassle"[128] and was quoted in an RKO press release that "actors are always a target for [a] belligerent type of guy who thinks he is tough and movie he-men are softies."[129] Mitchum initially
denied kicking the soldier in the head, and then later admitted that he (Mitchum) was "the
aggressor."[130] In an era before lawsuits came into vogue and men routinely settled differences
in bars with their fists (and feet), nobody really cared that much anyway. Howard Hughes and
the moviegoing public assumed that the rugged actor was simply behaving like the tough guys
he played on screen. Mitchum, who grew up poor, escaped from a chain gang and rode the rails
during the Great Depression, was assuredly no softie — on or off the screen.

As the apparent instigator, McGraw was constrained to add proper perspective to Mitchum's
PR image. Asked later by a reporter about what type of man his co-star was, Charlie put his
tongue firmly in cheek and advised, "He's wonderful. He writes to his mother every day."[131]

The combat in the barroom involving the actors was more compelling than the ostensible
Korean War action captured on the screen. *One Minute to Zero* was released to universally tepid
reviews. The battle sequences staged in Colorado by Tay Garnett were unrealistic and a poor
match to the second unit combat footage. The script had evolved into a recitation of clichés
and the romantic scenes between the "Mutt and Jeff" duo of Ann Blyth and Mitchum were

Robert Mitchum and McGraw racked up a barroom body count off screen during the filming of *One Minute to Zero* (1952) in Colorado Springs.

difficult to take seriously. *The New York Times* described the picture as "ripely synthetic ... another war picture that smells of grease paint and studios."[132]

The picture attracted little attention beyond a controversial scene where Colonel Mitchum orders a column of what appeared to be Korean civilians—later revealed to be North Korean soldiers in disguise—strafed for the greater good of prosecuting the war. *One Minute to Zero* sank like a stone at the box office as RKO reached the nadir of its history as a major Hollywood studio.

15

RKO Studios as Andersonville

RKO Studios under Howard Hughes had evolved from the "biggest little major" to a focal point of concern over the self-preservation of the entire studio system. While all of the majors were struggling to adapt to a new era, no other studio committed the outright professional hari-kari witnessed at 780 Gower Street.

Sid Rogell, promoted to executive production head by Hughes, had to endure Howard's late-night telephonic monologues as part of his new duties. Hughes was an insomniac and naturally assumed those in his employ would maintain identical hours. After a series of interminable early morning phone calls, Rogell finally told Howard where to go. The tough-minded production chief disappeared through a corporate trapdoor on May 18, 1950, and was replaced by veteran producer Samuel Bischoff. Bischoff lasted about a year before he couldn't endure working any longer for the man that Robert Mitchum nicknamed "The Phantom." Hughes was like a ghost. He would not return telephone calls, was unavailable for meetings or consultation, never even came to the studio. When Howard did communicate, it was via cryptic notes or rambling post-midnight phone calls. Hughes refused to delegate and did not make decisions. Gridlock reigned at RKO.

Hughes' next move set Hollywood on its collective ear. He hired the independent production team of Jerry Wald and Norman Krasna on August 14, 1950. Wald was a screenwriter who successfully trod in the large footprints left by Hal B. Wallis as the singular producer at Warner Brothers in 1943. He racked up a impressive production record for Jack L. Warner that included such seminal film noirs as *Mildred Pierce, Dark Passage, Key Largo, The Turning Point* and *Caged.*

Wald had a hail-fellow personality, a Jack Carson character playing a used-car salesman or song-and-dance man. He was an ex–newspaper writer with considerable talent who "already knew every yarn in the story department and came up with a better idea every five minutes."[133] Whoever reached a final consensus with Wald frequently needed to be the last person in the room to talk with him. Krasna, his ostensible partner, was a witty screenwriter, playwright and scenarist who penned *Fury* (1936) *The Devil and Miss Jones* (1941), *Mr. and Mrs. Smith* (1941) and *Dear Ruth* (1947). Wald and Krasna looked to be a talent-laded, prestigious production team. Both men eagerly accepted an unprecedented Hughes deal of $50 million over the next 5½ years to produce 60 features at RKO with the promise of complete creative autonomy. Hollywood was abuzz with the order of magnitude of this coup by Howard Hughes. It appeared that RKO was finally getting its house in order.

Of course, the worm quickly turned in the apple when Hughes reneged on the autonomy deal and handcuffed his production team, dubbed in the press as "The Whiz Kids." Why an executive would pay the considerable money to buy out both Wald and Krasna's contracts, provide them with a king's ransom to make films and then ineptly micromanage their efforts was beyond anyone's comprehension. The Wald-Krasna production company would have its name on a mere four features for RKO before Jerry Wald bought out Krasna, who immediately wanted out, followed shortly by Wald who also bailed instead of attempting to retrieve a lost game with a studio head who behaved like someone in the early stages of dementia. As a final touch of obtuse infamy, Hughes kept the film *Jet Pilot* in production for over half a decade with the picture finally being released as the studio was being sold.

RKO Studios was no longer a movie-making organization. The once-proud producer of such classics as *King Kong, Top Hat, Gunga Din, Citizen Kane, The Hunchback of Notre Dame, Crossfire, I Remember Mama* and *Out of the Past* was now a releasing company for independent production companies such as Walt Disney, Samuel Goldwyn, Argosy (John Ford & Merian C. Cooper), Winchester (Howard Hawks), The Filmmakers (Ida Lupino and Collier Young), Howard Hill, Royal Productions Inc. (Julian Lesser), Daiei (American distributor for *Rashomon*) and Theasquare Productions.

Hughes spent much of 1952 embroiled with lawsuits with screenwriter Paul Jarrico and actress Jean Simmons. The fight with Jarrico, one of the Hollywood Ten, was a typical Hughes knee-jerk attempt to purge Communists from the RKO payroll by denying the writer screen credit on *The Las Vegas Story*. Jarrico sued for breach of contract and the Writers Guild sued Hughes, who countersued both of them. The court found for Hughes against Jarrico because the writer was found to have violated the Morals Clause in his contract by not cooperating with HUAC. The Guild also found that there was no enforcement clause in their collective bargaining agreement with the studios and had to back down. Hughes won against Jarrico and the Guild, but his victory was pyrrhic. The amount of money spent litigating these unnecessary lawsuits drained the studio's coffers even further.

The Jean Simmons imbroglio became more than a contractual hassle. Hughes bought her contract from J. Arthur Rank with six months left to run and claimed he had an oral agreement with Rank that Miss Simmons would not be loaned out for other projects. He refused to loan out Simmons and did little or nothing to advance the career of a gorgeously talented actress who was being compared to Elizabeth Taylor.

According to previously published accounts, Hughes was obsessed with carnally possessing the beautiful British brunette and tried everything in his power to bend her to his will. Hughes reportedly became enraged because the married actress refused to have anything to do with him. Simmons and her then-husband, actor Stewart Granger, allegedly became mortally offended by the mogul's incessant blandishments.

This story about Hughes and Simmons was given wide circulation by Stewart Granger. The actor made it exceedingly clear in his memoirs that he hated Hughes with a passion and that he was certain that the tycoon had designs on his twenty-three-year-old wife. For her part, Simmons remembers little about the lawsuit other than she didn't understand it and was told to say certain things by her husband and the attorneys. Asked if Hughes had romantic inclinations towards her, the actress laughed and said, "If he did, I didn't notice."[134] Simmons claimed that Hughes acted like a perfect gentleman and tried to warn her at one point that her husband was after her money. She concluded, "My husband was very controlling and I think he made this up...."[135]

By whatever initiative, Simmons sued Hughes to have the right to work on loanout for other studios. In apparent retaliation, Howard continued not to let her work for any other studio, and put her in RKO films not designed to boost her career. *Angel Face* (1953), a compelling film noir helmed by that Teutonic prince of darkness, Otto Preminger, was a case in point. Preminger, captivating off the set, lacked only a spiked Saxon helmet and a riding crop when seated in the director's chair. He frequently selected a actor to be the object of his bullying during a picture, someone who wouldn't or couldn't fight back. In this case, it was Jean Simmons. According to the actress, she had met Preminger socially before production on *Angel Face* and found him charming. Once the filming began, Otto treated her contemptuously. During a brief scene where Robert Mitchum slapped Simmons, the director had Mitchum hit her again, and again, and again; "He did it in long shot, medium and close-up until I thought my jaw was broken."[136] Mitchum eventually confronted Preminger about his behavior in front of the crew and walked off. Otto had to dismiss the company for the day and backed off during the rest of the filming. Producer Stanley Rubin, who with Mitchum would be the chief feather smoothers between Preminger and Marilyn Monroe on *River of No Return* (1954), remarked, "Bob Mitchum was the one guy that Otto couldn't intimidate."[137]

After a year, the lawsuit was settled with Simmons remaining under contract to RKO for three years but winning the right to work on loanout to other studios. Hughes ended up paying Simmons $250,000 as well as her legal bills. It was a notable victory for the actress over a Croesus accustomed to having his own way.

By 1953, RKO was the Hollywood studio equivalent of Andersonville. There were approximately 450 employees remaining on the payroll out of the more than two thousand on board when Hughes bought RKO in 1948. While a certain downsizing of the studio was inevitable due the consent decree and television, the studio's ultimate fate was an object lesson of felonious mismanagement.

RKO lost over $10,000,000 in 1952 with only 32 releases. The shareholders were in rebellion and Hughes had become both bored and annoyed being the owner of a movie studio. He finally unloaded RKO in September to a group of Chicago investors who made the inner circle of Enron executives look like the Disciples. The deal was orchestrated by Chicago mob fixer Sidney Korshak, who represented the new board of RKO that gave true meaning to the word "syndicate." The new studio owners included Ray Ryan, a business partner of underworld chieftain Frank Costello; George Uffner, a former convict and underworld associate; and Abe Koolish, who pioneered sapping non-profit charities and was indicted in 1948 for insurance fraud. Korshak's "end" was being hired as a "consultant" at $15,000 per year by the new board. Shortly after the sales agreement was signed, the whole deal flew apart. Somebody leaked details about the buyers and their true résumés to *The Wall Street Journal*. Once the ownership group's links to various scams and relationships with gangsters were publicly exposed, and the media went crazy with headlines, the new RKO board of directors scattered like cockroaches under the beam of a flashlight.

After an en masse resignation of the board, Hughes got his RKO stock returned in February 1953 and appointed a new board of directors. Much to the chagrined fury of Sidney Korshak, Howard was entitled to keep the $1.25 million down payment from the group, making a tidy profit out of the non-sale of his studio.

Korshak had good reason to be incensed. He emphatically believed that Hughes was the person who leaked the details of the RKO deal to *The Wall Street Journal* in the first place. This version of events is corroborated by several Hughes associates including one who commented:

> Howard Hughes knew the type of people he was dealing with; he knew their backgrounds and he knew their associations. That was the way he operated.... He took their down payment and waited. At the right time, he leaked the story to the press.[138]

What, if any degree, Korshak's involvement in Ted Briskin's messy divorce of Hughes ingénue actress Joan Dixon, who was under personal contract to Howard, motivated treachery by Hughes is unknown. However, Hughes was never shy about exacting vengeance on anyone who failed to meet his elastic standards of loyalty. What there was no doubt about was that Sidney Korshak never forgot or forgave Hughes' apparent double-cross and bided his time. Revenge would be exacted when Hughes' Las Vegas casino empire was mercilessly skimmed to tune of over $50 million by the Mob during the following decade.

RKO was made to twist in the wind only somewhat longer. By 1954, the studio was down to 15 releases and Hughes sold the studio for a final time in July 1955 to General Teleradio Inc., a subsidiary of General Tire, at a tidy profit of $6 million. After a final spasm of production, RKO's film library was sold to a television concern and the Gower Street lot was purchased by Lucille Ball and Desi Arnaz for television production in 1957. Hollywood veterans were stunned that RKO was no longer a movie studio. When Hedda Hopper drove down Gower Street in early 1958 and looked at the *Desilu* sign that replaced the RKO lightning bolt above the studio walls, she bitterly mumbled, "That bastard, television."[139]

Like a doctor who specialized in malpractice, Howard Hughes owned RKO little more than half a decade until the plug finally got pulled and the patient was declared dead. Hughes walked away with millions and the studio ceased to exist. Howard might have bankrupted RKO, but he was always the bottom-line businessman when it came to increasing his personal fortune. Hughes' money wasn't based on the movie business anyway, so he felt free to leave a trail of truncated careers, exposed film and ruined dreams at Gower and Melrose before moving on to his next obsession.

16

Freelance Actor

One of the numerous departures from RKO before Hughes' corporate denouement was Charles McGraw. The actor rightly concluded that he was wasting his time remaining contractually tied to a studio that was no longer committed to making movies. He was an established commodity and sensed that the work would now find him. McGraw's tenure at RKO lasted exactly two years. Charlie left the studio in January 1952 and immediately signed a one year contract with Douglas Fairbanks, Jr., to star in a new television series that would be filmed in England. After arriving in England via the *Queen Mary* in April 1952, McGraw played the lead role of Sergeant Flint in the pilot of a new television series titled *Foreign Legion*. Unfortunately for both Fairbanks and McGraw, NBC balked at buying the completed pilot and the deal collapsed. NBC made amends by picking up Fairbanks' anthology series, *Douglas Fairbanks Jr. Presents*, in 1954 while signing up McGraw to star in *The Adventures of Falcon* the same year. While the *Foreign Legion* pilot was reportedly incorporated into Fairbanks' television series that aired in the U.S. until 1957, a search for a viable print of McGraw's first television show has, to date, proved unsuccessful.

McGraw's first movie as a newly independent actor was *War Paint* (1953), a stark, gripping Western filmed on location in Death Valley. This picture was the initial entry from Bel-Air Productions, a company formed by Howard W. Koch and Aubrey Schenck, who worked out a distribution deal for their films with United Artists. Both of these men were astute commercial filmmakers who would thrive in Hollywood.

Koch, in particular, would experience spectacular success. He would move on from "B" Westerns and horror movies to major film productions in the 1960s. *The Manchurian Candidate* (1962), *The Odd Couple* (1968), *Airplane!* (1980) and *Ghost* (1990) are some of his more notable credits. Koch headed up Frank Sinatra's production company for a time and rose to become head of production at Paramount and president of the Motion Picture Academy. Koch was a movie lover — he began as a film librarian — who never lost sight of his professional roots ["W]e really *cared* what we were making, we really *tried*"[140]) and wasn't changed by the dazzle of Tinseltown success. He never forgot his friends from the early days, whether it was actor pals like Marie Windsor or low-budget directors who worked for him during the 1950s such as Reggie LeBorg and Lee "Roll 'em" Sholem.

War Paint had McGraw as a tough, pipe-smoking cavalry sergeant in support of Robert Stack's tightlipped lieutenant. The two soldiers lead a miserable expedition through Indian country to deliver a peace treaty. The journey rapidly degenerates into a survivalist search for water. Charlie has to contend with a mutinous detachment of troops (comprised of Peter Graves, Robert J. Wilke, Paul Richards and John Doucette, among others) who are getting picked off by a stalking Indian and his paramour, who want to sabotage the treaty. Joan Taylor, who played the fulsome Indian maiden in *Warpaint*, was the sole female in the company out in barren Death Valley and valued McGraw's awareness of her situation. Taylor remembered, "Charlie was

As insurance agent Gus Flavin, McGraw drives Barry Sullivan round the bend in *Loophole* (1954).

very protective of me on location. I was the only gal in the cast and I appreciated his watching over me. He was gruff at times—truly a man's man, and always a gentleman." McGraw's taciturn ruggedness on screen made him a natural for the plethora of Westerns still being resolutely churned out by the studios for theatres and television. Like a familiar, worn saddle, Charlie's distinctive visage would grace episodes of *Gunsmoke, Wagon Train, Bonanza, The Deputy, Laredo, The Virginian* and similar Western series during the coming years.

McGraw appeared in another popular Western, *Thunder Over the Plains,* a neatly crafted Andre de Toth–helmed picture starring the rugged star Randolph Scott. Scott, as natural out west as sagebrush, produced and starred in a plethora of successful horse operas during the 1950s. His pictures, particularly those directed by Budd Boetticher, were distinctive, popular and returned substantial profits that the actor poured into his real estate and oil investments. Scott retired after appearing in Sam Peckinpah's *Ride the High Country* (1962). Discounting Bob Hope, he was arguably the wealthiest actor in town.

In *Thunder Over the Plains,* Charlie plays a character that is a hybrid Quantrill-as-Robin Hood, a rebel leader who takes on swinish post–Civil War carpetbaggers who are swindling the good burghers of the Lone Star State. In one amusing sequence, Charlie and his gang rob a conniving Elisha Cook Jr. and force him into a humiliating hike back to town in his long johns!

McGraw had his film noir chops memorably burnished in *Loophole* (1954), a "B" effort under the auspices of the former Monogram Studios at the reconstituted Allied Artists. McGraw was third-billed under Barry Sullivan and Dorothy Malone. The film was produced by the veteran Lindsley Parsons, who had spent his entire career at Monogram. Lindsley Parsons Jr., who worked on several of his father's pictures as an assistant director and production manager, candidly remarked that casting call for the hard drinkers (including Parsons Sr.) appearing in *Loop-hole* might have been "held at AA."[141] He further observed that since this picture had a budget of $150,000–$200,000 and a two-week schedule, the elder Parsons typically used actors who were either on their way up or on their way down.

Regardless of liquor or production values, *Loophole* is a frequently overlooked film that contains one of Charles McGraw's more relentless characterizations. When bank teller Barry Sullivan gets framed for embezzlement by a clever bunco scheme, the blind alley of film noir opens up and swallows him whole. Despite no evidence of guilt other than his teller's cash drawer being mysteriously short of money, Sullivan is subsequently let go by the bank. The police turn his life inside out, but they finally have to give him a pass. Unfortunately for Sullivan, bank insurance bond investigator Gus Slavin (McGraw) is just getting started. McGraw proves to be the ultimate bureaucratic sadist. He obdurately refuses to consider that Sullivan might be innocent and makes the unemployed teller's existence a living hell in order to break him down. McGraw's reign of psychological mayhem prevents Sullivan from finding work and he ends up losing his house. The former bank teller cannot support his wife (Dorothy Malone) and struggles to find any type of employment and shelter due to Charlie's ceaseless campaign of scurrilous gossip to prospective landlords and employers.

Sullivan ultimately has to clear himself by finding the actual thieves (Mary Beth Hughes and Don Beddoe; a wonderfully degenerate film noir couple for the ages) and bundling them up for the police. McGraw remains unrepentant, however. The film concludes with a close-up of Charlie hovering outside the bank, still shadowing Sullivan after he has been cleared and rehired.

With the Blacklist was at its somber apogee — Senator Joe McCarthy would soon slide into oblivion through a pile of empty whiskey bottles after overreaching by taking on Eisenhower and the Army — the thematic thrust of *Loophole* concerning the consequences of the officious abuse of power by those who can wield it remains powerful, particularly in the shadowy netherworld of noir.

However, by the mid–1950s, that Hades of film genres, film noir, reached a decisive fork in the evolutionary Hollywood road. The post–World War II realism that had injected a nihilistic jet stream into film noir movies was dissipating to cloudless vapor and beginning to peter out.

17

Small Screen Evolution

As the 1950s evolved from the Blacklist to bomb shelters, the studio "B" programmers that comprised so much of what would be labeled film noir began to disappear from theatre marquees. Film noir pictures increasingly relied on contemporary themes with criminal exposé storylines about organized crime based on the Kefauver Crime Commission hearings. These formulaic pictures including *Hoodlum Empire* (1952), *The Big Combo* (1955) and *New York Confidential* (1955) had a brief heyday and then began to disappear altogether.

Instead of hard-boiled cops and femme fatales, a new generation of "B" films frequently starred giant arachnids and irascible dinosaurs. These creatures, spawned by atomic mushroom clouds or white-jacketed scientists involved in arcane experiments, invariably woke up in a malevolently cranky mood and wreaked havoc on people, cities and a varied assortment of Matchbox trucks. Much of this mayhem occurred amid scientific techno-babble dialogue with the occasional revving of hot rod engines as background theme music. The staple protagonist was usually an older actor like Morris Ankrum, outfitted in an Army colonel's uniform from Western Costume, charged with sole supervision of the nation's entire military might against a multi-legged threat. Younger actors increasingly abstained fedoras and ties. Many of the new generation on screen sported combed-back pompadours and leather jackets, aping James Dean, while eyeballing an assortment of blowsy buxom bimbettes. American-International and other nascent companies pioneered this new wave of cheap, sensational horror and science-fiction pictures that were successfully integrated into theatres and multiplying drive-ins that were no longer controlled by the major studios.

Noir was always a minimalist style from a pictorial perspective: bars, hotel rooms, back alleys shrouded in fog and terse exchanges in the rear of coupes. The content was always in the story, lighting, acting and dialogue. It was an inevitable progression of cinematic Darwinism that the film noir movement would evolve to television. Television was the replacement for "B" studio features that comprised much of film noir. A review of the early television fare indicates that noir wasn't simply a victim of sudden death in the mid–1950s. The genre merely moved indoors to the small tube and morphed into a different type of entertainment. Formulaic shows including *Dragnet, Danger, China Smith* and *City Detective* were the forerunners of programs that emerged later in the decade like *M-Squad, Perry Mason, Johnny Staccato* and *Richard Diamond, Private Detective*. While these and like programs would be categorized as either "action-adventure" or "police dramas," one could clearly discern the dark roots of film noir in many of these small-screen stories. An emblematic example was Charles McGraw's television series bow that maintained the look and feel of a period film noir albeit frequently in an international setting.

The Adventures of Falcon (1954) was a syndicated 30-minute television series produced under the auspices of Federal Telefilms at Paramount for distribution by NBC. McGraw's new series had nothing to do with the old Falcon detective series at RKO starring Tom Conway.

The series of adventures of an international intelligence agent combating foreign intrigue around the globe was a thematic continuance of an earlier radio program of the same title. In 1950, Charlie had formed Collier-McGraw, a business partnership, with a man named William "Buster" Collier Jr. Collier was a former actor who appeared in over 80 films from 1916 to 1935. After living in England for a time, Collier returned to produce several early episodic television series including *Mr. and Mrs. North* with Richard Denning and Barbara Britton as a husband-and-wife sleuthing team episodically solving murders. Collier was the nominal producer of *The Adventures of Falcon* that was packaged and sold to NBC for a single season run. How their partnership worked out financially for McGraw is not clear; however, television offered another opportunity for him and other film actors who were no longer under contract to make a living.

McGraw starred as Mike Waring, alias "The Falcon," an ex-detective working as a government troubleshooter. Waring worked alternate assignments for the Senate investigating committee, the FCC, the Treasury Department, the Immigration Service, etc. The identity of McGraw's government employer was solely dependent on the weekly scriptwriter's imagination. Each episode would begin with a McGraw voice-over narrative against the visual backdrop of a spinning globe that summarily paused on episodic postwar locales such as Vienna, Italy, Paris and Taipei or the more prosaic New York. A quick disgorgement of a 24-minute story of international intrigue would follow.

With episodes directed by experienced hands like former Universal film cutter Paul Landres, *The Adventures of Falcon* was an archetype series of early television. The program was characterized by fast-paced action with solid performances by actors disciplined by the movie studio system. The scripts, several penned by the reliable Gene Wang (the leading scribe behind the later *Perry Mason* series), verged from credible to laughably camp. The acting and action proved a welcome distraction from the show's production values which were reminiscent of the cheapest Poverty Row offerings from the previous decade.

McGraw got the opportunity to clip off some pithy dialogue lines and he didn't end up face down in the gutter for a change. As the hero, he came out on top, usually exiting with the crooks rounded up and the girl on his arm before the final commercial break. Charlie enjoyed strong support as the series seemingly employed every working character actor in Hollywood: James Flavin, Nancy Gates, Robert Armstrong, Douglas Fowley, Barry Kelley, Philip Van Zandt, Peter Brocco, Ted de Corsia, James Westerfield, Tristram Coffin, Pamela Duncan, Myron Healey and a host of other familiar faces.

Cold War tensions played a prominent theme in many *Falcon* episodes as a topical reflection of the times. McGraw was either parachuting into Soviet Czechoslovakia to steal missile secrets and escaping into the American zone of Germany — still under postwar occupation by the Allies — or breaking up a black market ring in Austria selling phony medicine (shades of Harry Lime in *The Third Man*). Stateside episodes frequently opened with a bit of business such as Charlie leaning against a building in San Francisco reading a newspaper with a double bold headline screaming REDS FLOOD U.S. WITH DOPE. The plots were not complex and didn't need to be. A memorable episode about a U.S. nerve gas facility that had an espionage agent releasing the deadly substance proved to be more than a bit distressing. Although McGraw satisfactorily resolves the situation, it probably wasn't reassuring for viewers to observe the perpetually nervous Percy Helton as the scientist in charge of the U.S. nerve gas arsenal. Some of the period dialogue, now politically incorrect, is amusing. One surviving gem set in Italy has McGraw berating ethnic character actor Tito Vuolo as a "pizza-brained intellectual."[142]

With Laura Mason from his NBC television series *The Adventures of Falcon* (1954) (courtesy Mildred Black).

Other episodes were more traditional, after-the-bad-guys crime noir potboiler stuff: McGraw roaming the streets of New York breaking up a phony stamp racket and rolling up an underworld chieftain; on a train from Chicago chasing down stolen diamonds; or in Detroit when all the employees in his hotel are switched around to cover a major heist. Through it all, Charlie was cool, unflappable and tough with a voice-over patter that kept the program moving along at a rapid clip. *The Adventures of Falcon* was an entertaining program that was unfortunately not renewed after 39 episodes.

When the Falcon played out, McGraw donned a white dinner jacket and bow tie as saloon owner Rick in *Casablanca,* a small-screen spin-off of the legendary 1942 screen classic. Produced at the Warner Bros. nascent television unit headed by Jack L. Warner's son-in-law, William T. Orr, the series laid an immediate egg. The venerable movie studio wasn't sure what they were doing with television anyway. Veteran actor and filmmaker L.Q. Jones, then a Warners contract player starring in *Cheyenne* (1955–56), recalled, "Warners was just testing the television thing back then. Jack L. Warner didn't believe in television."[143]

Neither did Harry Warner, who ran the business end, even though he did apply for an FCC television license for the studio back in 1949. The only person at the Burbank studio who apparently noticed the exploding sales of television sets was J.L.'s majordomo Steve Trilling, who ran the studio's day-to-day operations but couldn't get Jack to listen. The daily reality that Jack, the head of production, and Harry, the titular studio president, hated each other's guts and were barely on speaking terms didn't aid in the development of a cohesive business strategy at Warner Brothers.

While television represented a new revenue stream for the studios, the money going to the artists was a mere trickle. This was particularly true at Warners where Harry Warner was observed walking around the lot picking up nails while Jack still kept tabs on the arrival times of producers and sent out blustery memos reminding employees about keeping the lights turned off. Television was regarded as a bush-league operation at WB according to L.Q. Jones:

> Warners was buying four or five scripts at a time during the writers' strike and wasn't paying anybody any money on television. I was making $550 a week when I was working and that was highest price of the whole bunch. Clint [Eastwood] was only making $250.[144]

On the *Casablanca* program, McGraw was certainly no Bogart, but his acting exuded confidence and he looked great in mufti on the sumptuous "Rick's Café" set. The show's main problem was the hackneyed teleplays that discarded Rick's world-weary cynicism (Charlie's character was renamed Rick Jason and his bar was now the Club American) and replaced it with McGraw acting as a referee for different characters who wandered in and out of the stories. The handsome set and expansive camerawork (for early television) were really wasted by the trite stories. In the episode "Siren Song," McGraw attempts to prevent a retired bullfighter friend (James Mitchell) from returning to the corrida in order to show off for Amazonian femme fatale Mari Blanchard. What this foolishness had to do with wartime intrigue in North Africa was not readily apparent. The legendary movie simply didn't translate well to an episodic television series. Despite playing a debonair man of action on a highly visible television show, McGraw was still McGraw. Mickey Knox visited Charlie on the set and observed the star taking a pull from a fifth of vodka that he kept in his dressing room. McGraw's reaction to being cast opposite the Swedish bombshell Anita Ekberg in the debut episode of *Casablanca* was also typical. He was made aware of a tryst that Ekberg reportedly had the night before with a Great Big Star. When the straight-laced McGraw had to kiss Ekberg during a close-up during the next day's show, he reportedly demurred, stating afterward that he "did not drink from a public fountain."[145]

In a vain effort to recapture past glories and the dollars that went with them, Warner Bros. recycled some of the original cast members into the mercifully brief series. Massive character actor Dan Seymour, who played a doorman in the 1942 film classic, took over the Sydney Greenstreet role. The croupier in the original film, Marcel Dalio was assigned to play Captain Renaud, who was first immortalized by Claude Rains. Ludwig Stossel, who played a refugee in the original, got the "Cuddles" Sakall part, etc. None of it worked. The show was yanked off of ABC after eight episodes.

Despite off-the-record misgivings, McGraw pitches woo to bombshell Anita Ekberg in the debut episode of the television series *Casablanca* (1955). The show was canceled after eight episodes (courtesy Mildred Black).

The postscript at Warner Brothers was a perverse display of Hollywood familial love. Jack Warner stage-managed the sale of the Warner Brothers studio in May 1956, convincing his older brother Harry that it was time for both of them to cash in their chips and retire. Harry reluctantly agreed only on the condition that neither of the two brothers would remain in control of the studio. When Harry Warner read in the trade papers that the sale went through and Jack made a secret deal to retain his stock and become the new president of Warner Brothers, the elder brother fell on the floor of his dining room with a stroke. Much diminished, Harry Warner finally died in 1958. Jack Warner, who was vacationing on the French Riviera, declined to leave the Monaco gaming tables in order to attend his brother's funeral.

18

"Where Do We Get Such Men ..."

During the middle of the the the 1950s, Charles McGraw reached the high point of his career on screen. Into addition to starring in two television series, the actor landed notable parts in top-tier studio productions, the first of which poised him on the cusp of stardom.

McGraw's work in *The Bridges at Toko-Ri* (1955) was one of many distinctive performances in a huge "A" production with an all-star cast including William Holden, Fredric March, Grace Kelly and Mickey Rooney. Directed by former RKO editor Mark Robson, the picture was based on James Michener's bestseller about the Korean War. An entertaining drama about the dedication and challenge faced by Navy carrier pilots, as epitomized by reluctant warrior Bill Holden, *The Bridges at Toko-Ri* remains one of the singular war movies of the 1950s. Charlie plays Commander Wayne Lee, the Carrier Air Group Chief (CAG) to Holden's conflicted Naval Reserve jet pilot who is recalled to active duty to serve In the Korean War with ultimately tragic results. Clichés are refreshingly absent from a compelling portrait of the ambivalent, tragic complexities on why men do what they must do during wartime. McGraw is ruggedly handsome in the Technicolor production. His piercing blue eyes and neatly combed brown hair were nicely complemented by his pressed khaki uniform and flyer's jacket. His performance as the war-weary veteran pilot who tries to look after the men that he is responsible for putting in harm's way was extremely well-conceived.

McGraw more than holds his own in two key scenes with the legendary Fredric March, who plays the task force admiral. After becoming irked after Charlie sees him in an unsuccessful attempt to bypass the carrier's commanding officer to halt the perceived abuse of his squadron's aircraft, March pigeonholes Charlie as an opportunistic "chain-of-command jumper" who is unworthy of future promotion. In the final scene with Holden dead, and March despondent, McGraw has another tense exchange with the admiral on the carrier's bridge. This time, Charlie locks his frosty baby blues directly with March's and goes on the offensive: "[M]aybe he was your boy, admiral, but he was my boy, too."[146]

McGraw exits the bridge with his pride intact, leaving March's admiral with his mouth slightly agape. March admits that he was completely wrong about his earlier assessment of McGraw as an officer before movingly reflecting on Holden's legacy: "Where do we get such men...." Where indeed.

There was talk in the industry about a Best Supporting Actor nomination for Charlie but it wasn't to be. In an extremely competitive year, *The Bridges at Toko-Ri* was only nominated for two Oscars, film editing and special effects, winning for the latter.

By the mid–1950s, McGraw was such a respected actor that he could become publicly crotchety over a newer generation of actors who lacked the desire or opportunity to master their craft. McGraw fulminated about the changes in the movie business and took stock in his own success shortly before *Bridges* wrapped at Paramount:

The Bridges at Toko-Ri (1955): Mickey Rooney, Earl Holliman, McGraw, and Robert Sherry (courtesy Mildred Black).

I'm all for new faces. And I'm not sore at the producers. They give a kid good direction and custom-written parts and sometimes the kids click. But I get my dander up at the way some of these kindergarten actors put on the dog. They let their hair grow long if they're a man or cut it off if they're a woman. They start giving out with their theories on picture-making and the theatre in general, when most of them haven't been closer to the stage than the one in the high school auditorium. They get interviewed and they say unusual things—and they make me sick....

Show business has been good to me. I have money in the bank, a home that's paid for, a swimming pool and three French poodles. I have a wife too. But it all came hard. I never studied drama at school. But I sure studied it in the theatre. We read about acting and we acted. Bits in plays. And in flops. Touring companies. Bits in pictures. But we didn't pontificate on the theatre to disc jockeys who interviewed us. We didn't set ourselves up as experts and put up a big front. Trouble with kids today [is that] they don't want to be actors half as much as they want to be stars. The craftsmanship, the joy of doing something well hasn't half the exciting appeal as the dollars or the phony glamour.[147]

McGraw certainly had some valid points about the changes in the business. There was a new generation of actors who didn't treat acting as a craft or progress through the school of hard knocks because they didn't have to. One didn't have to pay their dues if they were the newest twenty-four-year-old face on a television show or record label. One can only wonder how Charles McGraw would react to the modern cyberworld of instant celebrity and the heavyweight talent of "stars" like Paris Hilton.

Charlie followed *Bridges* with two more, top-tier military-themed pictures, *Away All Boats* (1956) and *Toward the Unknown* (1956).

Away All Boats was filmed on location in St. Thomas in the U.S. Virgin Islands by Joseph Pevney, Charlie's old stage partner from the Ivoryton, Connecticut stock company days. In the intervening two decades since treading the boards with McGraw, much had changed for Pevney. His abbreviated screen acting career had been confined entirely to noir: *Nocturne* (1946), *Body and Soul* (1947), *The Street with No Name* (1948), *Thieves Highway* (1949) and *Outside the Wall*

(1950). Aside from a cameo in his directorial debut of *Shakedown* (1950), Pevney moved exclusively into directing and stayed there until his retirement in 1985. The still voluble Pevney recalled the transition: Acting was very difficult for me: I always worked hard. But I always was a director on the stage. Wherever they needed a director, I always wanted to direct.[148]

Pevney helmed a flurry of distinctive films at V-I during the 1950s including *The Strange Door, Female on the Beach, Man of a Thousand Faces, Six Bridges to Cross* and *The Midnight Story* before moving into television where he directed fourteen of the original *Star Trek* episodes. The native New Yorker developed a reputation as an actor's director with a brambly sense of humor, but had little patience for people who wouldn't work hard.

According to Jill McGraw, who visited her dad with Freda on St. Thomas during the filming, Pevney needed vast reserves of both humor and patience. Members of the company who enjoyed surveying the island scenery from a barstool included Lex Barker, Richard Boone, Bobby Hoy, a young David Janssen, Charles Horvath, *and* Charles McGraw. A large segment of the nearly all-male cast struggled to get on the set every morning in a filmable condition. Recalls Jill, "Pevney had to have the assistant director swing by all of these waterfront dives every morning to round up a number of the actors!"[149]

Jill was 15 years old and was put under close supervision by her parents when a U.S. Navy flotilla of 19 ships came in to support the production and the sailors took over the hotel pool and lobby. The fun-loving Charlie Horvath took particular delight in playing practical jokes and once showed up at a cast party dressed in a large diaper. William Reynolds, who was in the cast, remembered a bus trip with Horvath and McGraw on a stopover in Texas during the long plane ride from Los Angeles to St. Thomas:

> Charlie Horvath was a large actor I had known for some time as a stuntman and he and I would have a few drinks together over the years. He was a decorated Marine and the toughest man in the world but, happily, he had a sweet disposition. He was also a real joker. We worked together, along with actor Charles McGraw, on the film *Away All Boats*, and in transit to the Virgin Islands for the filming we stopped over in Texas. As we were bussed in from the airport, Charlie Horvath stuck his head out of the window and yelled, as loud as he could, "My name is Charlie McGraw and I am staying at the Rice Hotel and I can whip any Texan who ever lived!" And he repeated it all the way to the hotel. It cost McGraw a fortune in tips to the staff at the hotel to make sure that if anyone came looking for Charlie McGraw they never heard of him.[150] [Note: It is impossible to read this anecdote without recalling an earlier one involving McGraw on *Border Incident*.]

Bobby Hoy recalled the St. Thomas shoot fondly. The stuntman remembered a bar owned by an American near the waterfront that catered to "a select number of the cast including Dick Boone, McGraw, Lex, Charlie Horvath and yours truly."[151] The barkeep reputedly served up prodigious amounts of Old Granddad for 15 cents a shot to the hard-drinking cast members.

Joe Pevney's recollections of *Away All Boats* are more prosaic. The veteran director related that Universal-International originally mandated that the extensive ocean sequences be filmed at nearby Santa Catalina Island. After dismissing that time-worn locale as impractical for the large-scale Naval saga called for in the script, Pevney scouted locations in Hawaii and elsewhere before deciding on St. Thomas. The director has pleasant fond memories of a cast and crew that exhibited the utmost teamwork and professionalism while working on a large, complicated picture, saying, "Moving around those large, heavy cameras we used in those days on board ship was a challenge."[152] Pevney recalled some of the bacchanal atmosphere that infected the company's more macho participants. Bobby Hoy took to diving into the hotel pool from the balcony of his room. According to Pevney, the dive was 18 or 20 feet, with all the stuntmen taking turns showing off.

Not too surprisingly, Pevney expressed weariness working with McGraw on this picture;

McGraw is decidedly out of uniform in *Away All Boats* (1956). L to R (foreground): Keith Andes, Richard Boone, Jeff Chandler, McGraw, George Nader, Lex Barker.

the actor was having so much fun that he was not easy to get on the set. While the director respected McGraw as an actor, whatever closeness existed between the two men suffered a permanent rupture during the production. "Charlie upset me in many ways as a human being," said Pevney. "I didn't feel that he was as honest in his approach as he could be."[153] According to the director, he and McGraw were simply cut from two different bolts of cloth. Nonetheless, Pevney admired Charlie's work, particularly in an early scene when Jeff Chandler takes command of the ship and McGraw, as the lieutenant in charge of small boats, shows up for a formal meeting dressed in pajamas. Charlie's character gets killed in combat about half way through the picture. Pevney didn't elaborate whether McGraw's early departure from the film was an occasion for grief or relief.

While the gripping saga of a Naval combat vessel during World War II might have taken on the characteristics of a liquor-soaked Mardi Gras behind the scenes, the film that ended up in the can was an extremely effective war drama with Chandler and George Nader as the two male leads.

The carnival atmosphere that prevailed in St. Thomas was noticeably absent during the filming of *Toward the Unknown* (1956), a picture that was filmed at Edwards Air Force Base in the Mojave Desert by veteran director Mervyn LeRoy. *Toward the Unknown* was a high-quality production, curiously overlooked and virtually unmentioned in contemporary accounts of William Holden's career and film history books. Based on a first-rate original story by Beirne Lay Jr., who penned the epochal *Twelve O'Clock High*, the picture boasts a stout cast of Holden,

Lloyd Nolan, McGraw, Virginia Leith, Murray Hamilton and L.Q. Jones. The film also featured the screen debut of James Garner, who played a young test pilot.

Holden is a test pilot who was captured over Korea, brainwashed and forced to disavow the Code of Conduct. No traitor, but tainted, the returned P.O.W. wants to climb back into the cockpit, but is blocked by the always reliable Nolan, the hard-driving test base commander. Nolan is personally testing a prototype jet while concealing an encroaching blackout problem at high altitudes that would ground him and jeopardize the program. Nolan believes that Holden might be damaged goods, but knowing he was once the best, grudgingly lets him back in the test program at the junior achievement level. The two spar about the vagaries of the mission and over the trophy woman, Nolan's secretary, smoky-voiced Virginia Leith, who remains one of the interesting "what-ifs" from 1950s Hollywood.

The actress was briefly placed under contract by Warners shortly before the studios dumped most of their contracted players in the late 1950s. Leith resembled a brunette Lizabeth Scott that might have lived down the block in the suburbs and been mooned over by, say, Tony Dow. She also had acting talent, but, like so many other performers on the Hollywood scene, never got the big break and suffered a truncated film career. Leith remains best remembered for playing that infamous living head in a lasagna pan ("Jan in the Pan") in the grade–Z camp horror movie, *The Brain That Wouldn't Die* (1962).

McGraw was again cast opposite William Holden, this time as a contemporary Air Force buddy who is the executive officer of the base. In a role that was not as well-written as *The Bridges at Toko-Ri* but was still prominent. Charlie did his usual competent job, solid and credible. The all-smiles finale to the picture has Lloyd Nolan retiring from the base and being kicked upstairs to Washington; McGraw lands Nolan's job with Bill Holden getting both Virginia Leith and his self-respect back.

L.Q. Jones, who played a bumbling Air Force lieutenant in the picture and would go on to work with Charlie on several other films, remembered McGraw with fond respect:

> Charlie was like other people during that era. Just an extraordinarily good actor. He didn't need someone to tell him how to do it or why. Charlie was kind of a shy individual, kind of wary initially. He had many working friends, but not that many good friends. He didn't need many friends. He had been screwed over a number of times. There was no talk about motivation or this type of thing. Charlie's philosophy was to hit his marks, say his lines and pick up his check. That was what it was about. It wasn't easy either. Charlie was just extraordinarily good.[154]

McGraw shed his uniform and returned to the now-disheveled world of B films at Allied Artists with *The Cruel Tower* (1956). As a working actor, Charlie would never look down at any role, particularly a choice part like this one, but he must have realized this picture would not come close to replicating the production or marquee values of his previous two features. *The Cruel Tower* was ostensibly an adventure about the travails of a group of steeplejacks. What remains is a campy film that is part soap opera and part adventure with a dash of film noir.

As with *Loophole* (1954), the picture was produced at Allied Artists by the veteran Lindsley Parsons Sr. whose career in B pictures began back in 1937 making Westerns at (yes, seriously) Boots and Saddles Productions Inc. Parsons had the dubious distinction of producing both *King of the Zombies* (1941) and *Revenge of the Zombies* (1943) along with a seemingly endless series of migraine-inducing but profitable Bowery Boys films. Parsons was still providing his expertise in cut-rate film production as a damage control consultant to modern filmmakers—there isn't a Monogram proving ground around anymore to imbue young filmmakers with the twin virtues of speed and economy—shortly before he passed away at age 87 in 1992.

Charlie frequently played the role of on-set jokester. Here he breaks up William Holden during *Toward the Unknown* (1956) (courtesy Mildred Black).

Parsons' son, Lindsley Jr., was the assistant director on *The Cruel Tower*: "In those days," he says, "the AD did everything including being the Production Manager."[155]) The younger Parsons scouted locations for the film by renting an airplane and flying over greater Los Angeles. He eventually decided on a water tower near Huntington Beach (still standing) and a smokestack in Burbank (long gone) near St. Joseph's Hospital to use for the extensive filming of the steeplejacks at work. Photo plates and scaffolding were used for the close-ups of the actors on the job. Parsons' budget couldn't afford the high rates demanded by union stuntmen to work off the tower and smokestack for the long shots. He ended up hiring the actual electricians who periodically went aloft to change the aircraft warning lights at the top of the structures to rig the scaffolding and ropes, climbing up so the director could shoot the footage.

The director of *The Cruel Tower* was Lew Landers, nee Louis Friedlander, perhaps the most prolifically skilled helmsman of low-budget serials and B features in movie history. Landers compiled a voluminous directing résumé of over 150 features, none of which probably had a budget of over $200,000. The director consistently achieved credible results through mastery of always having to do more with less. According to Lindsley Parsons Jr.:

> Lew was terrified of unemployment and was pulling out what was left of his hair. He was usually on the phone to his agent attempting to line up his next job while saying, "Cut, print."[156]

In this particular film, the artfully lean production values did nothing to impede an interesting story with an amusingly clichéd script.

When iterant John Ericson gets rolled and thrown off of a freight train by a pair of predatory hobos, he is taken in by a group of steeplejacks led by Harry "Stretch" Clay (McGraw). Only Charlie at 5'10" could credibly portray a character named "Stretch." McGraw appears to be bedding — the story is not wholly clear about this — the unbelievably statuesque Mari Blanchard, whose character is aptly named Mary "The Babe" Thompson. Blanchard, taller than "Stretch," is inexplicably traveling around in a steeplejack trailer with McGraw, Steve Brodie, Alan Hale Jr. and Peter Whitney. The boys get turned on watching Blanchard strut around in a variety of tight-fitting slack and blouse combos and then alternate getting into a series of obtuse fights with each other. What Blanchard gains from this curious arrangement is left to the viewer's imagination. "The Babe" either gets turned on by the phallic symbolism of the water tower that looms out of every other camera shot as the jarring musical soundtrack crescendos or she simply digs watching a group of macho brain donors suspended in midair, risking their lives hanging off of ropes while fighting over her attentions. The romantic fireworks start immediately when Blanchard decides to change her clothes in the trailer in front of the slack-jawed Ericson and then becomes startled when he immediately comes on to her. Pressurized fuel is added to the fire when McGraw discovers that co-worker Steve Brodie is fooling around with his wife, conveniently at home, while McGraw is pursuing Blanchard on the road. Murder, business rivalry and overlapping double crosses are thrown in as the film churns along like a high-speed blender.

The Cruel Tower gave Charlie plenty of opportunities to chew scenery with vigor. He mashes a cigarette out on his hand, overturns tables, starts a saloon brawl and leads an exciting fight denouement on top of that perpetual water tower. John Ericson, who was in the process of being packaged by the film industry as a template of James Dean, complete with blue jeans and leather jacket, remembered McGraw fondly.

> I took things so seriously as an actor — I wasn't having much fun at all. Charlie was a real prankster. He would be telling a joke or a story on the set and then go right into character when it was time. He taught me how to loosen up.[157]

By the second half of the 1950s, Charles McGraw concluded his film noir appearances as the style transitioned out of the popular culture and became homogenized into television crime dramas. While the dark-shaded rhythms of noir became diluted and finally extinguished by the sensibilities and tastes of a different environment and coming-of-age generation, the actor was near or at the peak of his film career. McGraw's personal journey into noir was yet to come.

19

Family Tensions

By the summer of 1956, Charles McGraw had ample reason to be satisfied with his decision to leave RKO. He was at the apex of his career with an acclaimed supporting performance in an all-star film, plenty of choice cinematic roles and two television series under his belt. He and Freda celebrated with a vacation to England, France and Italy during the summer of 1956. For his wife, it was a welcome break from Charlie's propensity for hanging out with his friends in the saloons of Studio City. Charlie also brought his family with him on location when he was appearing in *Away All Boats* (1956) with Freda going to Hawaii for *Twilight for the Gods* (1958) and Japan for *Joe Butterfly* (1957).

Charlie and Freda's social life revolved around visiting friends, going out for cocktails, or an occasional dinner out on the town at Jack La Rue's restaurant or a similar venue. Charlie enjoyed going to downtown L.A. for the Tuesday night fights at the Olympic Auditorium or to Wrigley Field to catch an Angels game. After 1958, it was the Dodgers. "Charlie was a man's man"[158] said one of the actor's boon companions. Indeed. Charlie loved hunting, fishing, boxing—in short, participating in a myriad of masculine activities with his pals that were bound together by drinking. A singular example of the esteem with which the actor was held by his comrades was when he was elected vice president of the *San Fernando Laurel Room Fish Head and Split Infinitive Society* aboard the fishing vessel *Blue Fin* out of San Pedro. Many of these activities truncated the time that he spent with his wife and daughter when he was home in Studio City.

McGraw's drinking and nocturnal absences exacerbated a growing dysfunction within the small family. According to Jill, parenting was a vocation that both her parents appeared to have minimal interest in. Charlie had the movies and his pals. Freda had the house, her two poodles and the garden. Jill increasingly felt like the odd one out. Even as a young child dining out with her parents, she was allowed to order anything on the menu she chose, but sat in silence during the meal while her mother and father retreated to sharing a newspaper at the table amid minimal communication.

"You have to understand that I was raised by 'Marcellus.'"[159] The reference by Charlie's daughter to her father's memorable performance as the cruel gladiator instructor in *Spartacus* was humorously tongue-in-cheek, but the comment contained more than a trace of sadness. The remark in no way meant to indicate that her father was unkind or mean; he wasn't. It was directly aimed at the rough-hewn exterior characterized by the pursuit of masculine leisure by the elder McGraw. As a young girl, Jill accompanied her father to the fights, ballgames and like activities to the point where the daughter once wondered aloud if her dad would have been more comfortable with a son.

McGraw would often head down the hill to Ventura Boulevard for a newspaper and would frequently end up in Herbert's Drive-In where he could sip cold beer and chat with Dick Martin and other cronies. Daughter Jill's school bus stop was across the street on the southern side

Freda McGraw and Dick Martin at a pool get-together at Reklaw Drive in the mid–1950s (courtesy Mildred Black).

of Ventura Boulevard; she remembered waiting in a booth at Herbert's for her father to take her home.

For all his drinking, McGraw was a virtual teetotaler around the house with Freda. The actor normally didn't keep much liquor besides beer at home and confined most of his heavy imbibing to bars. At home, the McGraws regularly had swimming pool parties and guests over to their house. Charlie also quasi-adopted a well-known eccentric named Peter the Hermit, who had been roaming around Hollywood since the 1920s. Peter Howard was reportedly born in Ireland during the "year of the wind," affected white clothes and long beard and rode a burro in Hollywood parades. He lived for years in a tent on a vacant Laurel Canyon lot before finally being evicted. While a strapping athlete in his youth, Peter the Hermit was now an old man, gnarled and stooped. Charlie loved him and installed him in the spare room on the ground floor of his house for a time. There is no record on how Freda felt about sharing her hillside abode with Peter.

From the late afternoon into the evening, McGraw pretty much resided in Herbert's or O'Brien's Bar, or Keith's and perhaps the Blarney Stone. Charlie was an enigmatic guy who people gravitated to. He was simply fun to *be* with, his rough spontaneity of humor, debate, and adventure drawing in all types of characters. The barroom camaraderie in Studio City between the actors, stuntmen, and locals took on the characteristics of a fraternal lodge with Charlie anointed as the king. One barroom bard penned a verse that aptly summed up the barroom milieu along the Boulevard

Ventura Boulevard in the Spring

A bunch of the boys were shootin' the shit
Down at O'Briens bar.
They had discussed the merits of various broads
And refought the bloody war.

Then in through the door with a blast of light
And into that dimlit place
Came Charlie McGraw and with a raspy craw,
Says "How 'bout a little blast?"

Ventura Blvd in the spring. Charlie and the boys out on the town in the mid–1950s. The gent with his hand on Charlie's shoulder is Wilson Bridges (Willie) Geiger. Others are unidentified friends of McGraw (courtesy Mildred Black).

The bullshit artists gathered around
And exchanged admiring looks.
Les the lawyer — Freddie the Fox
And even Bathhouse Brooks.

Highschool Harry and Big Bad John
Moved to join the ring
For a title well earned where bullshit's concerned
Was Charlie McGraw, the king.

The news got out and round about;
And eventually reached the home
Of the other artists on the boulevard
Up at the Blarney Stone.

Dago Dick and Little John
Were among the rist to cut
Then Indian Boy and Billy Boy,
And finally Len the Gut.

The meeting was called to order
And the previous bullshit read
When King McGraw discovered a flaw —
Little Caesar must still be in bed.

This threw the meeting into a panic
As each bullshitter vied for the floor.
"Begone with your quarrels," bellowed King Charles,
And headed forthwith for the door.

"But hold up, King Charles," they cried as a group,
"Stay and have just one more!"
"Nay!" said King Charles, "the meeting's adjourned
And I'm now on me way to the store."
God Bless[160]

Although a reasonably attentive father when Jill was a child, McGraw ran into difficulties in trying to parent an increasingly restless daughter in the mid–1950s. A major problem was that Charlie's drinking became excessive as Jill entered her critical teenage years. The negative outcomes for a child being raised in a household with an alcoholic parent are not a new phenomenon. Add to it growing up in the fishbowl world of Hollywood with a recognizable celebrity for a dad and the situation became a recipe for heartbreak. Fifty years later, Jill believed that her father "wasn't the person he was meant to be" as she "watched him change."[161] From the standpoint of fairness, it must be noted that the perspective of Jill's childhood years lacks any corroborative balance from her parents or other family intimates. What is apparent, though, is that the pain of Jill's upbringing, even after the passage of more than half a century, remains preeminent and undeniable.

Charlie relaxes at home with Peter the Hermit (courtesy Mildred Black).

Even as a fourteen-year-old, Jill wasn't happy with her dad. In an episode tinged with humor, an account of taking her father to task about his famous voice made it into Earl Wilson's Broadway column:

"Can't you do something about it? When my girl friends come over they think you're angry — even when you smile." ... "Without the voice," he told Jill fatherly, "we'd be living in a two room flat somewhere." Charley recalled that he and his wife once had a swimming party at their home which was attended by many of Hollywood's handsome young leading men.... "I swim a lot better than most of them. But Jill didn't like that. She got mad, accusing me of deliberately showing off." ... Recently the McGraws had another party.... A lot of big men important in show business attended. Later he asked his daughter if she better understood his position as an actor. "You can't be important," replied his daughter, "or else I wouldn't know you."[162]

Freda McGraw had her hands full attempting to manage her day-to-day existence around

Charlie and Freda McGraw in 1956. They loved each other passionately until McGraw's drinking made their life together unendurable (courtesy Mildred Black).

Charlie's roller coaster lifestyle. According to Jill McGraw, her father's behavior "drove my mother crazy." McGraw's wife gradually became a nervous wreck dealing with the chaotic habits of a cherished husband who would arrive home all smiles with a new puppy or car and then would subsequently disappear without phoning for a day and show up later, unshaven, bellicose and ready to sleep off a drunk. Due to her anxious devotion to her husband or for whatever other reason, Jill McGraw believes that Freda withheld the affection from her that any child would normally take for granted, that her own birth was unplanned and the birth of other siblings was something her mother assiduously avoided. Well kept and provided for, but emotionally bereft, McGraw's daughter claims that she grew up in a lonely household.

Charlie's career continued at a steady clip, but the actor wasn't investing or saving his money like he should have been. McGraw didn't have a comprehensive, long-term financial management plan other than spending his pay and putting some of the excess money in the bank; there would always be another check from a television show or film. Jill remembers a tail-finned Caddy being driven up the driveway with a flourish—and that it disappeared just as quickly several months later. Charlie was always generous with friends, even casual acquaintances. Much later, when McGraw was really struggling financially, he saw fit to give away nearly an entire paycheck from a television appearance to a drinking buddy towards the purchase of a set of false teeth. For the present, the actor continued making a good living while maintaining his relentless lifestyle.

20

Character Actor

While accepting that he was never going to be a leading man on screen, McGraw continued to land choice character roles in prestige films. He had his hair dyed white as Lieutenant
Joseph Vosnick in *Slaughter on Tenth Avenue* (1957), a talent-laden waterfront crime film. The
picture is an obvious attempt to replicate the smash success of *On the Waterfront* (1954) along
with the incorporation of a *Dragnet*-style warning that precedes the opening credits:

> The picture you are about to see is based on fact, but to ensure the safety of people still alive, certain
> modifications have been made.[163]

More social editorial than film noir, *Slaughter on Tenth Avenue* stars Richard Egan as a
young assistant D.A. who takes on a dockside murder case that is emblematic of underworld
infiltration of a longshoremen local and official corruption. The picture is bolstered by a terrific
ensemble cast headed by Egan, Jan Sterling, Julie Adams, Walter Matthau, Dan Duryea, McGraw
and Sam Levene. Although the film plods at times, the realistic depiction of big city justice as
a bureaucratic and politically slanted affair until someone in power finally decides to take a
stand remains a compelling message. Sterling, playing the conflicted wife of a slain longshoreman is particularly effective. Sam Levene, eschewing his typical eyebrow-lifting performance,
also performs yeoman work as a realpolitik Manhattan district attorney, forced to temper the
hard-charging idealism of assistant Egan who inevitably triumphs in the end. McGraw is
extremely effective as a rough-hewn, honest cop with a world-weary "been there-done that"
attitude over taking on underworld crooks.

The picture was also memorable for pairing McGraw up with the great Dan Duryea in a
tense courtroom scene. It was the film noir dream match-up of "King Kong vs. Godzilla."
Duryea, elegantly turned out with a mustache and ornate watch fob, exhibits his usual sleazy
elegance as a former D.A. turned high-powered attorney defending the waterfront mobsters
headed by Matthau. Duryea bests Charlie by a TKO. His irresistible legalese fractures the stolid
John Law granite of McGraw on the witness stand. The clever attorney makes the hard-boiled
detective appear as an avenging wraith who coerced false testimony through a personal connection to the murdered longshoreman. Charlie departs with his credibility damaged but with
jaw resolutely set. Julie Adams recalls McGraw as a wonderfully professional actor and a great
guy on the set. Adams appeared in three movies with Charlie, but had no major scenes with
him and didn't get to know him particularly well. She vividly remembers being struck by the
charismatic presence of newcomer Walter Matthau who played the principal heavy ("No one
knew who he was and look at what Walter Matthau turned out to be!"[164]). Matthau was part of
a new generation of actors who would start with live television in New York and go on to a legendary career in Hollywood.

McGraw went to Japan for *Joe Butterfly* (1957). The picture, a spin-off of *Teahouse of the
August Moon* from the previous year, featured the unusual casting of Audie Murphy and Burgess

The Film Noir equivalent of King Kong vs. Godzilla: Dangerous Dan Duryea takes on Charlie McGraw in *Slaughter on Tenth Avenue* (1957).

Meredith as a Japanese con artist. Meredith, after several hours in makeup and coaching from a Japanese actor, was startlingly effective as a Nipponese character. The comedic backdrop of the picture concerns the staff of *Yank* magazine (Murphy, George Nader, McGraw and John Agar) impossibly tasked to put out a magazine in 72 hours. They enlist the aid of Meredith and matters immediately start falling off the turnip truck. McGraw played a funny Army sergeant; he brought Freda over to Japan for the location shoot.

Surviving 16mm home movies shot by Freda and Charlie on the *Joe Butterfly* trip include brief sequences of Burgess Meredith, Audie Murphy and other cast members relaxing on the long flight to Japan. Some of the home movies show a rural-looking Japan that was still recovering from the devastation of World War II.*

No different than any other actor, Charlie missed out on several choice roles that went to other performers. He was under consideration by Billy Wilder for the part of "Duke" in *Stalag 17* back in 1953, but lost out to authentic war hero and consummate heavy, Neville Brand. McGraw also was on the short list to play a sheriff—a role that he would become mind-numbingly familiar with—in *Gunfight at the O.K. Corral* (1957), but the role went to veteran character actor Frank Faylen. The picture ended up being one of the biggest box offices successes of the mid–1950s. Despite the near-misses, the work for Charlie kept on coming.

In a moody MGM Western, *Saddle the Wind* (1958), McGraw portrayed a memorable heavy.

*The McGraws' home movies are from 1955–1959. The films range from backyard pool parties, to a vacation to Europe and visits to locations including the Virgin Islands, Connecticut, Colorado, and Hawaii. Many of these films show the couple having fun and clowning with various friends and guests. This period was the apex of Charlie's career and personal life before the gathering dark clouds began to coalesce.

As gunslinger Larry Venables, he rides into town during the opening credits seeking vengeance against retired gunslinger, now rancher, Robert Taylor. After abusing a sad-eyed saloonkeeper in a filthy shirt (Jay Adler) and stealing his breakfast, McGraw's character quickly ends up in a barroom showdown with Taylor's hot-headed brother, John Cassavetes. When Taylor enters the barroom at a key moment, Charlie becomes distracted and is fatally plugged by Cassavetes. *Saddle the Wind* was shot in the Rockies near Canyon City, Colorado. Character actor Richard Erdman, also in the cast, retains two (actually three) principal memories of the shoot: "Charles McGraw and Julie London's tits!"

> Robert Parrish was the director and a close friend. He was in absolute awe of McGraw and couldn't wait for him to show up. He arrived at the airport dead drunk off the plane and nearly knocked over two people in the baggage area.[165]

Erdman enjoyed working with Charlie immensely, but didn't care much for Rod Serling's script or McGraw's truncated appearance: "I thought we were going to have this great heavy for the balance of the film."[166]

Charlie was reunited with his buddy Bobby Hoy on Stanley Kramer's paean for racial equality, *The Defiant Ones* (1958). As the lead stuntman on a picture that was essentially a chase sequence from beginning to end, Hoy had his hands full on this production. In addition to being responsible for the execution and staging of the numerous stunt "gags," Hoy kept an eye on Charlie to ensure that the older actor's drinking didn't interfere with his work.

Producer-director Stanley Kramer tasked Hoy to locate an African-American stuntman who was an adept swimmer to double Sidney Poitier during an arduous river-crossing scene while chained to Hoy, who was doubling Tony Curtis. This particular talent acquisition was no easy feat in Hollywood circa 1958. Hoy came through and hired a young man named Ivan Dixon, who would go on to forge a distinguished career in Hollywood as an actor and television director.

McGraw was cast as a State Police captain in pursuit of the escaped duo of Tony Curtis and Sidney Poitier. Charlie responded with a captivating performance of curmudgeonly, bureaucratic malevolence. Adorned in a uniform of redneck proletariat (a Smokey the Bear hat with dark jodhpurs), McGraw verbally spars with the county sheriff (Theodore Bikel) over jurisdictional and tactical issues relating to the hunt to recapture the two escaped convicts. Bikel enjoyed working with Charlie and, like many others who spent extended time with McGraw away from the barroom bluster, was struck by the inherent contradiction of the tough guy facade and the actual man: "He was fun to be with. I just recall that there always seemed to be a contrast between his rough, raspy voice and the basically gentle nature of the man."[167]

Charlie also carries on an intermittently amusing repartee of irritated looks and lifted eyebrows with actor Carl Switzer, a member of the posse who insists on playing a portable radio while McGraw is trying to bark out orders like an amateur General Patton. *The Defiant Ones* turned out to be Switzer's final screen appearance. The former child star, etched in the public consciousness as "Alfalfa" from the Our Gang shorts of the 1930s, had eked out a career as an adult character actor while attempting other enterprises including managing a bar in North Hollywood. Contemporaries who knew the adult Switzer remember "Alfie" as an obstinate person who followed his own bent regardless of consequences. In 1959, Switzer had the terminal misfortune to physically confront a man at his domicile in Van Nuys over a reported $50 debt for a hunting dog and was fatally shot.

Charlie was next reunited with director Joe Pevney on another location shoot. This time it was in Hawaii for *Twilight for the Gods* (1958). Pevney himself remembered very little about

McGraw and Burgess Meredith arrive on the Tokyo location shoot of *Joe Butterfly* (1957). Note the eye makeup on Meredith, who played the title role. Assistant director Terrence Nelson (wearing sunglasses) is at far right (courtesy Mildred Black).

this film and it is probably just as well; it's a creaky "soap opera at sea" about a weathered sailing ship en route from Honolulu to Mexico with a group of disparate passengers. Fulsome seascape photography and a wonderful supporting cast of Arthur Kennedy, Leif Erickson, Celia Lovsky, Richard Haydn, Wallace Ford, and Vladimir Sokoloff can't rescue the misguided casting of the two leads: Rock Hudson as a Hemingwayesque skipper who goes to pieces over a woman with a secret (Cyd Charisse). Both stars were completely out of place in these roles and it showed. The film was additionally betrayed by an endlessly talky script by Ernest Gann, based on his novel.

For McGraw, *Twilight for the Gods* was terrific fun. He had a meaty part as Yancy, the leading sailor under Arthur Kennedy, and his subordinate crewmates were two of his closest compadres off the set: Charlie Horvath and Bobby Hoy. Surviving McGraw home movies taken during the Hawaii sequences include a beachside luau with torches and hula dancers along with Joe Pevney barking orders to the crew of the sailing ship that was used during the location shoot. Hoy remembered an accident that occurred during the studio sequences for *Twilight for the Gods* that nearly impacted the production schedule. During an impromptu get-together at Horvath's house up in the Hollywood Hills, Arthur Kennedy fell down a flight of stairs and broke his arm. Hoy had the thankless task of phoning director Pevney at home in the middle of the night to inform him of the accident. After an initial reaction of fury, Pevney figured out a way to shoot around Kennedy with his arm in a sling for the remainder of the scheduled sequences.

When McGraw traveled to Thompson, Connecticut in June of 1958 to film *The Man in the Net* (1959) starring Alan Ladd, he returned to the New England locale where his career began in the 1930s. McGraw waxed philosophical during a newspaper interview.

McGraw is assuredly not sizing up Carolyn Jones' hand for a wedding ring in *The Man in the Net* (1959).

Charlie as he preferred to be called, claimed that "acting is more fun than hard work. Every picture is like Christmas morning," he says.... [I]t's the most fascinating profession in the world." ... McGraw's best friends are stuntmen, bartenders, jockeys and horse trainers because, "these are nice people because they are sincere." ... When asked if he suffers any frustrations in his profession, McGraw replied that his biggest frustration is that "... I've never become a good stuntman."[168]

Frustration was an apt description of the results of his latest picture. Despite a marquee director in Michael Curtiz and a fine writer in Reginald Rose, *The Man in the Net* was a major disappointment. The film was a murder mystery about Ladd being framed for the murder of his liquor-soaked, trampy wife (Carolyn Jones). Ladd is an artist living in a small town who is helped by a group of local children who believe in his innocence after most of the adults become convinced that Ladd is a murderer. Charlie is in top form playing a disagreeable town sheriff who was also diddling with Jones before she was done away with. The picture is dragged down by Ladd's leaden performance and a poor script that possessed holes wide enough to accommodate a Mack truck. The finale, with the surprise murderer being unmasked in a group setting, was reminiscent of a Monogram Studios Charlie Chan movie. *The Man in the Net* was a critical and box office failure. Its lack of success was not unexpected by some of the participants. Actor Michael McGreevey played McGraw's ten-year-old son in the film; he recalled the location shoot in Thompson, Connecticut, as an extremely unpleasant situation due to Alan Ladd's poor health and the tyranny of director Michael Curtiz. It was my first film and I was terrified of Curtiz. Alan Ladd was a sweet guy, but gave nothing to the kids, he was distant.[169]

McGreevey remembered that Ladd was so ill that he couldn't run very far at all and had to be extensively doubled. The group of child actors in the cast who formed an alliance with Ladd's character was the crux of the storyline, but Michael Curtiz, near the end of a very long career,

Charles McGraw helped his "son," actor Michael McGreevey, through a difficult moment during the shooting of *The Man in the Net* (1959). L to R: Tom Helmore, McGraw, McGreevey, Patrick Miller.

was grouchy and impatient, growling behind the camera about goddamn Hollywood kid actors. It was an extremely discomfiting situation that initially seemed worse when the young actor was introduced to his screen "father" played by Charles McGraw.

> Initially, Charlie sort of scared me. It was the voice and that jaw. You know, he had a very big head. There was something I liked about him. Charlie reminded me of an actor that I worked with later, Jack Warden. Charlie was not a warm and fuzzy guy, he was actually very nervous on the set, but when you acted with him, you felt good.[170]

McGreevey vividly recalled a disastrous situation that occurred during the filming of *The Man in the Net* between Michael Curtiz and McGraw:

> This made a distinct impression on me at a young age. We were filming out in a dump, trash and everything. Charlie and I had to find something there that linked Ladd to his wife's murder in the story. Curtiz had this involved master shot with a lot of camera movements. It was not uncommon for Curtiz to go 25 takes when things were going well. Charlie had a *lot* of dialogue. He was missing words, blowing lines and getting more and more frustrated. Instead of calling a break, Curtiz just kept on going. After about 45, 46 takes, Curtiz dressed Charlie down publicly, just humiliated him in front of everybody.[171]

According to McGreevey, McGraw was reduced to tears, but quietly walked off the set, composed himself and came back in a short while to deliver his lines flawlessly. To his credit, the actor didn't return and punch Curtiz in the mouth.

Soon afterward, it was young McGreevey's turn to be anxious and Charlie came to the rescue during a scene where the young actor had to cry and didn't think he could do it:

> I threw up in the bushes because I didn't know if I could do it and was going to mess up and have Curtiz come down on me. Charlie saw I was having trouble, took me aside and asked me what was

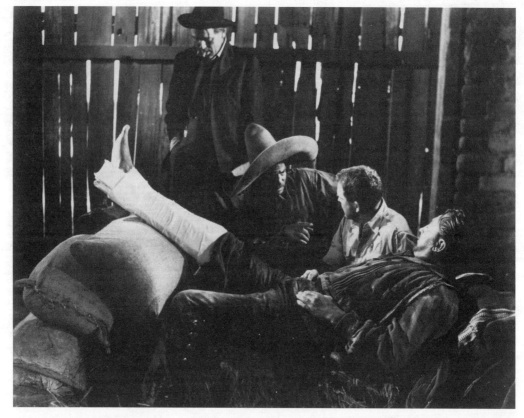

Charlie as cigar-chomping Dr. Herbert J. Stovall, admiring his recent handiwork on Robert Mitchum's broken leg as Jay Novello kibitzes with Max Slaten in *The Wonderful Country* (1959).

wrong. I said, "I'm scared." Charlie said, "Use that." I did and went back and got it done. You know, that was the first time as an actor that someone, another actor, bailed me out, helped me. I've never forgotten it."[172]

After the ordeal of *The Man in the Net,* Charlie was ready to blow off considerable steam in his next location shoot. He was given ample opportunity when he was reunited with his old RKO drinking pal, Robert Mitchum. *The Wonderful Country* (1959) was filmed in Durango, Mexico. The fact-based story of an ambiguous outlaw who works as a hired gun on both sides of the Rio Grande and becomes a pawn between a ruthless Mexican governor and his murderously ambitious brother, it was a perfect vehicle for Mitchum. Beautifully directed by Academy Award–winning editor and John Ford acolyte, Robert Parrish, the picture was made by Mitchum's production company, released by United Artists and remains one of the star's best, if least remembered, pictures. Mitchum, whose movie career had soared as his one-time RKO "rival" McGraw became consigned to character roles, was as committed to this project as anything he had made since *The Night of the Hunter* (1955). Mitchum stocked the cast with an eclectic mix of old friends and drinking buddies (Tony Caruso, McGraw, stunt double Chuck Roberson), veteran Hollywood hands (Gary Merrill, Albert Dekker, Pedro Armendariz, Jack Oakie) and new faces (Julie London, Mike Kellin). Easily the most improbable actor was legendary baseball star Leroy "Satchel" Paige, who played the leader of a black cavalry regiment and arrived in Durango with a youthful female in tow.

As Dr. Herbert J. Stovall, Charlie was a crusty frontier sawbones who ministers to Mitchum's broken leg with a something less than a genteel bedside manner. McGraw chats enthusiastically to the writhing Mitchum about the pain level of the imminent bone-setting procedure while taking a deep swallow from a whiskey bottle meant for his patient. In another scene with the town barber, played by *Wonderful Country* writer Tom Lea, giving Mitchum a shave and a bath there was a typical McGraw-contrived gag. Charlie ensured that it was chilled ice water that the barber used to douse Mitchum's genitals in the bathtub. The star's genuine eye-popping reaction was nicely captured by the camera.

The Wonderful Country was a location shoot that Freda wasn't invited along on, and with good reason. According to Anthony Caruso, the still rustic mining town of Durango was "full of bars and hookers."[173] Indoor plumbing proved to be an intermittent luxury at the lone hotel in town housing the company with Mitchum recommending that everyone drink plenty of tequila to internally disinfect themselves. McGraw reportedly arrived in a coma from drink after a leapfrogging flight (from Mexico City to Juarez, then Monterey, Torreon and finally Durango) after visiting a bar during each stop. Charlie made room for traveling companion Chuck Roberson by berating an ill passenger boarding the plane at Mexico City for the nervy inconvenience of requiring an oxygen tank that was taking up an extra seat. McGraw kicked up such a fuss that the man left the plane and his empty seat was claimed by Roberson. McGraw's raucous behavior on *The Wonderful Country* would be an appropriate dispositional bridge to his next cinematic role, a distinctive characterization that would be among his most memorable.

21

Spartacus

At first glance, Kirk Douglas' concept of making a gigantic blockbuster of Howard Fast's novel appeared to be another imitative notion from the stream of Biblical-tinged epics that Hollywood had revived since *The Robe* in 1953. The star decided to produce and star in *Spartacus* as a matter of prideful pique over not landing the title role of *Ben-Hur* the previous year. Only Kirk Douglas possessed the chutzpah to show everybody in Hollywood that he could top the biggest picture ever made. The fact-based saga about a slave who leads a spirited revolt that threatens Rome's hegemony of the ancient world circa 70 B.C. was a compelling story. It would be expensive, but Douglas had cash after *The Vikings* (1958), which grossed close to $15,000,000, and his production company, Byrna Corporation, partnered with Universal for use of their lot and additional financing along with distribution.

The initial budget for the film was quickly blown out of the water. Douglas spent whatever it took to fulfill his pictorial vision. The sole extravagance that he was talked out of was building an exact replica set of the Coliseum. Douglas declined building a duplicate stadium only because the infamously blood-stained venue wasn't around during the historical period of the story. Little else was spared. From handmade armor and uniforms to the immense battle scenes staged on the plains outside Madrid, using 8000 men from the Spanish Army, the gigantic production included 30 stars, eight assistant directors, 130 bit parts and nearly 5,000 extras. *Spartacus* would come in at a stupendous $12 million, the most expensive Hollywood production to date. A revealing perspective of the financial order-of-magnitude of the picture was the sale of Universal Studios to MCA Inc. for $11.5 million that transpired during the film's production. *Spartacus* cost more to make than the entire studio was worth.

Spartacus premiered a month short of a year after *Ben-Hur* with comparisons between the two spectacles proving inevitable. William Wyler's thunderous epic had swept through the 1959 Academy Awards like a tsunami, capturing 11 Oscars. *Spartacus* would win only four statuettes, even though it clearly was the superior film. There was speculation at the time that the dearth of awards was due to a right-wing backlash against the involvement of blacklisted writers Howard Fast and Dalton Trumbo. While the famous chariot race sequence in *Ben-Hur* remains a classic of cinematic action, *Spartacus* remains the "secular spectacle," a story of good and evil against a backdrop of ancient power and passion that eschews the hackneyed Biblical potboiler theatrics that were ceaselessly recycled by Hollywood. Despite the adulation and subsequent box office windfall, one can't help but wonder how the mammoth spectacle would have turned out if the original director of *Spartacus*, Anthony Mann, was left in place to direct the entire picture.

Before the start of production, Kirk Douglas acceded to Universal's entreaties and agreed to have Mann direct. Mann, whose directorial technique was honed in the shaded film noirs of the late 1940s, had moved on to a series of distinctive Westerns during the next decade, establishing his considerable reputation as a filmmaker. During the first half of the 1950s, Tony Mann and James Stewart combined on *Winchester '73, The Naked Spur, Bend of the River, The Far Country,* and *The Man from Laramie.* These picturesque classics of the Western genre were big earners and made Stewart the number one male box office star in Hollywood. Mann appeared to be an inspired choice as the director of *Spartacus.*

It didn't work out. Douglas and Mann immediately clashed. Both men were convinced of the righteousness of their artistic vision and neither was a shrinking violet. Mann further alienated Douglas when he attempted to act as a peacemaker in a disagreement between the producer-star and Sir Laurence Olivier. The legendary actor was cast as the patrician general, Crassus, who finally brings Spartacus to heel. Olivier reacted irritably to Douglas' gravitational propensity for micromanaging every aspect of the production including the British star's wardrobe. Although the two stars patched things up, the relationship between the executive producer and director deteriorated rapidly. Several weeks into the shooting schedule, word filtered out that Mann had been fired from the picture. Mann said afterward that he quit the production because Douglas was insistent on telling the story through what the director considered to be an excessive amount of superfluous dialogue. Mann was a firm believer in allowing the visual action, rather than the script, to lead the story.

The apotheosis of pagan villainy. Charles McGraw as Marcellus in *Spartacus* (1960).

Over three decades later, Kirk Douglas claimed that while he believed Mann was wrong for the picture, it was the Universal studio brass that came to him and demanded that Mann be jettisoned. Producer Edward Lewis offered that Mann wasn't fired, but quit under the weight of dealing with what amounted to four additional directors and screenwriters (Douglas, Olivier, Charles Laughton, Peter Ustinov). None of it mattered. Kirk Douglas was the producer, it was his picture and Tony Mann was not his guy. The only Mann-directed sequences that remained in the film were the initial scenes shot in Death Valley, California. Some measure of the challenge of working with Douglas as a star-producer on a film project was chronicled by the late Richard Fleischer, who commented after directing *The Vikings,* "You don't make pictures with Kirk. You survive them."[174] In fairness, Fleischer also pointed out that if it wasn't for Kirk Douglas, there wouldn't have been a picture to make.

Douglas replaced Mann with Stanley Kubrick, a young director with whom he had one of his finest critical successes, *Paths of Glory* (1957). The determined 31-year-old, thrust into a super-complicated, expensive production with an all-star cast of immensely delicate egos, won the respect of the company by imposing his will to get the film in the can while keeping the stars contented despite the myriad delays and disruptions. The problems were considerable. Charles Laughton immediately clashed with Olivier and Douglas over the script and according to Peter Ustinov, "would loiter about waiting to get insulted…. Laughton became extremely difficult."[175]

Upon request, Ustinov ended up rewriting the dialogue for a lot of the scenes he and Laughton shared. Production was delayed when Tony Curtis tore his Achilles tendon playing tennis with Kirk Douglas and Jean Simmons required surgery during the shoot. Kubrick clenched his teeth, worked through the problems and got it done.

Kubrick was a peerless technician who was determined to do it his own way. The young director bossed veteran director of photography Russell Metty around as if he were a film can jockey. The DOP, claiming he was being treated like a lackey, threatened to quit. The complaints became considerably muted when Metty later won the Oscar for Best Cinematography for *Spartacus*.

Kubrick also realized that there were certain windmills that couldn't be tilted at. Despite expectations that he could work with the executive producer to reshape the literate but elephantine script (Dalton Trumbo generated over 1600 pages with the endless rewrites and revisions with Olivier and Ustinov composing their selected passages), he quickly discovered that Douglas was immovable on this subject. Kubrick was stuck and could do nothing other than finish the picture. The young *wunderkind* was certainly mindful that a resignation from the biggest project in Hollywood would damage his professional reputation. Despite the challenges, for three hours and thirty minutes, there is hardly a dull moment in the film.

Kubrick later publicly disowned the completed picture because it wasn't "his," but the results of the director's inspired work are evident. *Spartacus* remains a considerable achievement that is clearly the best of its type. A control freak to a greater extent than Anthony Mann or Kirk Douglas, Stanley Kubrick soured on Hollywood after *Spartacus* and relocated to England. There would be no more compromises to executive producers who were also movie stars, or to anyone else, on future Kubrick projects. Working at the pace of a Galapagos tortoise, the often brilliant and deliriously lionized Stanley Kubrick would exercise complete creative control over his sparse output of eight films during the next 39 years.

Fortunately, Charlie's casting as the gladiator trainer Marcellus, was not trifled with, even after Mann was fired. As the sadistic "drill sergeant" of Ustinov's gladiator academy, Charlie gave a performance that was the apotheosis of villainy during the first third or so of the film. When McGraw snarls, "I like you, I want you to be my friend"— perhaps the most insincere gesture of fellowship in movie history — to Douglas and a new group of slave recruits, it is clear that this guttural majordomo is a diabolically evil bastard who will have to be reckoned with. Charlie's subsequent tormenting of Douglas is reminiscent of the campaign of misery that he waged on Barry Sullivan in *Loophole* (1954). This time, though, the techniques of his sadism encompassed a lot more heavy-handed paganism than even a mid–20th century insurance investigator could muster. McGraw initially hands Douglas a sword, but the weapon is quickly returned when the rugged but unskilled slave realizes that it would be suicide to take on the master gladiator. "You're not as stupid as I thought. You may even be intelligent — that's dangerous for a slave," intones Charlie.

Douglas declines to ravish the beautiful slave Virinia (Jean Simmons) during a nighttime "training" interlude as McGraw and Ustinov look on through the barred ceiling of his cell like leering voyeurs at a medieval stag show. Spartacus falls madly for Virinia, but is forced to admire her from a distance.

McGraw uses the couple's mutual attraction as a vehicle for added humiliation. Simmons is ushered into Spartacus' quarters for a surprise conjugal visit. As Douglas springs forward with ardor as his lady love enters, McGraw steps through the doorway and leads Simmons back out with a smirk: "No, she goes to the Spaniard. Have a good night's rest, Spartacus." The pressure builds after Douglas and Jabba (former Olympian Woody Strode) are picked to fight to the

Bobby Hoy, Charlie and Jill McGraw on the set of *Spartacus* (1960).

death by Olivier and his entourage, who arrive as guests at the gladiator school. After Strode gets a spear in the back for his trouble, his body is suspended like a rack of freshly killed venison in the gladiator quarters as the mutinous students file in. McGraw rasps: "He'll hang there till he rots!"

The inevitable rebellion is ignited by a final spasm by cruelty from McGraw. As Simmons is being driven off in a wagon, Charlie takes care to make it known that the departure is permanent:

McGraw: "Take your last look, Spartacus, she's going to Rome. She's been sold."

Douglas (disbelief) "She's been sold?!"

McGraw (lashes Douglas viciously across the face with a whip):

"No talking in the kitchen, slave."[176]

What happened to Charlie next was truly unfortunate. Kirk Douglas grabbed him by the throat after his "no talking" line and the two men had a choreographed struggle. Douglas quickly got McGraw in a half nelson and viciously forced his head down in a vat of soup, ostensibly drowning him. Too viciously, according to producer Edward Lewis, who related that Charlie's jaw got broken when jammed into the soup pot. Jean Simmons, who was on the set that day, remembers watching the scene and hearing the crack of McGraw's jaw hitting the iron pot. She remembered: "Kirk certainly didn't mean to do it, but Charlie was furious and they took him straight to the hospital."[177] McGraw complained privately afterwards that Douglas was an unprofessional "pipsqueak"[178] who took advantage of the situation to treat him roughly. It is also notable that despite the pain of his injury, Charlie professionally finished the scene until the director cut it.

Charlie and one of his closest friends, stuntman-actor Johnny Daheim (courtesy Mildred Black).

Kirk Douglas said years later that Charlie resisted during the staged fight and made the scene so difficult that a double was required to finish staging the struggle properly. Douglas then appeared to contradict himself with the blasé rationalization "[S]ometimes people get hurt."[179]

Bobby Hoy, who performed stunts and bit work on *Spartacus*, was also made to suffer by Douglas. During a battle scene, Douglas rammed a fake sword into Hoy's side so roughly that he cracked one of the stuntman's ribs. Douglas was apparently a man who was prone to being physically rough off the set as well. During post-production, Douglas became momentarily enraged at an editor whom he erroneously believed was siding with Stanley Kubrick and editing the film behind his back. After grabbing the man around the throat and tearing his shirt, the star-producer sent the editor a letter of apology and three new monogrammed shirts the following day.

These repetitive episodes, dating back to his rough handling of Jane Greer in *Out of the Past* (1947), along with his high-octane arrogance, helped enshrine Kirk Douglas as an unpopular figure with many actors, stuntmen and nearly everybody else on a movie crew who wasn't named Burt Lancaster.*

Aside from the injurious fight scene with Douglas, Charlie had a rollicking good time while working on *Spartacus*. Marcellus was a meaty, high-visibility role in the biggest Hollywood film to date and a good payday. There was again talk about an Oscar nomination for Charlie, but nothing happened. Ad-hoc entertainment on the set was provided by the effervescent Peter Ustinov. The erudite actor was a superb mimic who would answer the flashing set phone with an uproarious variety of foreign accents that baffled incoming callers. Jean Simmons remembered having to dig her nails into the palm of her hand to halt the laughter while playing scenes with Ustinov because he was so uproariously funny, "even when he wasn't trying to be."[180] *Spartacus* employed almost every stunt person and bit player in Hollywood. Along with Bobby Hoy, Charlie was reunited with a plethora of his old working pals and drinking buddies: Yakima Canutt, who directed the second unit stunt work, along with his sons, Tap and Joe; Johnny Daheim, Richard Farnsworth, Chuck Roberson, Dale Van Sickel, Charlie Horvath and a host of others. There was even a bit part for Jill McGraw as one of the slave girls at the gladiator school. These were some righteous times for Hollywood's working class. Keyes and O'Brien's Bar on Ventura Boulevard were packed every night during the long production.

Five years later, on the set of In Harm's Way *(1965), Douglas was mysteriously and roughly held down underwater during a large shipboard battle scene that had a large number of stuntmen and actors in a flooded compartment. The stunt people and extras in the scene became scarce when the smoke cleared and the furiously sputtering star surfaced. In Hollywood, what goes around, comes around ... sometimes even for a superstar.*

22

"Good Evening ..."

As the 1950s concluded and Charlie began his third decade as a Hollywood actor, he remained busy primarily with episodic television guest shots between feature film appearances. He typically played a crime heavy, cop or frontier sheriff without too much in between. McGraw appeared in four different episodes of *The Untouchables* and popped up regularly on *Wagon Train, Laramie,* and *The Dick Powell Show,* among many others. There were occasional variant portrayals that broke the monotony of television typecasting. *87th Precinct,* a gritty New York cop series based on Evan Hunter's famed "Ed McBain" police procedural novels, was a case in point. Charlie plays a shoe factory owner who believes his son is kidnapped. Charlie's stressed-out wife is played by none other than Nancy Davis Reagan. This episode was Mrs. Reagan's second-to-last professional acting gig before assuming her permanent role of a lifetime as *aide de muse* and gate keeper for her husband Ronald Reagan. Another memorable guest spot for McGraw was on the noir-tinged, but unfortunately short-lived *Johnny Staccato* series starring John Cassavetes as a jazz stylist-as-private eye. Charlie was memorable as a jive talking pianist-composer whose penchant for plagiarism garners him a personlized slab at the morgue.

Charlie's next feature reunited him for a final time with director Tony Mann: *Cimarron* (1960) was the second cinematic send-up of Edna Ferber's sprawling Oklahoma saga chronicling the opening of the Cherokee Strip to the oil boom, and it fared poorly. More a historical soap opera than a true Western, the film suffered in comparison to Mann's superbly crafted oaters of the previous decade. Mann attempted to change the story's plodding characterization of the two lead characters (Glenn Ford and a miscast Maria Schell) and lobbied incessantly to film the picture on the Western plains instead of the Metro back lot. After several quarrels with producer Edmund Grainger, Mann quit the production with Charles Walters directing the rest of the film. Anthony Mann had begun his final transition as a film director. After being one of the pioneers of the noir style and making some of the most beautifully composed westerns, Mann was now ready to embark on direction of spectacular epics, a genre that had grown exponentially in Hollywood. Mann would helm both *El Cid* (1961) and *The Fall of the Roman Empire* (1964), two gigantic projects that would consume the balance of his directorial career before his untimely death in 1967.

In *Cimarron,* McGraw played Bob Yountis, a character L.Q. Jones termed "a dog heavy." It was a part that Charlie could now do in his sleep. Jones played an acolyte thug to McGraw's character: "I got to carry Charlie's gun around for him in that one and was proud to do it."[181] McGraw's character indulges in bullying, arson and lynching, kind of an all-around pestilence, before being dispatched by Glenn Ford.

Charlie went to MGM to appear in a wartime farce, *The Horizontal Lieutenant* (1962), the final of four films starring the elevated romantic duo of Jim Hutton and Paula Prentiss. With a veteran Metro team of Joe Pasternak and Richard Thorpe, one would think that this film would have more redeeming elements than Charles McGraw but it simply doesn't offer too

Two old pros on the set of *Cimarron* (1960), Robert Keith and Charles McGraw (courtesy Mildred Black).

much more. While Prentiss was (and remains) a talented comedic actress, Hutton's character simply isn't funny; he comes off as detached, as if being cast in another lightweight comedy had become a fearful bore. Fortunately, McGraw is at his comedic best. As an irascible colonel commanding an isolated Pacific outpost, he gets to officiously browbeat the hapless Hutton who is tasked with a deadline to capture a Nipponese spy after multiple failures. Several of McGraw's

Colonel McGraw's unexpected materialization puts a damper on Jim Hutton's nocturnal notions for Paula Prentiss in *The Horizontal Lieutenant* (1962). L to R: McGraw, Prentiss, Hutton and Jack Carter.

lines are uproarious such as when he unexpectedly spots the beleaguered Hutton at a military social function and makes him feel less than welcome by clipping off:

> Well, lieutenant, I see you're wearing a side arm which in your case can only mean that you're planning to shoot yourself. At this point, it's not a bad idea.[182]

In between shows, Charlie continued to have fun with his friends and companions. One memorable escapade included Bobby Hoy and a small group of friends taking off for an international junket aboard a private plane from Los Angeles. Concerns by aviation authorities over the safe piloting of the aircraft were expressed in New Orleans shortly after the plane landed in the Crescent City. When McGraw briefly exited the plane, he was accompanied by a cascade of empty beer cans that fell through the open crew hatch onto the tarmac. Once it was understood that the actor was a passenger and not a pilot, the plane was permitted to refuel and take off.

After a stop in Boston where Hoy departed to visit friends, the plane touched down in Newfoundland for refueling. There, McGraw received a frantic message from his agent: Could he please return to Hollywood immediately? Alfred Hitchcock wanted McGraw to appear in *The Birds* (1963) with production starting forthwith. Charlie immediately turned around and began the long journey back to California on a commercial carrier. The junket airplane took off from Newfoundland and ended up going down over Africa. McGraw's luck continued to hold up ... in spades. He just missed getting himself killed so he could go to work with the most renowned filmmaker in Hollywood.

By 1962, Alfred Hitchcock had ascended to an unequalled plateau of success achieved by no other filmmaker. In addition to classic films including *Rear Window* (1954), *Vertigo* (1958), and *North by Northwest* (1959), Hitchcock's television series, *Alfred Hitchcock Presents*, with his funnily pithy introductions, transformed him into the first director-celebrity who was instantly recognizable to millions of people. His last production before *The Birds* was the epochal *Psycho* (1960) whose opening half-hour was reminiscent of a fulsomely plotted film noir before wickedly veering off into something much more troublesome. The Master of Suspense was a stand-alone entertainment industry, exquisitely crafting uniquely profitable films while his television series, on the air since 1955, was recently expanded to an hour-long format. Hitchcock's production company was given carte blanche at Universal, a studio now ruled by his former agent, friend, and Hollywood *éminence grise*, Lew Wasserman. Hitchcock typically received absolute deference and awed respect from his cast, crews and sponsors. No one was better prepared. Hitchcock managed preproduction with the precise storyboarding of each scene to the point where the actual filming of the picture became an anticlimactic bore. For the great director, the creative process was concluded when the film went into production.

The shooting of the picture became a necessary but tiresome task. Asked about this predilection, Hitchcock stated that while he would just as soon not shoot the picture after a script is done and the film is visualized, he always did so because if somebody else filmed his work, "They might screw it up."[183] Farley Granger, who worked with the Master in *Strangers on a Train* and *Rope*, remarked:

> So many of these directors are unprepared or they want to ask the actors what to do. What a crock! [Hitchcock] planned everything in advance and knew exactly what he wanted to do. Hitch was the best director I ever worked with, bar none.[184]

Hitchcock's meticulous attention to detail included casting with McGraw's selection for *The Birds* being an emblematic example of the director's methodical process.

McGraw also starred in an Alfred Hitchcock television episode. Titled "Diagnosis: Danger" and directed by Sydney Pollack, the program was a solid entry in the prestigious suspense series. Charlie played a harassed chief health officer who managed an incipient anthrax epidemic by dispensing wry counsel while chug-a-lugging antacid. McGraw's characterization was a neatly drawn portrayal that transcended his usual entourage of televised cops and gunslingers. Hitchcock previewed and approved all of his Shamley Production television shows and must have appraised McGraw's work in this episode. While it would be tidy to conclude that this program was why McGraw was cast in *The Birds*, there was more to it. McGraw was one of 16 actors recommended by casting assistants Joe Reich and Jere Henshaw in a memo for Hitchcock and his assistant, Peggy Robertson, to consider for the part of Sebastian Sholes in *The Birds*. The other candidates for the credited supporting role included such character stalwarts as Robert Simon, Simon Oakland, Telly Savalas, John Larkin, Royal Dano, William Conrad, James Gregory, John Doucette, Edward Binns and Michael Constantine.

Each of the actors was carefully reviewed by Hitchcock and Robertson with the finalists having a sample film or television episode screened in the Revue Studios projection room at Universal for the Master's ultimate casting decision. Simon, Conrad, Savalas, Larkin and McGraw were culled from the original list of 16 names. This group was reduced to three finalists after the initial session in the projection room. Hitchcock sat through two screenings of a 1960 *Route 66* television episode in which McGraw guest-starred, "Layout at Glen Canyon." Charlie portrayed a case-hardened contractor, honchoing the construction of a dam in the Southwest, who is compelled to relive the tragedy of his dead child and a broken marriage. It was an exceptional performance and it closed the deal with Alfred Hitchcock. Charlie was hired for *The Birds* at $2500 per week with a two-week guarantee and co-star billing on April 30, 1962.

A weathered McGraw, playing a fisherman in *The Birds* (1963), appeared right at home in a diner.

McGraw's Sebastian Sholes, a weatherbeaten fisherman, skeptically declines to join Rod Taylor's call to arms against the "bird invasion" of Bodega Bay, California. McGraw proved to be a complementary addition to a superb character ensemble of venerable Ethel Griffies as a scoffing amateur ornithologist, Karl Swenson as the town drunk predicting the end of the world, Joe Mantell as a traveling salesman, and Lonny Chapman as a cook, among others.

The principal scenes with McGraw and the others were shot in a diner set with the group being either apprehensive or scornfully dismissive (notably Griffies) about the recent avian attacks. The tension escalates to terror when the birds wreak fiery chaos on downtown Bodega Bay. This harrowing sequence added considerable heft to Hitchcock's fabled reputation as a master of cinematic mayhem. In retrospect, it seems incredible that *The Birds* didn't win an Oscar for Best Visual Effects or any other type of formal award. For Alfred Hitchcock, the omission of public acclaim was nothing new.

The officious dismissal by Hollywood's award bodies of Alfred Hitchcock and his work was a long-term, inexplicable insult. The director was five times nominated for the Best Director Oscar, three nominations by the Directors Guild and two from the Emmy Awards for his television series, and nary a statuette to take home. It was small wonder that when Hitchcock finally accepted the Irving Thalberg Award from the Motion Picture Academy in 1968, he simply said, "Thank you," and exited stage right. As director Peter Bogdanovich speculated, there were certainly more than a few people watching who could have conjured up a more brusque response by the Master after being jobbed by Hollywood during his entire career.

McGraw's experience with Hitchcock had a mixed outcome. While his performance on screen was admirable, the working relationship between the actor and famed director reportedly veered off track. Charles McGraw and Alfred Hitchcock were as alike as inhabitants of separate planets. Although the director would occasionally josh a performer with the expectation of a deferential response, Hitchcock was a shy, fastidious man who shrank from emphatic confrontation. McGraw was prepared and professional, but could be extremely sensitive to criticism with reactions ranging from humor to umbrage. Hitchcock reputedly made a remark that got under Charlie's skin. McGraw's blunt riposte, which included a sarcastic comment on Hitchcock's girth, created a moment of icy silence on the set with the director ominously intoning, "McGraw, your part will *not* appear in this picture."[185] Despite the remark, McGraw's footage remained in the final cut. How much of McGraw's footage, if any, was edited is unknown; however, Hitchcock never put anything, especially a quarrel with a mere actor, ahead of the integrity of his work. Charlie finished his guaranteed two weeks on *The Birds* and never worked for Alfred Hitchcock again.

Dismissed by one legendary director, Charlie was subsequently embraced by another. Stanley Kramer welcomed Charlie for his all-star comedy extravaganza *It's a Mad Mad Mad Mad World* (1963). The picture was shot in Cinerama and featured a veritable army of comics, stunt men and physical gags; there were two huge, separate shooting scripts for the film, one for dialogue and one for the unrelenting action and stunts. The humongous, unwieldy picture was critically panned, but the public didn't care. Even though Kramer's comedic opus was shut out at the Oscars, it was a huge earner at the box office and has developed a passionate cult following over the years. Even now, it is well-nigh impossible not to laugh out loud at some of the hilarious antics of Don Knotts, Phil Silvers, Jim Backus, Ben Blue and Terry-Thomas, among others.

Charlie played a police lieutenant in support of Spencer Tracy's Captain Culpepper. McGraw makes the most of a small part with some effective, amusing reaction scenes with Tracy. Tracy coordinates the surveillance of a wild chase after a stolen $350,000 that was left by a dying crook (Jimmy Durante) who was found by the roadside by Milton Berle, Sid Caesar, Edie Adams, Mickey Rooney, Buddy Hackett et al.; they are joined by Phil Silvers in a hunt for the money, and they in turn are followed by … well, you get it. Charlie was reunited with Bobby Hoy and a number of his old pals and associates including Chuck Hayward, Mike Mazurki, Jimmy Flavin and Howard Da Silva. Da Silva had finally returned to mainstream movie work with *David and Lisa* (1962) after a decade-long absence due to being blacklisted for his Communist Party affiliation.

Although McGraw didn't realize it, behind the scenes, he was also off the hook. The FBI's intermittent investigation of him as a Communist-under-alias finally ended for good by 1960. In a summary of his file conducted in 1958 when the actor applied for a passport, the FBI noted that McGraw was totally unknown to anyone having any knowledge of the Communist Party in Los Angeles. Despite this repetitive conclusion on a specious allegation dating back seventeen years, his file was forwarded to authorities in London and Paris when McGraw went on a European vacation in 1959 … just in case. To anyone who knew him either slightly or well, McGraw was the last person on the planet one would associate any type of subversive political activism. Whether or not Charlie was "Vance Adkins" back in 1943 (he almost certainly was not) is irrelevant.

He and so many others who were investigated, and had case files maintained by J. Edgar Hoover's FBI, never posed even a theoretical risk to national security. That such a threadbare, unsupported allegation against Charles McGraw could endure for so long is a moral indictment of an internal bureaucracy that lacked both appropriate oversight and common sense. In a perverse way, McGraw was fortunate. Other performers had been blacklisted and denied work based on even more specious rationale.

Stanley Kramer attempted to cram every comedian and funny character actor drawing breath into his comedic epic and nearly succeeded. He shot a lot of the film during the summer to free up performers tied to television. In addition to the well-known comedic names in nearly every lead role and innumerable character bit parts, there were cameos by the Three Stooges, Jack Benny, Jerry Lewis, and Buster Keaton, among many others. Kramer even found room for Minta Durfee, the wife of silent comedian Roscoe "Fatty" Arbuckle, whose screen career dated back to 1916. Several well-known comedy stars turned down roles in *World* for various reasons: Groucho Marx, allegedly because his price couldn't be met by Kramer; Stan Laurel, who retired in 1951 and couldn't see himself back on the screen as either an old man or bereft of his late partner, Oliver Hardy; and Bob Hope and George Burns, who were unavailable. Don Rickles wasn't even asked, to his eternally irritated chagrin.

A sad note amidst the comedic whirlwind was the condition of the great Spencer Tracy. The most accomplished of film actors appeared shockingly aged and dissipated.

Tracy was in bad shape at this point, physically and psychologically, and had to be handled with kid gloves. The years of binge drinking and depression had evolved into ill health and premature old age. Stanley Kramer and Tracy were extremely close, with the actor making four of his final five screen appearances in Kramer's films. Tracy trusted Kramer to "protect him from himself" so the veteran star would not be put into a position of embarrassment. This compassionate oversight was not always 100 percent effective.

According to several McGraw intimates, Charlie was asked to keep an eye on Tracy at one point during the production so the bender-prone star would remain on the wagon. It was an ill-advised request. Expecting McGraw to keep Tracy away from booze was like having the fox guard the henhouse. After the two actors spent an evening running their lines in a tavern, other arrangements to ensure Tracy's sobriety during the production were quickly made. While Tracy struggled with his health during the shooting of what would be his second-to-last motion picture — he would die on June 10, 1967 — Charlie's life and career also began to sag under the combined weight of personal and professional challenges.

23

Golden Age Dissolution

McGraw's lifestyle of incessant excess continued unabated, but the due bill was becoming visually apparent. In less than ten years, the strikingly handsome Carrier Air Group commander from *The Bridges at Toko-Ri* had been transformed into an assortment of craggy-faced sheriffs, cops and saddle tramps in his recent television appearances. Although Charlie kept his weight under control, always knew his lines and could still faultlessly hit his marks, the chiseled McGraw profile began to resemble a relief map of strip mine furrows—a visual chronicle of his nightly forays to favored watering holes along Ventura Boulevard.

Matters were reaching critical mass at home. As his daughter advanced into her teenage years, relations between Jill and her parents became strained past the breaking point. Jill proved to be more than a match for her father in terms of stubbornness. Freda could barely manage coping with Charlie, much less a troubled teenager who required attention that hadn't been forthcoming since she was a toddler. After Jill experienced disciplinary problems at several schools, including running away from a private institution near Glendale, McGraw sent his daughter back to his parents to attend his alma mater high school in Akron; "If I could walk through the snow to high school in the winter, then you can too."[186] The temporary relocation to Ohio, away from the Sodom and Gomorrah temptations of Hollywood, in an attempt to resolve his daughter's problems didn't work. Nothing would. Jill left her parents' home on Reklaw Drive in the late 1950s, had a baby and married a film editor. Her contacts with her parents lessened as the years advanced.

McGraw's movie career began to stall during the mid–1960s. After the release of *It's a Mad Mad Mad Mad World* in November 1963, Charlie did not have another legitimate feature film appearance until he played a henchman to crime boss Robert Ryan in William Castle's oddball comedy *The Busy Body*, which came out in March 1967—a dry spell of nearly 3½ years. Other actors were in the same situation, bereft of work due to the final dissolution of the old studio system. The huge studio overhead in employees and infrastructure no longer had the revenue to prop it up.

Film production had slowed to a steady crawl in Hollywood. Average weekly movie attendance decreased by 20 million between 1950 and 1960 as the U.S. population increased by 30 million. Total film releases decreased from 622 to 387 during the same period. There was no longer a requirement for seven-year contracts to front-load a conveyor belt of talent into a huge filmmaking factory that ejected endless feature films like so many plastic buttons. The once-thriving market for "B" crime pictures and Westerns was completely sewed up by television and the lurid drive-in pictures geared for teens now became more wholesome ground for the majors. New releases were carpet-bombed into thousands of theatres simultaneously. There simply weren't many low-budget films made any more by the studios. Going to the movies was increasingly a special occasion rather than a reflex action. The big-budget blockbusters of the 1950s shattered box office records, but the secondary features that were previously supported as overhead product and given a chance to sink or swim like *The Narrow Margin* were financially unsustainable now that the studios didn't own the theatres. Filmmaking had become more of a financial crapshoot instead of a self-sustaining business that possessed large economies of scale.

The moviemaking empire controlled by the moguls and the power they wielded had degenerated with the mortality of the original overseers. Columbia mogul Harry Cohn died in 1958, reportedly apoplectic over reports that his last female superstar, Kim Novak, was having a clandestine love affair with Sammy Davis Jr. Metro's L.B. Mayer, deposed in 1951, died six years later, unafraid of anything other than "making a bad picture."[187] Dore Schary and a parade of lesser mortals proceeded through an executive revolving door at MGM as a brief resurgence in movie musicals spiked and quickly receded. The consummate insider symbol of Metro omnipotence, Eddie Mannix, was knocked down into a figurehead position until his death in 1963. The once-proud studio, renowned for having "more stars than there are in heaven," had a mere two actors under contract by the mid–1960s with a subsequent fire sale of assets by new owner Kirk Kerkorian to finance his Las Vegas interests beginning in 1969.

Jack L. Warner would have his last hurrah with *My Fair Lady* (1964). Directed by George Cukor and personally produced by Warner, the picture was a final spasm of unalloyed critical acclaim (Best Picture among eight Academy Awards) and a box office success for the veteran mogul. Jack L. was now an old, battle-scarred tiger with nobody left to fight with or outmaneuver. He was the last brother standing. After producing the box office flop *Camelot,* he finally sold the studio and the source of his power in 1967. Only at Fox did the old guard still have a death grip on the power levers. Darryl F. Zanuck emerged from the reverie of an extended midlife crisis spent in Paris bedding a series of untalented ingénues that he tried to make into movie stars. After running the table with his hit war extravaganza *The Longest Day* (1962), Zanuck would reclaim supremacy at Fox in an attempt to rescue a studio that effectively bankrupted itself with the grotesque extravagance of *Cleopatra* (1963). To pay the bills, Fox sold off its legendary back lot that would become Century City. In another perverse Hollywood version of *Family Affair,* Zanuck would enter into retirement and premature senility after engaging in an ugly proxy fight to depose his own son, Richard, as Fox production chief early in the next decade.

In a role reversal from the old studio guard, Arthur Krim, head of United Artists, was a shining example of a Hollywood executive who understood the new realities. Krim used his lessons learned with independent production at Eagle-Lion as a springboard into ultimate control and success at UA. Studios *per se* became a relic of the past with their facilities now being rented by the independents or used for television. The new money in film production was backing proven independent directors and producers with financing and distribution deals. After careful deals with talented filmmakers, Krim allowed free rein to people such as Billy Wilder, Otto Preminger, Albert Broccoli and the Mirsch brothers to make their movies. It worked. With the James Bond franchise in ascendancy, United Artists became a spectacular success throughout the 1960s and '70s. UA would remain ascendant before being tripped up by the next bugaboo of the movie industry: corporate ownership of studios starring executive dilettantes who attempted to impose their business models on the motion picture industry. Krim, an exquisitely talented man, would become a close personal advisor to presidents Kennedy and Johnson and would return from retirement to bail out UA one more time.

While the flame of Old Hollywood flickered, the alluring myth of Tinseltown became a brand in and of itself. Hollywood looked inward and began to market itself as much as it used to sell movies. To witness this promotional paradigm, all one had to do these days was walk down Hollywood Boulevard and glance down at the sidewalk.

According to Johnny Grant, long-time honorary mayor of Hollywood, there were eight original stars selected in 1958 for the Hollywood Walk of Fame. The remaining 1539 celebrities were elected in 1960 by local merchants who put up $1.25 million for the extensive sidewalk refurbishment. The Walk of Fame was a "welcome wagon" notion to pump the glamorous linkage of Hollywood with the entertainment business, particularly as the Hollywood Boulevard area had begun to deteriorate. Hollywood Boulevard in its heyday was laden with classy specialty shops and movie theatres. The shops had increasingly given way to souvenir kiosks and hole-in-the-wall bars with the theatres starting to run down.

While the current cost for a Walk of Fame star award is around $30,000 and the induction ceremony has assumed the trappings of a religious consecration, none of the original stars received any kind of public recognition. Even though it was less of a big deal almost half a century ago, Grant witnessed the discussions between the local merchants who chose the original 1539 stars and recalled that the debate could be politely described as "contentious."[188] Charles McGraw was awarded a star for achievement in television on the new Hollywood Walk of Fame in 1960. According to Millie Black, McGraw had a merchant friend along Hollywood Boulevard who successfully lobbied for his inclusion. (According to Millie, "Charlie had a friend who was a bartender...." Then she paused and amended her statement: "Well, what bartender wasn't a friend of Charlie's?")

Even though Charlie's television star was located directly in front of Grauman's Chinese Theatre on Hollywood Boulevard, the actor didn't land another lead role in a TV series after *Casablanca* folded in 1955. During the mid–1960s, McGraw survived on a dozen or so television appearances. He also picked up some commercial radio and voice-over work where he could. It was the lowest point of his career since immediately after World War II.

Although most of his television guest spots were the usual roll call of sheriffs and heavies, a bright spot in the professional gloom was an entertaining *Kraft Suspense Theatre* television episode helmed by a future directing icon, Robert Altman. "Once Upon a Savage Night" was adapted by Altman from crime writer William P. McGivern's novel, *Death on the Turnpike*. Produced by the estimable Roy Huggins (*The Fugitive*), the program was a forerunner of what would become a Hollywood staple: the hunt for a demented serial killer. A weathered-looking McGraw dons a battered fedora in essaying what had become an authentic world-weariness while tracking down the psycho named "Georgie-Porgie," played by Philip Abbott. The program was so well-received that it was expanded into a movie-for-television, *Nightmare in Chicago*. There was also a serendipitous *Run for Your Life* Christmas episode where Charlie was cast as a small town bartender in a nearly deserted tavern on Christmas Eve. McGraw becomes humorously drunk and gets into a lighthearted barroom brawl with co-star Ernest Borgnine, who plays a taxi cab driver. Charlie's character had a wife and six kids so he ends up taking home a bicycle from Borgnine as one kid's Christmas present. The sentimental Yuletide finale to this show was assuredly not a case of art imitating life for McGraw.

McGraw's marriage to Freda finally imploded in the late 1960s. Charlie's drinking was now put ahead of everything else, even his cherished wife. Freda and Charlie had an intense union that was marked by ardent affection and equally passionate quarreling. Charlie was gone all the time and Freda was jealous. Whether she had specific reason to be is unknown even though McGraw did not have a reputation as a skirt chaser. While it was noted that there had always been "a sense of tension"[189] between the couple, after more than two decades of marriage, they still cared about one another. However, the years of emotional scar tissue from the accumulation of discordant scenes over Charlie's erratic behavior, drinking, Jill, and money, among other domestic firefights, had done its work. Freda was past the point of despair as McGraw obdurately refused to acknowledge that he had a drinking problem. The couple lived separately in their own house as the bills began to pile up.

At length, McGraw moved out of the hillside house on Reklaw and into an apartment on Magnolia and Colfax in North Hollywood. He would frequently drink himself sodden at O'Brien's, stumble into his apartment after closing time and pass out, sometimes leaving the door open and the television blaring. It was here that Millie would come by to look in on him, turn off the TV and close the door.

24

A Glorious Time

Mildred "Millie" Black can't quite pin down when she initially glimpsed Charles McGraw while on duty as a cocktail waitress on Ventura Boulevard. McGraw had seemingly always been around. There are conflicting stories about their initial meeting.

On a Saturday night in the early 1950s, a driver came into O'Brien's claiming that he was waiting for stuntman and McGraw chum, Johnny Daheim. Daheim was dead drunk, staggering by the juke box, and didn't know from anything. "The bar was crowded that night and it was all stuntman and cowboys," Millie recalled. The main cowboy himself, Gene Autry, took Millie aside and told her, "Better call Charlie so he can take care of Johnny." "Charlie who?" she replied. Autry gave her McGraw's phone number, she phoned him at home and he hurried down to the bar. He got Daheim home and then, according to Millie, "naturally, stuck around the bar and got loaded."

The other version of their meeting is more prosaic: "One night, several people at the bar said, 'Turn on Channel 7, McGraw's on, McGraw's on ...' I wondered who the heck they were talking about." The short-lived ABC *Casablanca* program, with McGraw sartorially turned out in white jacket and bow tie, gave Millie her first glimpse of Charlie. The actor looked quite nice, she thought. McGraw knew everybody and everyone knew Charlie. Knowing Charlie McGraw was akin to being in the eye of the virtual party along Ventura Boulevard. "Charlie would come down the hill while he was baking and would have some drinks while the bread was rising," Black remembered. A true penchant for the culinary arts by McGraw would be misconstrued. The actor took advantage of any opening to leave his house and shoot down Laurel Canyon for a cold pop with the accompanying bar chatter serving as a stimulating chaser. Asked how she and the actor finally got together, Black responded; "That was much later. He was married, I was married.... Boy, it was a mess!"

By the time she and McGraw became an item, Black was a wary, but resolutely upbeat veteran of the L.A. club, restaurant and bar circuit. Millie's employment history encompassed a veritable telephone directory of nightclubs, restaurants, and taverns in the greater Hollywood and Studio City area for over 35 years. As she put it, "I never liked to stay in one place too long." Although her employment habits might have been that of a leap frog, Millie was more reticent about the pitfalls of male companionship by the late 1960s. Freshly divorced, she certainly realized what she was getting into with Charlie. While she enjoyed a good time, Millie always could control her drinking but was fated to spend a great deal of her life in relationships with men who couldn't. "I always thought that I could reform them," she laughed without too much regret.

Millie and her twin sister arrived in Hollywood during the early 1940s after escaping from a dreary convent in the damp Northwest. Millie was the brunette and Marge was the blonde. Descended from French-Canadian stock, the bookend knockouts seemed destined for work in the movies. While a photo from *Since You Went Away* (1944) with the sisters linking arms with a nautically attired Joseph Cotten was displayed on a wall over the couch, Millie and her sister quickly realized that they couldn't cope with languishing for hours around a movie set waiting to be called. They also believed that talent-wise, they were fish out of water. Both the sisters preferred the invigorating routine and steady pay of the Hollywood nightclub beat.

Millie started out at the legendary Florentine Gardens on Hollywood Boulevard. She remembered: "The first celebrity I waited on was Lupe Velez.... I was really nervous." She and Marge moved on to the Palladium. The twin showgirls would ride scooters around ringside as a diversion for the patrons during band intermission, and then split up to work different joints. Millie was employed in nightclubs along the Sunset Strip, rubbing elbows with the famous and infamous at Earl Carroll's Vanities, the Trocadero, the Blue Room, the Ready Room, Ray Bourbon's joint, The Rendezvous and other headliner night spots.

Millie's professional arrival in Hollywood occurred during a time when the term "the Strip" was less about geography and more of an epochal definition of the heyday of glamorous Tinseltown night life. Her youthful immersion into the golden age of Hollywood Nocturne provides an observation window into an era of big band music, movie celebrities, radio shows, dancing and headliner entertainment amid a whirl of glamour and excitement.

While the working class rode the Pacific Electric red cars to work, the swells dressed up to the nines and rode in open automobiles to go nightclubbing. It was a glorious time. Everyone got dolled up to go out on Sunset at night. Closing time during the war years was at midnight. Following last call on the Strip, it was on to the after-hours joints. It was an era when men rarely ventured outside their residence in a collarless shirt and only the women wore earrings. Beneath the veneer of sleek elegance, however, all was not just cashmere, wide lapels, and gilded camaraderie on the Strip.

The term "evening wear" amongst the rougher trade meant somebody was heeled. Benjamin "Bugsy" Siegel was a hidden owner of the Mocambo, perhaps Hollywood's most glamorous nightclub, until getting a 30–30 slug between the eyeballs. Gangster Mickey Cohen kept busy, lining his pockets with money from club shakedowns and other rackets while the L.A.P.D. remained on the pad or clueless. It took a long-running series of gunfights and bomb explosions between local Cosa Nostra boss Jack Dragna's borgata and Cohen's gang during the "War on the Sunset Strip" for control of the rackets to get the Feds mobilized. Cohen was toppled off his throne for income tax evasion in 1950. At the same time, reform-minded Police Chief William H. Parker began to put cops walking a beat in patrol cars to keep them away from the hoi polloi with the proffered temptations. This important management decision might have distanced the foot patrolmen from the easy graft, but it also served to separate the Los Angeles police force from the public they were supposed to serve. The slow transformation of the L.A.P.D. as an elite force of well-trained mercenaries had begun with the ultimate cost of their alienation from the community not coming due until many years later.

Millie's recollections of 1940s Hollywood are a kaleidoscope of drive-by memories with the forgotten and the famous. She became friendly with headliners like Sophie Tucker. She dated bandleader Jimmy Dorsey and capped off a close relationship with actor Lawrence Tierney by being arrested with the actor after he took on three comers on the sidewalk outside an after-hours joint. She shared a late dinner with Anthony Quinn, a booth with Cary Grant, and jumped off the Redcar into Max Baer's convertible on Sunset so the ex-heavyweight champ could chauffeur her to work. Millie spent an entire evening into the wee hours consoling a distraught Robert Walker after his wife Jennifer Jones dumped him for David O Selznick. Both the famous, infamous and the obscure melded together on the Strip. Hollywood was a small, convivial place where most anybody was approachable and the town was flooded with men in uniform on their way to war.

Bookend knockouts. Millie Black and twin sister Marge flank Joseph Cotten on the set of *Since You Went Away* (1944) (courtesy Mildred Black).

During one memorable evening in Dave's Blue Room, Millie introduced Lawrence Tierney and Max Baer to actor Robert Mitchum. This trio of bacchanal buccaneers was a potentially volatile tripartite pact that could have wreaked barroom carnage on an urban scale worthy of a Godzilla epic. Affable congeniality reigned, though, with Baer and Mitchum waxing philosophical over Tierney's frustration about being repeatedly braced by obnoxious drunks who wanted to fight *Dillinger*. It is impossible to determine how many saloon fights involving Tierney were engendered by the actor's starring portrayal in the 1945 film about the legendary Depression-era bank robber, but it had to be a considerable number.

Lawrence Tierney was a paradoxical denizen of the lost Hollywood night. Contemporaries of Tierney, ranging from Millie, the late Richard Fleischer, Robert Wise and others recall the frequently embattled actor as a nice guy who was picked on incessantly by drunks and showoffs. The way *they* tell it, Larry's reputation as a drunken brawler was overblown, amounting to a bum rap; he was charming, cooperative, quoted Yeats and Shakespeare and would stand the bar to many a round. While these accounts are no doubt genuine, the victimization routine doesn't fully square with the voluminous Tierney police record that became so laden with alcohol-fueled violence that the initial gloss of his 1940s film career became opaque before the end of the next decade. In fashioning an arrest record that would be the envy of the actual John Dillinger, Tierney evolved into an elemental force of nature, a brooding Mount St. Helens, trailing a plume of smoke, prone to erupt at any time. People familiar with the actor's dark side became scarce when his ire began to heat up. After becoming virtually unemployable as an actor, he eked out an existence in New York as a bartender, construction worker, and hansom driver, living virtually by his wits. Down, but never out, Lawrence Tierney cleaned himself up and returned to Hollywood to engineer a remarkable acting comeback beginning in the 1980s. Director Quentin Tarantino made him a celebrity again with a starring role in *Reservoir Dogs* (1992). By this time, Tierney lost his hair, put on considerable weight, and looked even more intimidating. Like a simmering Golem, the actor prowled around what was left of the old nocturnal haunts (primarily Boardner's on Cherokee) still taking umbrage at actual and imagined slights yet conversely companionable and fiercely loyal to a new generation of friends. Tierney's death on February 26, 2002, just a few weeks before his 83rd birthday, was akin to the last Tyrannosaurus who roamed through Old and New Hollywood, finally taking his eternal rest.

Colorful characters aside, a voluminous array of photographs depicting Millie and her sister smiling with their co-workers, friends, and servicemen (and with celebrities such as Dick Haymes and Harry James, among others) provide emblematic evidence of a joyous lifestyle that was a tonic for the years of youthful servitude in the convent.

As the flush of the postwar years subsided into the suburban sprawl of the 1950s, Millie no longer rode the Pacific Electric trolley to her apartment in Hollywood after closing time. Like millions of others in L.A., she now drove a car, singing a song while coasting down darkened Laurel Canyon Blvd. to her apartment in the valley. Millie settled in to work at O'Brien's Bar on Ventura Boulevard. Another prime spot was Keith's Café, a food and drink joint that was strategically located on Ventura with a rear entrance into the alley that ran behind Republic Studios. There was an adjoining hotel next door for those who couldn't make it home or got lucky at closing time. The grips, stuntmen and actors would run over in between set-ups for the best French dip in the Valley. The dripping beef would be washed down with an ice-cold beer while jawing over the latest gossip.

Millie's long-term marriage with guitarist-composer-bandleader Stanley Black hit the skids by the late 1960s and although the couple eventually divorced, they remained friendly. She was

Marge and Millie with Charles Laughton at the wrap party of *The Night of the Hunter* (1955) (courtesy Mildred Black).

forever close to her twin sister Marge, who had married and lived in nearby Burbank. Millie had managed to save some money: She and her husband had bought a small house in North Hollywood in 1963, she remained there when he moved on, and kept right on working. And then she hooked up with McGraw.

Charlie and Millie enjoyed each other's company. McGraw remained a brusquely charming rogue. No one was more fun to hang out with for drinks with friends and sporadic nightclubbing. The couple would occasionally hit joints over in Hollywood like Steve Boardner's bar or Viscotti's Restaurant on La Cienega where Millie worked during the mid–1950s and catered the wrap party for *The Night of the Hunter* in 1955. One night Millie and Charlie walked into Viscotti's for a late meal. A young man at the bar nervously eyeballed McGraw and then left in a hurry after whispering to the bartender. It turned out that the youth believed that Charlie's mug shot resided on the local post office wall and the barkeep, a friend of McGraw's, decided to string him along for laughs.

For the most part, the couple stuck close to home, just over the bridge from Studio City. With the rest of Hollywood, the Studio City area had undergone major changes in the last decade. Republic Studios closed up shop in 1958 and the long-term presence of movie cowboys and stuntmen in the Valley had been greatly lessened. The venerable studio on Ventura Boulevard had been preeminent since Mack Sennett shot two-reel comedies on what was the Keystone lot during the 1920s. After "The King of Comedy" went belly up during the Depression, the studio was picked up by Mascot Pictures. A small moviemaking firm, Mascot was coupled with Monogram and Liberty Pictures by a savvy businessman named Herbert J. Yates, who owned Consolidated Film Laboratories. Starting in 1935, the newly named Republic Studios began to crank out Westerns and serials with sustained rapidity. While the early Republic pictures were sustained in part by the presence of Gene Autry and John Wayne, the studio became renowned for action pictures and serials—lots of them. Director Spencer Gordon Bennet remembered the lightning-fast pace at the studio where directors would frequently increase camera speed on running horses or similar action in the middle of a scene:

> [A]t Republic, we could turn out serials at a bewildering rate, 'cause all personnel, all the equipment were geared to that fast-pace production style. Everyone whom Republic placed in the serial productions, for instance—assistant directors, cameramen, sound engineers and others—were capable of doing the work under pressure, doing maybe forty or more set-ups per working day.[190]

After the war years, Republic financed a number of high-budget films with the always-bankable John Wayne in *Sands of Iwo Jima* and *The Quiet Man*. The steady profits continued to roll in with oaters, serials and a series of hayseed comedies starring Judy Canova. It seemed like the studio would go on forever, but when the end came, it was a typical Hollywood transition for many of Republic's employees: nasty, brutish and short.

The market for serials and low-budget Westerns that sustained Republic evaporated with the shuttering of movie theatres due to the boom of television by the late 1950s. "Papa" Yates either was too obtuse to attempt the transition into television Westerns that his organization appeared uniquely qualified to do; or, more likely, at 80 years of age, he already had enough loot and the rocking chair beckoned. Whatever the reason, Yates abruptly ceased film production at the studio in 1958 and many Republic long-term employees were out looking for work.

Industry cynics speculated that the only silver lining to the production shutdown at Republic was the forced retirement of Yates' wife, former ice-skater Vera Hruba-Ralston. Ralston's repeated forays at motion picture stardom were the equivalent of dramatic root canal. An actress whose thespian technique was in the tradition of George Raft, Ralston compounded the absence of any discernable talent with a wooden personality in front of the camera. One insider observed, "Her films just didn't make any money and the minority stockholders at Republic finally raised hell."[191] It was almost a comfort to know that with the studio's demise, Yates could no longer use his spouse to inflict further cinematic felonies on the moviegoing public.

In the immediate gloom in Studio City, there was ample cause for some optimistic hope. Even though Republic went dark, the studio facilities remained busy, though employing less people. MCA had paid big money to use part of the Republic lot for its Revue television productions since the early 1950s. Revue moved on to Universal after Robert Kennedy orchestrated an anti-trust initiative that forced the monopolistic talent conglomerate to drop its talent agency and go into movie production by buying Universal Studios outright in 1959.

CBS leased some of the Studio City property from Republic in 1963 and subsequently bought the entire property. Television production took over.

Instead of movie cowboys and stuntmen from serials and Roy Rogers oaters, it was now television cowpunchers from *Gunsmoke*, *The Wild Wild West* and *Rawhide* who frequented the bars along Ventura Boulevard. Millie distinctly remembers a young and pensive Clint Eastwood, then popularly known as Rowdy Yates from *Rawhide*, quietly nursing his beer in O'Brien's, saying little to anyone.

25

Single Actor, Needs Work

McGraw was pretty much on his own. Since Jill had left home, Charlie had seen precious little of his daughter with the exception of a visit here or there with a new grandchild. Jill was the mother of two daughters and was on her way to a second marriage with more children on the way. She and her father were radically different, independent people who went their own way and lost whatever closeness that they once had.

McGraw saw Freda more often. Freda finally served Charlie with divorce papers on July 9, 1968, with the final dissolution occurring on October 3 of the same year. There are two anomalies on the McGraws' final divorce decree. Even though Freda was the petitioner and Charlie the respondent, the names on the form were annotated in McGraw's distinctive cursive handwriting. Also: although the final divorce decree is appended that the final judgment of marriage dissolution was entered on October 3, 1968, the Los Angeles County Clerk's official stamp for officially entering and filing the divorce did not occur until March 29, 1977. It is unknown if Freda held off filing the papers for nearly nine years in the hopes of a possible reconciliation, or if it was an administrative oversight. It really didn't matter: The marriage was over and Charlie didn't contest the divorce. Millie Black remembers Freda being driven by her house by a friend or via taxi cab. Charlie would get in the car and sit next to his wife, review and sign some papers, and Freda would leave. That Freda still cared deeply about her husband is undeniable. A cordial note forwarding an unpaid medical bill to her husband is signed "Love, Freda." She simply couldn't live with him any more. As far as it can be determined, McGraw's wife never had an intimate relationship with any man other than Charlie.

There were bills to pay and not enough money to pay them. The Studio City hillside house was sold. Freda got a reported $85,000 sale price for the house and moved into an apartment in Hollywood. Although the divorce and losing the house must have been traumatic, in one way, it was probably a liberating event for the former Mrs. McGraw.

Due to McGraw's frequent absences, the "dream house" on the hill became a domestic prison. Freda never learned how to drive and she never was formally employed for the duration of her marriage. Although she had a circle of friends, Freda was often alone with her poodles, the big backyard with a still-water swimming pool and empty lawn furniture. Unless someone visited her, drove, or a taxi was summoned, she was stuck at home. With McGraw seldom around, life became an increasingly solitary existence characterized by chain-smoking and despair over an absent husband and a failed marriage.

From her new apartment on Hudson Avenue, just off of Melrose, Freda could walk to the stores, go to a show and not feel like a caged bird. It is also possible that readier access to people, shopping and entertainment also made her more apprehensive of her solitary status. Times had changed with the cultural nexus of Hollywood altering considerably since 1950 and not for the better. There was a new generation of nocturnal prowlers who eschewed fun in search of prey. Hollywood was no longer a safe place for an unescorted woman to stroll around during the evening hours.

Back in the Valley, McGraw chafed. He needed work. He needed it badly. The actor obviously had an urgent need for money, but it was more than that. Work validated him; it was what he did as a professional. Artistic unemployment in Hollywood is palpably more emotionally debilitating then anywhere else. Aside from the obvious pitfalls of not being able to earn a living, there is something inherently degrading about a successful film actor, director or producer becoming a has-been. The movie business was and remains coldly dispassionate. You hit the skids and people start shunning you as if your misfortune is a contagious disease. Charlie vowed that it wasn't going to happen to him.

After the *Run for Your Life* guest shot shortly before Christmas of 1966, there was nothing until *The Busy Body* (1967) in February. The film was a low-budget hybrid of *Robin and the 7 Hoods* and *It's a Mad Mad Mad Mad World*. Sid Caesar is a wimpy doofus who becomes cross-threaded with an underworld boss (Robert Ryan) and his gang. McGraw played Ryan's chief henchman. The casting of the picture was a strange exercise. An oddball mixture of veterans (Ryan, Anne Baxter, Caesar, Ben Blue, and Georgie Jessel) was folded in with newer comedians such as Richard Pryor, Godfrey Cambridge, Arlene Golonka and Dom DeLuise. Ryan snarled, Caesar whimpered and nobody laughed. Producer-director William Castle excelled at scaring kids with gimmicky fright movies, but his foray into screen comedy was an unalloyed dud. One reviewer tabbed the film "a real horror."[192]

There would be no further film and television work for McGraw for at least six months. The cause for the dearth of roles is a subject for reasonable speculation. Hollywood had become increasingly hypercompetitive. More and more performers streamed into town in search of the holy talisman of any acting job, and the studios were concurrently turning out less product. Although Charlie was a veteran of nearly three decades in Hollywood, the jobs simply weren't coming in as in years past. Every professional actor experienced peaks and valleys; the job insecurity went with the territory. After the days of the long-term studio contracts played out, no one in town was sure of their next gig. In Charlie's case, though, there was also a more palpable reason why his agent didn't call.

McGraw was now fifty-three, and his long-term drinking habit, never a state secret, had become a problem that could no longer be ignored. It is uncomfortable to discuss an actor's substance abuse problem with peers, co-workers and others in the film business. Everyone knows it is there, but few want to acknowledge it publicly, especially to an outsider who is going to write about it. In addition to the reflexive "There, but for the grace of God, go I," any type of candid comment about a fellow performer, particularly a person as well-liked as McGraw, could be viewed as a dishonorable stab in the back. Better to take the high road and say little if anything. Despite the discreetness, there's little doubt that Charlie's drinking and the reputation that went with it affected his ability to obtain acting work by the late 1960s. One of McGraw's long-term strategies to keep his weight under control for the camera was to mix up a homemade diet drink of eggs and powder in a blender and scarf it down. He would lay off food, drink his concocted dietary mixture, exercise a bit and back off on the booze. The pounds would drop off and he would be ready to go. Without any acting gigs, McGraw picked up considerable weight and became bloated as his drinking was unchecked by the discipline of work.

At a point in his life when Charles McGraw needed a break more than at any other time, a big one was in the offing.

26

Cold-Blooded Comeback

It was a seminal event in publishing annals when *In Cold Blood* debuted in hardcover in 1966 after being first excerpted in the *New Yorker* magazine. The book became an immediate sensation. Journalism, non-fiction and the American novel had arrived at a literary nexus dubbed "The New Journalism." Although it remains debatable how much fiction Truman Capote injected into his five years of writing about the 1959 murder of the Clutter family in Kansas, there can be no question that his unique storytelling of a gruesome crime captivated the public.

In addition to becoming a behemoth of a best-seller, Capote's technique for writing *In Cold Blood* morphed into a historical benchmark that would be dissected in the best journalism schools. The book spawned a movie, a television miniseries and even a board game.

Nearly four decades after the publication of *In Cold Blood,* two different movies appeared, detailing Capote's odyssey of writing the book in Kansas with his childhood neighbor, Harper Lee of *To Kill a Mockingbird* fame. *In Cold Blood* was a literary brand name with an indefinite shelf life.

While much of this enduring fame couldn't be imagined when the book was initially published in 1966, it was clear that a film version of the book would be attempted sooner rather than later. Although John Huston wanted to make the film, the formidable Richard Brooks, along with Columbia Studios, bought the property. Brooks would write the screenplay, direct the film and serve as the nominal producer. It was an inspired choice. Brooks was one of the elite filmmakers in Hollywood. While it isn't injudicious to think that there have been enough films made about *In Cold Blood*, there is remaining grist for another distinctive and untold tale: the story of Richard Brooks' filming of the best-seller. It was a seminal professional chapter in the career of a memorable filmmaker.

Ruben Sax, later to be known as Richard Brooks, began as a sportswriter at the *Philadelphia Record*, moved on as radio journalist and then, a nascent screenwriter for "B" pictures starting in 1942. After serving as a combat Marine during World War II, he returned to Hollywood and got tapped by Mark Hellinger, first with an assist on the script of *The Killers* (1946) and penning the screenplay for *Brute Force* (1947). Continuing his predilection for realistic drama, Brooks turned his searing novel *The Brick Foxhole*, about a sadistic Marine beating a homosexual comrade-in-arms to death, into the screenplay for *Crossfire* (1947). For censorship reasons, the film was converted into a treatise on anti–Semitism with the homosexual victim becoming a Jew. Edward Dmytryk, the director of *Crossfire*, subsequently quipped that the Breen Office apparently thought it was acceptable for a film to show it was okay to have a Jew beaten to death so long as he wasn't a homosexual. After *Crossfire*, Brooks never looked back. He wrote the screenplay for *Key Largo* (1948) and directed his first feature *Crisis,* starring Cary Grant, in 1950.

Conventional Hollywood wisdom allowed that Richard Brooks learned to direct on the set of *Key Largo* perched at the elbow of John Huston. Brooks privately gave credit to the veteran cinematographer, Karl Freund. Freund gave Brooks a two-reel stag film to screen that he had made in Germany in the long ago as an object lesson in cinematic succinctness. Many years later, Brooks recalled: "To this very day, I remember Karl's advice: 'Get to the fucking point!' I position the camera where the story is; I don't try to be arty."[193]

By the time Brooks was ready to commence production on *In Cold Blood*, he had directed sixteen feature films with the biggest stars in the business including *Blackboard Jungle, The Brothers Karamazov, Cat on a Hot Tin Roof, Elmer Gantry* and *The Professionals.*

Brooks was a tough customer who could indulge the overweening egos of movie stars or a glitterati writer like Truman Capote but refused to compromise on core creative issues that he believed in. The steel-wool–haired director had taken on the famously ferocious Burt Lancaster over creative control on *Elmer Gantry* with the prevailing rumor that the former Marine scored a one-punch kayo on the ex-acrobat after a heated argument between the two turned physical.

Brooks also spurned the high-pitched entreaties of Capote as well as Columbia Studios who fervently wanted "name" actors like Paul Newman and Steve McQueen to portray the two losers who wiped out an entire family in a botched home robbery. Brooks knew that the story, not actors, would be the star of *In Cold Blood.*

Casting Scott Wilson and Robert Blake as Dick Hickok and Perry Smith was a masterstroke. Not only did the two actors physically resemble the infamous actual killers, they were not stars, and both gave the performances of a lifetime. Wilson's Hickok was the essence of the smooth-talking Midwest con man who proves to be the weaker of the pair, immediately caving to the police when both men are arrested. Hickok becomes honest only when he is counting the days before his execution. Queried by a reporter about his views on the death penalty, Wilson drawls, "Sure, I'm for hanging … so long as I'm not the one being hanged." If there is a singular character focus in the film, it is Robert Blake. His Perry Smith is a disarming sociopath who recognizes the difference between right and wrong, but simply doesn't possess a moral compass to act on his thoughts. With his childhood fantasies about locating buried treasure in Mexico (with a neat insider line by Blake about *The Treasure of the Sierra Madre* worked into the script) used as a backdrop to explore his horrifically troubled childhood, Smith is a quizzical victim of his own soulful malaise. When he knows all is lost and finally confesses his crime to the police, Blake appears totally earnest when he states, "I thought Mr. Clutter was a fine gentleman …" right before he slit Clutter's throat with a hunting knife.

Richard Brooks refused to film the picture in color. By 1967, this decision took a considerable amount of grace under pressure, but again, the filmmaker was absolutely correct. Never was a story more suited for the stark coldness of glorious black & white. The lonely chill of the Kansas plains, the face of Blake filmed through a rain-streaked windshield and the impersonal bureaucracy of police squad rooms and prisons were all elegantly captured by cinematographer Conrad Hall. *In Cold Blood* was perhaps the most striking picture ever lensed by the legendary Hall, who would be nominated for an Oscar.

Brooks understood that a screenplay adaptation of such a detailed story must be focused on a finite number of elements. His screenplay concentrated on the dysfunctional and ultimately deadly relationship of the two ex-cons who drove 400 miles to Kansas to rob rancher Herb Clutter of $10,000 due to Hickok's muddle-headed certainty from an ex-con that the farmer maintained a house safe loaded with cash. There was no safe, no ten grand; the two men horrifically executed the entire Clutter family for $40 and a portable radio. Brooks omitted Capote's capacious details about the Clutter family, portraying them solely as salt-of-the-earth victims. He would also introduce a new character in the story, "the reporter," played by that veteran smoothie, Paul Stewart. While Stewart does his usual professorial job, his role as an ad-hoc narrator introduces the sole element of moralizing into the picture. Brooks used Stewart's character to inject a statement about the futility of capital punishment into the film by comparing the two killers' execution to their murder of the Clutter family. Interestingly, Capote never looked at Brooks' script — he didn't want to see it. His faith was rewarded. Brooks' wife, Jean Simmons, recalled Capote telephoning her husband in "floods of tears"[194] after he first saw the finished picture, congratulating the director for perfectly capturing the vision of his book.

To aver that Richard Brooks strove for realism in his film is a gross understatement. With a 125-day production schedule, the director filmed on the actual Midwest locations where all of the key events involving the principals and the crime occurred. The exhaustive location shoot included the Clutter house in the actual rooms where each murder occurred, and the hardware store where Hickok and Smith bought the tape and rope used to hog-tie their victims. The actual pawnshops, clothing stores, bus terminals, restaurants, etc., were all similarly included. Jean Simmons visited her husband during the filming at the Clutter house and remembered the somber mood of the company: "Very, very down and depressing."[195] One of the few locations that Brooks couldn't get into was the Kansas State Prison where the two men were held for five years and finally executed in 1965. Brooks settled for filming the prison sequences at the Canon City penitentiary in Colorado. He staged the trial sequence, with a Bible-thumbing Will Geer as the prosecutor, in the same courtroom where the Hickok-Smith murder trial was conducted. The director seated the actual jurors and judge from the trial as actors to watch Geer deliver his summation. Brooks strove to use so many ancillary real-life participants and locations that he even included Nancy Clutter's horse in a brief sequence.

Using the same systematic attention to detail with his supporting cast, Brooks cast John Forsythe as the chain-smoking lead Kansas Bureau of Investigation detective. Forsythe was excellent: measured, detached, yet relentlessly focused on capturing the perpetrators of a senseless atrocity. Forsythe recently watched *In Cold Blood* for the first time in many years with his wife. Nearly four decades after the film was released, the veteran actor remarked, "What a pleasure it was to work on a picture that was so well-written and so well-produced."[196]

Forsythe's law enforcement acolytes were a trio of accomplished actors: Gerald S. O'Loughlin, John Galludet and James Flavin, Charlie's old prowl car partner from *Armored Car Robbery* (1950). Gallaudet and Flavin had over 600 screen appearances between them at this point. These two grizzled veterans of one-week character parts hit the sweet spot with *In Cold Blood*, signing on for a minimum of 25 weeks of contracted work.

Rounding out the cast was Jeff Corey, one of Charlie's co-stars from *The Killers* (1946). Corey, who became a legendary Hollywood acting teacher due to the Blacklist, continued the reclamation of his acting career as Hickok's father. Brooks added silent movie pioneer Raymond Hatton, whose first film appearance was in 1909, to the cast in what would be his final role as an elderly hitchhiker.

The flashback sequences that featured Perry Smith's troubled childhood included some powerful familial scenes. Perry's parents were erstwhile rodeo performers whose marriage disintegrated in a cloud of alcohol and abuse. The striking Native American stuntwoman and actress Sammy Thurman was another example of perfect casting by Brooks as Perry's mother. No woman in Hollywood could ride horses like Sammy Thurman.

What Brooks still needed was the appropriate character actor for the small but seminal role of Tex Smith, the father of Perry Smith. How Charles McGraw earned (that is definitely the correct word) the role ended up to be quite a story in itself.

By early 1967, Charlie was in a debilitated physical state from the combination of liquor and idleness. How bad off McGraw actually was became retrospectively flashed around the world by UPI's syndicated Hollywood correspondent Vernon Scott on October 4, 1967, in his column.

Entitled "Comeback Rare in Show-Biz," the piece opened with some superfluous comments about the difficulty of comebacks in Hollywood and then launched into discussing McGraw with varying degrees of accuracy:

> Charlie is a garrulous Irishman who would almost rather debate and argue any subject on earth — and he's pretty well-versed on most — than act. But he is an actor to the core. A fine one. No pretty boy, he wasn't considered a leading man type. But he worked regularly, made big money and once was nominated for a best supporting actor Oscar.

Scott certainly knew McGraw and had the noted aspects of his personality down pat, along with the enduring myth of his Irish ancestry. However, the UPI writer evidently never watched *The Narrow Margin* or *Roadblock* where McGraw assuredly was the leading man. "Big money" might be a subjective term but while Charlie earned a comfortable living during the 1950s, he never made big money. Also: McGraw was never nominated for an Academy Award. The story continues:

> McGraw, not adverse to a bit of the grape, became a two-fisted drinker. He could use his dukes in brawls as well as any actor in the business.... Somewhere along the line convinced that he could dispatch all of the distilled spirits in California — and maybe part of Nevada. Word got out, as it always does among producers, directors, studios and secretaries that Charlie had a problem. He did. Alcohol nearly killed him a year ago. He was given the last rites— against his will — in a hospital.

So, there it was, Charlie was a drunken brawler who nearly died from booze. The statement about Charlie's drinking was correct with his self-nurtured PR rep as a brawler typically overblown. It is the report about McGraw's near-death and the last rites that is a startling admission to see in print. *Did* Charlie nearly die from drink and receive the last rites in 1966? Forty years later, this revelation proved impossible to verify. Even though nobody interviewed for this book had intimate knowledge of the last rites allegation, no one who knew Charlie disbelieved it out of hand or otherwise refuted it. More significantly, there is no record of McGraw rebutting the Scott article.

> Thereafter, McGraw took the pledge.... Director Richard Brooks got wind of the Irishman's reformation and talked to him about a key role in *In Cold Blood*. Charlie had to lose his pot belly and hospital pallor. McGraw invaded Frank Van's health club near Universal Studios. The waistline diminished and McGraw regained his ruddy complexion ...

Richard Brooks had known Charlie since *The Killers* in 1946. McGraw with a five-day growth of beard would be perfect for Tex Smith. It was typical of Brooks to be tough-minded enough to insist that McGraw get himself fully in shape before signing him for the part. A review of the production files of *In Cold Blood* indicates that Brooks sequenced McGraw's performance to be among the last principal scenes that were filmed.

Production on the picture began on March 2, 1967, in Kansas and all location shooting, with the exception of the brief Las Vegas sequences, finished by April 30. McGraw signed his contract for $1500 per week with a two-week guarantee on May 17, 1967. His sequences were filmed on the Columbia lot from May 22 to June 1 with the exteriors of Tex Smith's trailer shot at a wrecking yard near Lankershim Boulevard in the Valley. The company wrapped production on June 12, 1967, an amazing 49 days ahead of schedule.

As for Charles McGraw getting into shape by working out at Frank Van's health club, there is no doubt about it. The diminutive Van, whose career as a bit actor dated back to W.C. Fields movies, parlayed his pugilistic expertise into a career as a technical expert for boxing movies, frequently portraying a referee. Van was an old chum who loved Charlie. His gym near Universal Studios was used by the famous as well as the obscure.

The physical turnaround and comeback by McGraw was remarkable. His success was a measure of both his personal grit and a determined realization to turn his waning fortunes around. Charlie's dedicated accomplishment was publicly recognized by his friends. The actor was presented with a poster of himself in cartoon caricature adorned in comic gym tights while hefting a miniature dumbbell. The picture is entitled "Frankie Van Athletic Awards—1967" and annotated in the upper left corner:

Charlie McGraw.... "Our Inspiration"

The bottom of the poster, inscribed "Lovingly the member," has 19 signatures including those of Frankie Van, Vernon Scott who wrote the piece on McGraw's come back and actor Robert Blake, who added "Your loving son" above his name. McGraw was certainly back in the game.

With *In Cold Blood*, Blake and McGraw dramatically plumb the depths of an abusive, but paradoxically loving relationship between Perry Smith and his father Tex. Through flashbacks, Blake recalls the good times of his childhood with his parents and siblings, riding on horseback with his mother Flo (Sammy Thurman). In a conversely nightmarish sequence, McGraw bursts into a fleabag hotel room to beat his drunken, philandering wife with a belt while the Smith children look on in benumbed horror. Blake sums up the paternal tragedy so central to the ultimately horrible catastrophe of the Clutter family when he is minutes away from the gallows. He recalls a serendipitous trip to Alaska that culminated with his father nearly killing him in a rage over a failed hunting lodge. Blake sadly summarizes his relationship with his dad: "I loved him and I hated him."

Tex Smith has similar feelings of ambivalent, lost love when he is queried by Forsythe and Flavin as the Kansas Bureau of Investigation begins to zero in on Smith and Hickok as the prime murder suspects.

The policemen visit Charlie in his shabby trailer in the back of a car junkyard. A 1937 rodeo poster promoting "Tex and Flo Smith" hangs on an interior wall of the cluttered trailer. After not recalling when he last saw his son, McGraw identifies a picture of Blake handed to him by Forsythe—"he gets his looks from his mother, part Cherokee"—and launches into a stern soliloquy about how the police won't have trouble with his son after his last stretch. "You won't be having more trouble from Perry," growls the grizzled rodeo rider. "He knows when he's licked. I taught all my kids the golden rule ..."

With the two cops watching him carefully, the elder Smith segues into the tragedy of his marriage to Flo: "She wanted the wild life. Took the kids away from me. Except Perry. She became a hopeless drunk. Choked to death on her own vomit...."

The father then becomes misty-eyed remembering the love of a young son before their relationship descended into tragedy:

I took him with me everywhere. How that boy loved me. I ... I was cold. He'd sleep down under ... and hang onto me with his little arms, so tight. I'd tell him stories about the great adventures we was gonna have. How he was going to strike it rich. Buried treasure. Gold. Alaska. That's where this picture was took.

John Forsythe tries to intercede with a question about whether Tex has seen his son, but stops. He obviously hasn't and never will. McGraw continues on, the tough man becoming almost mournful, "You just ask Perry if I was a good father, When I eats he eats. You just ask him." Forsythe and Flavin exchange glances and silently exit the trailer as McGraw, oblivious to their departure, wistfully concludes, "When I die, all my insurance goes to him. Yes sir, his life is all set." In a story laden with calamity and ruined lives, McGraw's performance movingly

McGraw as Tex Smith with his "son" Robert Blake, in a publicity shot from *In Cold Blood* (1967) (courtesy Mildred Black).

essays how emotional damage within a family perpetuates unintended, tragic consequences. In the denouement to *In Cold Blood*, that some believed to be over the top, Perry Smith mounts the gallows and sees his father (McGraw) as the face of the hangman.

McGraw's brief but powerful sequence as Tex Smith was a memorable *tour de force* for the veteran actor. One can only wonder if the role caused Charlie to reflect on his own unfortunate relationship with his daughter. More than likely, McGraw regarded the role as a choice professional opportunity and kept any inner thoughts opaquely private as was his instinct always.

27

Last Hurrah

McGraw's career renewal immediately after *In Cold Blood* was demonstrable. The word quickly got around about his rehabilitation and that he was capable of doing quality work. There were three television guest spots in quick succession: *Hondo*, *Judd for the Defense* and *The Man from U.N.C.L.E.* The writer-producer of *Hondo*, Andrew J. Fenady, sent a personal note to Charlie, lauding the actor's performance in the *Hondo* episode as "magnificent."[197]

In the *U.N.C.L.E* episode, Charlie plays the dictatorial head of a secret survival school, butting heads with Illya Kuryakin (David McCallum) who is trying to ferret out a double-agent embedded in McGraw's next graduating class of agents. A McGraw guest role on *Judd for the Defense* titled "Punishment, Cruel and Unusual" in 1968 contained a specific personal irony. In a dramatic episode about a closet-drinking judge (James Daly) railroading a reformed alcoholic (Jessica Tandy) on trial charged with drunk driving, Charlie plays an AA representative who delivers several worldly-wise speeches on the nature of alcoholics and their duplicitous habits! One can't help but wonder if this particular role caused any reflection by McGraw.

Although additional television episodes followed, what was more gratifying was the resurgence of roles in feature films. McGraw's current agent, Jerry Pam, began dialing Charlie's phone number with much greater frequency. The actor quickly reclaimed his niche in Westerns, a genre that was finally petering out. A few Westerns remained top-drawer entertainment, thanks mostly to the young and the old, Clint Eastwood and John Wayne.

In *Hang 'em High* (1968), McGraw saddled up opposite Eastwood, Inger Stevens and a gaggle of veteran character actors including Ben Johnson, Ed Begley, Pat Hingle, Alan Hale Jr. and L.Q. Jones. Charlie's portrayal as a crooked, cowardly Sheriff won praise from Jones:

Charlie was not heavy, but a *heavy*. He showed greed that scatters across his face.[198]

Eastwood's star in Hollywood had risen to great heights after exiting the television series *Rawhide*. He went to Italy and became a sensation in a series of "spaghetti Westerns" made by Sergio Leone, notably *For a Few Dollars More* (1964) and *The Good, the Bad and the Ugly* (1967). *Hang 'em High* was the first film rolled out by Eastwood's own production company and a Stateside response to the Italian Westerns in a final ripple of popularity for a time-honored film genre. The story was an action-packed polemic against capital punishment. In an opening sequence reminiscent of *The Ox-Bow Incident* (1943), Eastwood is lynched by a group of cowpunchers led by hard-bitten ranch baron Ed Begley who mistakenly think Clint is a murdering rustler. After being fortuitously cut down in time by passerby Ben Johnson, Eastwood survives the ordeal with vengeance now being the order of the day. He contrives to become a lawman and hunts down the gang of would-be executioners one by one. Audiences almost feel sorry for this wayward bunch; they had no idea what they were getting into with a vengeful Eastwood. L.Q Jones recalled that the production was not without some difficulty. "The script was being fought all the way. Charlie helped and got out of the way."[199] Also remembered was a younger actor in the cast who deigned to muse aloud about his intrinsic motivation for an upcoming scene. Charlie was thirty years removed from the Group Theatre and didn't have patience for coddling a neophyte at a broiling hot location in Las Cruces, New Mexico. "Just hit your fucking mark and let's get on with it," growled McGraw. At this point, it was still about the work … and getting it done as quickly as possible.

Pendulum (1969) was a refreshingly effective mystery-detective yarn that was filmed on location in Washington D.C. McGraw was fourth-billed behind George Peppard, Jean Seberg and Richard Kiley. Peppard is a D.C. police captain who is put on the spot when his philandering wife and her lover are murdered in his bed. Peppard has to elude his own police department and go on the run in a frantic search for the actual killer. McGraw is the conflicted deputy police chief who wants to believe in Peppard's innocence, but can't have it both ways. Charlie is wryly officious in essaying a balanced portrayal of a police official — honest, as far as it goes, but politically squeezed between his loyalty to Peppard and compliance to the bosses. McGraw even uttered a few garden-variety profanities that were included in the script. *Pendulum* remains an underrated, nearly forgotten picture that was reminiscent of a 1951 film noir, less its color photography, brief nudity and rough language.

With the tumultuous events of the late 1960s as a backdrop, motion pictures increasingly reflected a contemporary culture moving in a schizophrenic societal waltz. Certainly, there was a marked dichotomy among films coming out of Hollywood. While the Greatest Generation still queued up for John Wayne, who finally took home his Oscar for *True Grit* (1969), many younger viewers turned on and dropped into pictures such as *2001: A Space Odyssey* (1968) and *Easy Rider* (1969) and, naturally, *Woodstock* (1970). With the Vietnam War, drugs and the generation gap roiling the country, traditional values, cultural icons and other sacred cows were falling all over the place like bowling pins.

Tell Them Willie Boy Is Here (1969) was an emblematic film of the late 1960s. While most Westerns focused on a conventional Americana of the lonely idealist transfixed against the wide-open spaces of the frontier, *Willie Boy* marched to the beat of a different drummer. The picture used a factual story to adroitly puncture some of the heroic myths of the Western standard without resorting to cinematic proselytism.

The film's director, Abraham Polonsky, wasn't someone normally associated with traditional values, at least not the kind that were being prescribed during the early 1950s by the House on UnAmerican Activities Committee The writer-director didn't have a typical career path to Hollywood either. Polonsky was a brilliant man. He was an English teacher at CCNY and a law school graduate from Columbia University. After passing the bar, Polonsky started a legal practice, but turned to writing for radio full-time when he got paid $400 for several hours of work writing Gertrude Berg's radio program and compared it to a weekly check for $87.50 from his law practice. After coming to Hollywood in 1937 as a screenwriter, Polonsky subsequently became a member of the Office of Strategic Services (OSS) during World War II. He was also an unrepentant Communist who, despite his considerable intellect, remained a true believer in Marxist theoretical dogma till the bitter end. When he was called before HUAC in 1951, he adamantly refused to provide names of fellow party members and was subsequently blacklisted. Like Adrian Scott, Dalton Trumbo and others in similar straits, Polonsky wrote television screenplays, notably for the *You Are There* series, and performed script polishing jobs under an assumed name or fronts until he was able to work openly again by the mid–1960s. Given the opportunity and the subject matter, Abe Polonsky's writing invariably possessed the larger footprint of a higher moral imperative.

His Oscar-nominated original screenplay for *Body and Soul* (1947) was a compelling yarn of a boxer's (John Garfield) battle with his conscience over materialistic success and ambition. Polonsky's masterpiece was *Force of Evil* (1948) which he directed and wrote (again starring Garfield). The picture was an object lesson of the corrosive corruptness caused by the intersection of organized crime and big business with the angels and the devils becoming indistinguishable from one another. Polonsky's screenplay for *Odds Against Tomorrow* (1959), fronted by John O. Killens who received screen credit, was a noir-stained tale of a neatly planned robbery gone bad; it remains a sledgehammer paean for racial tolerance.

Tell Them Willie Boy Is Here was Polonsky's first opportunity to write and direct a film in over two decades. His adapted screenplay was based on Riverside, California, journalist Harry Lawton's novel, *Willie Boy: A Desert Manhunt*. Lawton obtained detailed anecdotal accounts from the participants of the Old West's last manhunt for a Paiute Indian who killed a medicine shaman in self-defense in a quarrel about marrying his 16-year-old daughter in 1909. Lawton dug deep and fashioned the recollections from Indians and members of the actual posse members into a considerable book.

Under Polonsky's light cinematic touch, Lawton's novel became a considerable film. The titular star, Robert Blake kills the father of his girl (Katharine Ross) in self-defense and the couple takes flight across the high desert into the mountains. The sage deputy sheriff (Robert Redford), who is bedding the reservation doctor (Susan Clark), leads an initially half-hearted chase for the young Native American. When a confused old Indian fighter (Barry Sullivan) is killed, the resultant press hysteria and institutionalized racism of the dying frontier whips up hysterical flashbacks of an Indian uprising. Blake resorts to his survivalist heritage in prolonging the chase merely to delay the inevitable.

All of the actors acquit themselves admirably, with Redford strikingly effective in one of his most authentic performances. The sparse, elegant dialogue from Polonsky modulates the pace and prevents the film from becoming a ham-handed "message picture." The sun-splashed action is accentuated by the beautifully stark high desert photography by ten-time Oscar nominated lenser Conrad Hall. For his part, Polonsky remembered afterward how he strove to highlight the symbolism of the love stories between the white and Indian protagonists. He also commented that he owed much to Hall for his use of desaturated color in the high desert. Polonsky further observed, not unkindly, that Robert Blake "was a good actor, but a pain in the ass. He tried to direct the film ... behind my back."[200]

For his performance, McGraw created yet another derivative of a frontier peace officer. This time, as Sheriff Frank Wilson, McGraw assays a suck-up, politico lawman who buys drinks for the press while ensuring that a concurrent, ballyhooed visit by President Taft to Riverside, California goes smoothly. Charlie's part was small, but vital to the story. The location shoot at Joshua Tree National Monument reunited McGraw with colleague Barry Sullivan and perhaps his closest friend, Johnny Daheim.

At the end of the picture, Katharine Ross commits suicide and Blake challenges Redford with an empty rifle, ending up a corpse. Redford allows the Native American brethren in his posse to cremate Willie Boy. McGraw, in a Smokey Bear hat reminiscent of *The Defiant Ones*, rides up with the hoi polloi, views the funeral pyre and immediately protests. "Who told you to burn him? ... God damn it.... We have to have something to bring back!" Redford fixes McGraw with a flinty glare and clips off, "Tell them we're all out of souvenirs."[201] McGraw's face in close-up alters from startled anger to bemused shame as the fire crackles and the scene fades to the closing credits. It was a fitting exclamation mark to an evocative tale of late-term frontier injustice.

Willie Boy would be Abraham Polonsky's motion picture valediction. There would be several more screenplays, none of which breathed his rhetorical fire, none of which anyone went to see. Interest in Polonsky and his career increased during his final years as he became sought after to provide living testimony of the Blacklist period. He remained unsparingly dismissive of his former friends and colleagues who, in his words, became "rats." Polonsky's ire peaked just prior to his death in 1999 at age 88. The great director Elia Kazan, perhaps the most noted HUAC cooperator who had informed on all as he repudiated Communism, was honored by the Motion Picture Academy for Lifetime Achievement in 1998. Asked to comment about Kazan and the upcoming Oscar telecast, Polonsky remarked, "I'll be watching, hoping somebody shoots him."[202]

As the decade rolled over into the 1970s, McGraw continued to work steadily. Most of his calls were quick television guest shots lasting a couple of days, but they kept him going. He appeared in a *Mod Squad* episode, "A Time for Hyacinths," alongside veterans Vincent Price and Warren Stevens in 1970. A novel introduction to this episode included one of McGraw's old film noir movies. One of the lead *Mod Squad* characters (Peggy Lipton) is in a beachside house watching *His Kind of Woman* (1951) on television (the sequence with Price and McGraw having a gun battle with Charlie being killed). The movie clip provided the lead-in to the story of Price as an old-time movie actor with a secret past who romances Lipton while his fellow thespian, Charlie, lives nearby as a beachside sketch artist. It turns out that both men are lying low due to a covered-up murder from twenty years ago that was actually committed by Stevens.

Stevens, still a working actor at age 87, recalled McGraw warmly. "Charlie was a really good guy. He was a friend and a fine actor."[203] The debonair Stevens, whose prolific career encompasses the entire history of television, also recalled that McGraw was having painful back problems during the filming of the *Mod Squad* episode.

A bad back wasn't a surprising malady for a man in his mid-fifties; however, Charlie's years of boxing, fight scenes, jumping, falling, riding horses, etc., had taken more than the usual toll on his once sturdy frame. McGraw had been an intensely physical man into his late forties. However, the rough treatment coupled with the fact that he took indifferent care of himself was becoming evident. McGraw had back problems, a bad knee, and his hips were starting to bother him. Cigarettes remained a long-term accompanist with his drinking. His pack of Camels always remained at hand, but now there was a smoker's cough after a long pull on a tar-bar. McGraw became periodically irritated about the aches and pains of aging but for the present, he kept up the pace between work, the bar and home on the couch.

1971 was to be a resurgent year for McGraw. He was reunited with director-producer Jack Webb for the two-hour pilot of his latest initiative, *O'Hara, United States Treasury*. A relentless dervish with a jet-black crew-cut, Webb stood out, even in a town filled with hard-core workaholics. An asthmatic Santa Monica kid who was a voracious reader, Webb drove himself savagely as a writer and character actor, then a director and producer. After appearing as a cop in the classic police procedural *He Walked by Night* (1948), Webb borrowed the docudrama format and melded it into the new L.A.P.D. paramilitary culture initiated by Chief William H. Parker. Webb's enduring police series, *Dragnet*, debuting first on radio and then television, was an inspired combination of brief, true-life dramas burnished by the businesslike, incorruptible L.A.P.D. image. The series captivated the public's imagination.

Webb, who starred as Sergeant Joe Friday, ran every detail on his shows. He was a dynamic innovator who pioneered the use of teleprompters for actors, markedly speeding up production time and lowering costs. Webb used a cadre of actors over the years that he remained intensely loyal to: Virginia Gregg, Harry Bartell, Jack Kruschen, Peggy Webber, Vic Perrin, others. Many of the performers in Webb's stock company reciprocated the dedication and tolerated his pow-derkeg temper that would periodically explode on the set. Webb had no patience with produc-tion delays caused by what he considered to be unprofessional behavior. James Doherty, a writer for Webb's *Dragnet 1968*, recalled, "Jack was an ogre on stage; very tough on actors, very tough on crews. There was no fooling around like on other shows. You could hear a pin drop."[204]

Webb had known Charlie for years. A charter member of the original *Dragnet* radio pro-gram that debuted on NBC in June 1949, McGraw played Chief of Detectives Ed Backstrand, but left four weeks into the program when his film career began to take off during that busy year. Webb was currently on the high side of a career rebound himself. After his spectacular success in television, he went into feature filmmaking with indifferent results and eventually ended up being fired by Warner Bros. He returned to television. After being let go again after an unsuccessful retooling of *77 Sunset Strip*, he subsequently produced an updated televised version of *Dragnet* in the late 1960s and a new hit police show, *Adam-12*. The Webb formula rarely varied: clipped dialogue laden with police jargon delivered by actors in a succession of huge close-ups within a tightly woven crime yarn. The stolid law enforcement lead (Webb) was invariably accompanied by a lower key partner (Ben Alexander, Harry Morgan) who provided minute doses of comedy relief to make the relentlessly taciturn tone a bit more palatable.

In *O'Hara, United States Treasury*, David Janssen (hot off his success as television's *The Fugitive*) starred as the undercover T-man, breaking up a dope ring and being backed up by McGraw as Agent Joe Flagg. The film was solid, if unspectacular, and the series got picked up for the 1971–72 television season. Charlie wasn't included in the transition of *O'Hara* into series production (aside from a guest appearance in a single episode), but he didn't miss too much. After 21 episodes, the flaccid show was cancelled. Webb later remarked that he erred in not giv-ing Janssen a sidekick to play off of. Janssen would have much better luck with his next series, *Harry O*, before shockingly dying of a heart attack in 1980.

A Hollywood version of Lazarus, Jack Webb weathered the failure of *O'Hara* and a succes-sive flop program, *The D.A.* The next series from his Mark VII production company, *Emergency!*, about the daily adventures of a Los Angeles Fire Department paramedic team, was a smash hit that stayed on the air for seven years. After burning his way through a trio of marriages and three daily packs of cigarettes, Webb would launch seven more television series before working himself to death via a heart attack in 1982.

While McGraw didn't have the financial legs of a Webb or the star power of a Janssen, he manufactured his own bit of good fortune. Instead of staying with *O'Hara*, Charlie landed a reoccurring role in NBC's *The Smith Family* for 1971–72. This program is a singular "what if ..." example of a network television show that was praised by the critics, but never found an audience. Produced by Don Fedderson of *My Three Sons* fame, the concept of a mature police detective with a wife and three kids who struggles to maintain proper balance in his life was unique. At a time when older movie stars like Glenn Ford and Jimmy Stewart were testing the waters of episodic television, the notion appealed to the legendary Henry Fonda, who signed on for the lead role. With Janet Blair as his understanding wife and Ron Howard as the teenage son — Opie now had long hair — the emphasis was on family drama instead of a by-the-num-bers police procedural. One can now easily visualize the topical 1971 scripts: Fonda busts a teen-ager for pot and then comes home and finds rolling papers in his son's windbreaker and turns him in ... or something like that. An okay idea backed up with considerable talent, but some-body was needed to round up enough people to watch the show. McGraw's reoccurring role in *The Smith Family* was another entry on Charlie's lengthy ledger of authoritative police admin-istrators: He played Fonda's boss, Captain Hughes.

Despite the presence of Henry Fonda and a talented supporting cast, the half-hour series endured for 39 episodes spread over two seasons before it was cancelled. The show couldn't commit to being either a family drama or a standard cop show. Evidence of the schizophrenic nature of the production was the dropping of the first year opening of a "feel-good" theme song with the second-year credits showing Fonda kicking a door in with his snub-nose .38 at the ready position.

Unfortunately, the program has completely disappeared from public view. Filmed just before the embryonic days of videotape, it may never have been shown in syndication reruns, recorded or otherwise retained. Unless someone stumbles over the missing thirty-four-year-old film cans, *The Smith Family* remains a fading footprint of early 1970s television.

McGraw was back on the big screen as a proletarian father-in-law in *Johnny Got His Gun* (1971), directed and written by Dalton Trumbo from his 1939 novel of the same title. An unremittingly grim story — a young man loses his voice, arms, legs in World War I but has an active brain that can't communicate — was successfully transferred to the screen, although the film was hampered by low production values. Trumbo, for all of his writing brilliance was not a film director; technically he was in over his head. A timely release during the long hot summer of 1971, the picture delivered a compelling anti-war message. McGraw has a roughly sympathetic part as the almost–father-in-law who reappears in flashback. Timothy Bottoms made his screen debut as Johnny with Marsha Hunt (another blacklisted artist), Jason Robards and Donald Sutherland the co-stars. The supporting cast included McGraw's former screen adversary and friend from the RKO "B" unit, Peter Brocco, and the diminutive Don "Red" Barry, whose credits dated back to *Night Waitress* (1936). A feisty performer who was envisioned as the dime store version of James Cagney while appearing in Red Ryder oaters at Republic, Barry would tragically commit suicide in 1980.

Johnny Got His Gun was another Blacklist product, this time by the most talented wordsmith of the Hollywood Ten, Dalton Trumbo. An avowed Communist Party member since 1943, a man of genuine depth and a true character, he was a terrific writer in any genre and the Blacklist actually served to increase his prodigious output. Trumbo wrote like a fiend for less money under pseudonyms and front names, churning out screenplays while sitting in his bathtub, chain-smoking, during exile in Mexico. After his name was restored to movie credits in 1959 (almost simultaneously for *Spartacus* and *Exodus*), Trumbo continued his prodigious work until his death from lung cancer in 1976. The writer belatedly received his screenwriting Oscars that were originally presented to fronts for *The Brave One* (1957) and another, posthumous, statuette for *Roman Holiday* (1953). After his professional resurrection, Trumbo contributed a fitting summation about the humanistic effects of the Blacklist in Hollywood with a stirring speech to the Writers Guild on the occasion of accepting the Laurel Award:

> [I]t will do no good to search for villains or heroes or saints or devils because there were none; there were only victims. Some suffered less than others, some grew and some diminished, but in the final tally we were all victims because almost without exception each of us felt compelled to say things he did not want to say, to do things that he did not want to do, to deliver and receive wounds he truly did not want to exchange. That is why none of us— right, left, or center — emerged from that long nightmare without sin.[205]

For Trumbo and the others who had been damaged by the Blacklist, a righteous corner of redemptive irony had been turned. In contemporary Hollywood, being a member of the Hollywood Ten had now become a badge of honor. For Charles McGraw, professionally untainted, but remembering so many of his co-workers and friends long out of work, it must have been gratifying to see Howard Da Silva and Morris Carnovsky, both on stage with Charlie in the opening night cast of *Golden Boy* in 1937, reclaim at least a portion of their lost film careers

Older actors were a prominent feature in *Chandler* (1971). Warren Oates is a down-and-out detective who has sunk to a new career low, working as a security guard. While he is brooding about his fate over a couple of jolts of Early Times, an old business associate (McGraw) offers him a shadow job for a mysterious lady arriving at Union Station the next day. After getting his belly gun out of hock from pawnbroker Richard Loo and drying out in Gloria Grahame's steam bath, Oates trails the mystery lady (Leslie Caron) from Union Station to Northern California, where she is kidnapped. It turns out that Chandler is being used by a shadowy group of baddies who are after Caron's boyfriend, a mob overlord. Oates falls for the mysterious Caron and events become complicated amidst numerous car chases and fistfights. The picture is a well-intentioned neo-noir effort that fails due to a superficial story about sinister government agents entangled with organized crime. Terse dialogue in a hardboiled story only accentuates a yarn when the basic premise is credible. Despite the best efforts of Warren Oates, a greatly underrated actor, *Chandler* doesn't succeed. Miss Caron is totally miscast as the femme fatale with a sordid past and much of the action has the slapped-together look of a television episode. McGraw's brief appearance wasn't good either. He appeared disheveled, old, and nervous. Now pushing sixty, Charlie was entering the final phase of his career.

28

Means of Descent

Instead of staying on the wagon after his 1967 revival, McGraw quickly reverted back to his habitual custom of excessive drinking. At this point, though, the thrill was gone and what used to be rollicking fun was becoming a downward, depressing spiral.

With his marriage to Freda over, McGraw took up permanent residence at Millie's house in North Hollywood. He enjoyed the domesticity and worked with Millie to plant a line of fir trees in the front yard, bordering the street, and to install a bountiful array of fruit trees in the backyard. McGraw's notion of household assistance typically entailed offering copious verbal advice rather than manual labor. For example, the actor's contributions to the fruit tree project were confined to recommending specific implantation locations while sipping a beer and ruminating over the benefits of fruit horticulture with the nurserymen who actually performed the work. McGraw could be a terrible nuisance with contractors, salesman, vendors or nearly anyone else of a business nature who dealt with Millie. Millie once made arrangements to have a Jacuzzi installed in the backyard. The contractor arrived to start work and quickly stormed out in a huff after a brief exchange with McGraw. The vendor had innocently asked Charlie where he wanted the electrical box for the spa installed. McGraw graveled back a response in classic style: "How the hell would I know where to put it! You're the frigging electrician, I'm a goddamn actor."[206] In another instance, Millie made an appointment with an insurance man to discuss a health insurance plan. Uninvited, McGraw joined the meeting and immediately started growling about "chiseling insurance companies that'll take your money, but don't take care of you when you get sick...."[207] (Note: It is impossible to recount this story without recalling a scene of McGraw chewing out an insurance agent in *Armored Car Robbery*.) Millie finally banished McGraw to the backyard so she could peacefully conclude her business.

McGraw was an unusual but well-liked fixture in the quiet neighborhood. He became quite close to the young children of a couple that lived several houses down the street. The kids and their parents would visit with Charlie and Millie and everyone became friendly to the point where Charlie would occasionally pick the children up at the local elementary school for the parents, who both worked, and bring them home.

One day, the school authorities refused to let the actor leave the playground with the kids due to a recently instituted policy of not permitting anyone to pick up kids without a designation note of permission from the parents on file with the principal. The neighbors gladly provided the note for McGraw. Parents and teachers continued to be intermittently startled when "Marcellus" would pull up in his Chrysler New Yorker at the schoolyard to give his small friends a lift home.

Charlie remained a socially engaging but argumentative contrarian. He read voraciously and loved to argue about history, literature, sports trivia, anything. Millie recalled leaving O'Brien's Bar one night and walking down the street to Dupars for a late snack after arguing with Charlie over the meaning of the word "ebullient," which he insisted was a synonym for

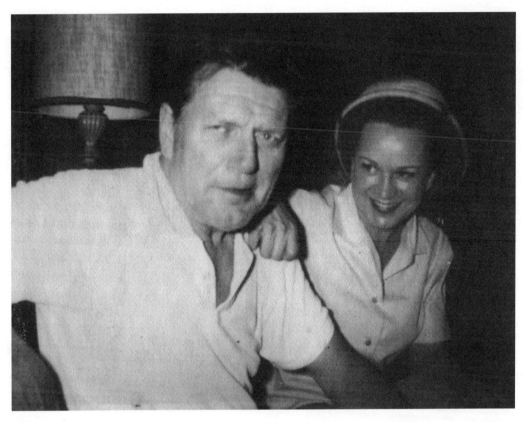

Charlie and Millie at home in the early 1970s (courtesy Mildred Black).

"excited." Even after she looked it up back at home in her Funk and Wagnall's and showed it to him, McGraw refused to give ground. The actor maintained that his definition was perfectly valid; it had simply had been erroneously omitted from the dictionary. Millie recalls McGraw as a protective and even jealous mate, but hardly a lothario, particularly as his libido became increasingly pickled by years and alcohol. The two frequently talked about getting married, but could never quite pull the trigger. On at least one occasion, the couple was en route to the courthouse for the nuptials, but somehow ended up in a bar. They continued to live as man and wife.

As the years and liquor accumulated, McGraw's old friends began to slip away from him. Bobby Hoy, who, "used to follow Charlie around like a little brother,"[208] had his personal epiphany in 1972. When Hoy became concerned about his own career, his close friend, actor Alan Hale Jr., pulled him aside in O'Brien's one day and gave him some frank advice about how the younger man's drinking was negatively affecting his life. Hoy left the bar and drove straight to Alcoholics Anonymous in North Hollywood. "When I walked in, I saw two old friends of mine, actors, who told me, 'Bobby, we've been waiting for you.'"[209] Hoy quit drinking permanently and became a mainstay of the North Hollywood Alcoholics Anonymous chapter while renewing his life and career. Hoy attempted to encourage McGraw to quit drinking — it was a low-key approach, not coercive — but his old friend either ignored it or brushed it off. Although Bobby would bump into Charlie occasionally, the close relationship between the two men, forged in the bars of Studio City nearly two decades earlier, was over. McGraw stayed in periodic touch with Bert Conway, his old pal from *Golden Boy* who lived in nearby Mission Hills. Charlie always said that Bert was the person who taught him how to dance back in New York.

Conway, who followed the rest of the Group Theatre to Hollywood, went back to New York after being tainted by the Blacklist while at the Actor's Lab during the late 1940s. After some mixed success, he returned to Hollywood doing local theatre and film bits. Charlie had main-

tained his friendship with John Mitchum, whose own career as a character actor had evolved with appearances in the *Dirty Harry* movies. The dual camaraderie was permanently put on ice after an intense argument at Mitchum's house after the consumption of a bottle or so of wine. McGraw apparently upbraided his host over having his young children within earshot of the men's increasingly ribald conversation. The disagreement became a heated quarrel with Charlie and Millie quickly departing. The younger Mitchum brother and McGraw never saw each other again. John Mitchum, who would later write an entertaining memoir which included some wild tales about McGraw, apparently decided to omit this particular story from his book.

McGraw as Lady Macbeth, clowning in Millie's backyard in the late 1970s (courtesy Mildred Black).

McGraw would occasionally invite friends over the house from local taprooms, people who had little or no connection to show business. One day, Millie came home to encounter Charlie running an impromptu acting class over drinks in the living room with several people she'd never seen before. More typically, Charlie and Millie frequently entertained neighbors and friends at parties or informal gatherings. McGraw also made time to drop his old friends and colleagues a complimentary note such as one to towering tough-guy Mike Mazurki for his appearance in *Challenge to Be Free* (1975). Charlie was particularly taken with the rugged outdoors yarn in Alaska helmed by the veteran Tay Garnett, who reclaimed his directorial career after quitting the booze. Mazurki wrote back, thanking Charlie and adding that he hoped McGraw "was being kept busy."[210] Unfortunately, McGraw's acting appearances were becoming increasingly confined to barrooms rather than sound stages.

By the mid–1970s, McGraw was arriving at either the Starlight Room or another bar near Laurel Canyon Boulevard as early as six a.m. He would stay there all day when he wasn't working. A perpetual early riser, Charlie would warm up his car at the crack of dawn and then take off for the bar. One morning, Charlie encountered former Our Gang child star Darla Hood sitting at the local bistro, drinking a martini before seven a.m. "No lady should be drinking in a bar with McGraw at this time in the morning,"[211] he growled, and sent her home to Millie. "Darla was a tiny, lovely gal, so talented and sweet," remembered Millie. By this time, Darla's career and marriages had flamed out. Any money she earned as Alfalfa's sweetheart in the Our Gang shorts of the '30s and '40s was long gone (reportedly siphoned off by her mother, an alleged ghastly stereotype of the horrific screen mother) and she was surviving on commercial voiceover work while making appearances at nostalgia shows. Hood was an endearing, dam-

Old thespians reminisce: Charles McGraw with Bert Conway in 1972 (courtesy Mildred Black).

aged person who had become a heavy drinker. She became very friendly with Millie and Charlie and was a regular guest at the house, particularly after becoming romantically involved with an engaging chap who managed the produce department at the grocery store around the corner. Both Charlie and particularly Millie were deeply saddened when Darla passed away from acute hepatitis in 1979 at the age of only 47.

Charlie still got calls to do television guest shots on shows like *Police Story* and *Adam-12*—roles that were little more than bit parts—as well as some radio and commercial voiceover work. It was getting progressively difficult for the actor to get it together for the camera and for the first time, he struggled to remember dialogue. The actor knew he had to right himself by abstaining from alcohol. Although his ability to stay on the wagon for extended periods might have been waning, Charlie was still capable of doing quality work. The Tracy and Locke Advertising Agency wrote to McGraw praising him for some radio spots for corn chips. Voiceover work helped, but the movie and television roles were drying up again.

It was unfortunate that Charlie's career faded away just as Hollywood began a creative renaissance period. In the early 1970s, the studios, though downsized and increasingly managed by lawyers and accountants, were giving increased latitude to a new generation of young directors and actors who brought renewed energy and creativity to the table. Certainly this emerging cohort of filmmakers had more creative freedom than most of their predecessors from the past era.

The old censorship office under Joe Breen with its Victorian hand-wringing over nonsense such as Marie Windsor's breasts in *The Narrow Margin* was long gone. After producer-director Otto Preminger's twin assaults on the Production Code of America (PCA) were tacitly endorsed by United Artists with *The Moon Is Blue* (1953), an amusing comedy about sexuality that was released without the MPAA seal, and *The Man with the Golden Arm* (1955), a drama tackled the subject of drug addiction that was expressly forbidden by the existing code, the old system was quietly tossed out in 1956.

With subsequent films like *Psycho*, more revisions and different enforcement czars making the Code irrelevant (Joe Breen retired in 1954), matters on screen became increasingly frank. The public and politicos began yowling for something, *any*thing to regulate movie content. In 1968, an alphabetic ratings system was developed by new MPAA honcho and political smoothie Jack Valenti; it mollified public opinion while reducing censorship to a pittance. Pulling the strings behind the scenes for Valenti was Lew Wasserman, who reigned omnipotent at MCA/Universal. Wasserman, perhaps the smartest person who ever set foot in Hollywood, pioneered the marriage of the new Hollywood's sophisticated relationship to Washington D.C. No one would be better than Valenti, LBJ's former troubleshooter and chief butterer, hand-picked by Wasserman to protect and guide the film industry through an unprecedented new era.

McGraw with Darla Hood (left) and neighbor (courtesy Mildred Black).

Operating in an environment of relaxed censorship, several of the new generation of directors became legendary filmmakers in their own right due to their innovative work and spectacular box office successes. Steven Spielberg, George Lucas, Martin Scorsese, Peter Bogdanovich, Francis Ford Coppola, and Hal Ashby, among others, all hit their stride with groundbreaking films in the 1970s. Unfortunately, none of these estimable filmmakers remembered Charles McGraw. Charlie would have been ideal for Roman Polanski's *Chinatown* (1974), a picture that elegantly depicted a late–1930s sun-drenched, corrupt Los Angeles that was largely extant when McGraw first arrived there. Another "might-have-been" role would have been Charlie playing a grizzled chief petty officer in Hal Ashby's brilliant *The Last Detail* (1973). It was also regrettable that while Francis Coppola offered the Luca Brasi role in *The Godfather* (1972) to the teethgnashing eccentric Timothy Carey (who inexplicably turned it down), he couldn't cast Charlie, even as a back-up "John Law" to Captain McCluskey (Sterling Hayden).

It was too late. After the box office success of *Jaws* (1975), the movie industry changed radically once again. All the major studios began "elephant hunting" for the big summer and holiday blockbusters featuring superheroes and larger-than-life themes. The creative Renaissance of the early 1970s became marginalized by a garishly hyped era of cinematic mercantilism focused on opening weekend grosses that only a handful of filmmakers, such as George Lucas and Steven Spielberg, would fully master. Hollywood had finally passed most of the older generation of working class actors like Charles McGraw by.

L.Q. Jones hadn't forgotten Charlie, though. When he cast his independent science-fiction picture, *A Boy and His Dog* (1975), he recalled McGraw immediately. "I went for the face and the voice," said Jones, who long admired Charlie's "completeness" as an actor. Despite his professional diversity, McGraw never had appeared in a film quite like this. Jones produced, directed and wrote the script based on a novella by the brilliantly eccentric writer Harlan Ellison. An eighteen-year-old named Vic (a young Don Johnson) roams the Earth's surface after nuclear Armageddon with a telepathic dog named Blood. The dog is a smart-assed intellectual (voiced by Tim McIntire) who scolds Vic about everything from his libido to his hunting skills with the pooch clearly the brains of a mutually beneficial survival partnership. Blood has a talent for sniffing out women for Vic to rape while the young man provides the hunter-gatherer services. When the pair locates the beautiful Quilla Jane (Susanne Benton), a lustful Vic is lured away from Blood down to the underground city of Topeka, a bizarre version of small town America reminiscent of a *Leave It to Beaver* rerun on LSD.

Quilla has enticed Vic to the subterranean burg for ostensible stud services in order to build up a dwindling population. What she actually has in mind is a double-cross of the star-chamber Topeka town committee led by Jason Robards, who condemns the rebellious duo to death ("… to the farm"). After escaping and killing the town's robotic enforcer (a shocking Hal Baylor), Vic and Quilla return to the surface to reunite with Blood, who is dying of hunger. Vic makes the no-brainer survival choice as summarized in the final scene of meat being cooked on an open fire after which Blood remarks, "Well, I'd say she certainly had marvelous judgment, Albert, if not particularly good taste."

Arguably misogynistic, but outrageously original, *A Boy and His Dog* scores with the satirical relationship between Johnson and the dog with the use of sarcasm instead of sappiness in L.Q. Jones' script about a post-apocalyptic world. The dog was the hands-down star of the picture. How many films have successfully featured an animal in a principal role that *never* appears to be staring at a trainer outside the frame of the camera shot?

McGraw, who played a white-faced preacher reciting unctuous Biblical platitudes to a line-up of veiled brides with "groom" Don Johnson strapped into a sperm-milking machine, probably wondered what was going on in this particular show. Whatever misgivings Charlie might have had about the film were doubtlessly trumped by his gratitude to L.Q. Jones for an opportunity to work.

A film much more attuned to McGraw's film noir roots was *The Killer Inside Me* (1976), writer-director Burt Kennedy's send-up of one of Jim Thompson's most twisted suspense tales. Thompson, tabbed by a *Washington Post* reviewer as the dark literary offspring of a union of "Raymond Chandler, Dashiell Hammett and Cornell Woolrich," was one of the least lionized of American pulp writers during his lifetime. His novels were unique, displaying more of a "what done it" than a "who done it" theme with a sparse, elegant writing style reminiscent of a slow-motion train wreck. Thompson's stories were usually set in a film noir environment that possessed all the glamour of an armpit; the rear seat of a car, a greasy diner or a seedy hotel room decorated with a half-empty whiskey bottle, a bra hanging over the bed post and a balled-up cigarette pack in an overflowing ashtray. This tawdry landscape was peopled by damaged characters who passed themselves off as normal with disturbing amounts of sociopathic success. Thompson was a brilliant, original writer who was also a binge-drinking alcoholic.

Despite working with Stanley Kubrick on *The Killing* (1956)—Kubrick later remarked that the critical success enjoyed by *The Killing* was due to Jim Thompson—and *Paths of Glory* (1957), Thompson toiled in relative obscurity for decades, turning out television screenplays and novels that were appreciated and then quickly forgotten. In a case of dark irony, a plethora of films were adapted from Thompson's novels shortly after his death in 1977, first in France (*Serie Noire* [A Hell of a Woman] [1979] *Coup du Torchon* [1981] [based on *Pop. 1280*] and then in America (*The Kill-Off* [1989], *After Dark, My Sweet* [1990], *The Grifters* [1990], two additional versions of *The Getaway* and *This World, Then the Fireworks* [1997].

Written in the first person, *The Killer Inside Me* was one of Thompson's most ungodly stories. Sheriff Lou Ford, the West Texas pocketbook edition of Horatio Alger, works hard, gets ahead and is the epitome of the trusted public servant. Inside, he is a seething, compulsive murderer spiraling out of control. The screenplay unfortunately lost Thompson's aroma of obsessive evil concerning the characterization of Ford's "sickness." An earnest Stacy Keach portrays the demented lawman as an intermittently amnesiac soul who inexplicably murders in a sort of Freudian fog. Burt Kennedy ended up helming the film after the initial director was fired by producer Michael Leighton with the production temporarily halted for a script rewrite. The hiatus didn't appear to do too much good. The failure to capture the dark élan of Thompson's story consigned the film to be an interesting, but routine potboiler. Charlie was Howard Hendricks, the D.A. running for mayor and a supporter of Sheriff Ford until too late. He has several effective scenes with Keach, including a fatal encounter while both men are out hunting. McGraw was joined on the Butte, Montana location shoot by a host of distinguished actors including Keenan Wynn, Royal Dano, John Dehner and John Carradine. With a world premiere in Peoria, Illinois, *The Killer Inside Me* was a seldom-seen and quickly forgotten blip on the Hollywood radar screen in 1976.

More prominent as top-drawer entertainment was McGraw's final big screen appearance, *Twilight's Last Gleaming* (1977). The picture was directed by Robert Aldrich, Hollywood's most muscular auteur. Aldrich's film was a continuation of his consistent thematic pattern about men under stress attempting to overcome circumstances that are adventurously dire. The dramatic hurdles depicted in an Aldrich film were characterized by honor, manliness, duty, ambition, greed, and pride all leading to interpersonal character entanglements.

Aldrich, the scion of a wealthy Rhode Island banking family, leveraged his connections into a job as a production assistant at RKO in 1941. He paid his professional dues and became one of the most sought-after assistant directors in Hollywood. As an AD, Aldrich worked under Charlie Chaplin, Abe Polonsky, Jules Dassin, Richard Fleischer, Joseph Losey, Lewis Milestone, Jean Renoir, Robert Rossen, William Wellman, and Fred Zinnemann, among others. Moving into the director's chair, he scored his first major hit with Burt Lancaster in *Apache* (1954). A diverse group of entertaining films followed: the late-term apocalyptic noir *Kiss Me Deadly* (1955), *The Big Knife* (1955)—made with his own production company—and *Attack!* (1956), one of the best war dramas of the 1950s. Aldrich made big money with *Vera Cruz* (1954), his Grand Guignol doubleheader *What Ever Happened to Baby Jane?* (1962) and *Hush ... Hush, Sweet Charlotte* (1964) and the ultimate macho World War II action picture, *The Dirty Dozen* (1967), which grossed a then-incredible $8 million in its first week of release.

By 1976, Aldrich was embarked on a rehabilitation of his directorial career after going bust with his own company. He had recently scored with *The Longest Yard* (1974) but needed more.

A robust liberal, he also desired to make a declarative statement about the Vietnam War that had eaten away at his psyche dating back to 1965.

Twilight's Last Gleaming starred a much-mellowed Burt Lancaster (in his fourth and last Aldrich picture) as a free-minded Air Force general whose uncompromising anti-war stance earns him a frame job upper berth on Death Row. He breaks out with three other inmates and the group takes over an ICBM silo in Montana. With his finger on the button, Lancaster threatens to start a nuclear holocaust unless the president (Charles Durning) comes clean about the perfidy of the Vietnam War. It seems that there are some top-secret documents revealing that a former president and his secret cabal continued to feed American G.I.s into the Southeast Asian meat grinder merely to demonstrate our anti–Communistic resolve to the Soviets. After an endless chain of accusatory dialogue is delivered over the telephone by Lancaster, Durning, Richard Widmark, and many others amid a plethora of split-screen gimmickry, Burt pushes the trigger and the missiles begin to rise.

Aged with a hairpiece but still wary: *The Killer Inside Me* (1976).

Although *Twilight's Last Gleaming* provided ample raw meat for the anti-war, government conspiracy audience, it was a disappointingly trite film. The story, set in 1981, is predicated on the idea that the disclosure of secret government papers will destroy the collective American psyche. Considering that the country had comfortably endured the multiple revelations of Vietnam, Watergate and a series of CIA scandals, the picture's linchpin premise was absurdly unbelievable.

Even worse was the script, a cliché-ridden disaster credited to Ronald Cohen and Edward Huebsch, screenwriter of *The Son of Dr. Jekyll* (1951) and *Cigarette Girl* (1947). The production values were also erratic. The armed take-over of the Titan missile base by Lancaster and his cohorts appeared laughably less onerous than a stick-up of a fast food restaurant in El Segundo.

Charlie joined a cast so replete with veteran performers that one reviewer unkindly stated that the film included actors "who look as if they'd passed through old age and gone on to the embalming room."[212] Although the geriatric criticism was a cheap shot, the remark was not numerically inaccurate. While Lancaster and Widmark were still vigorous, both stars were now in their mid-sixties, the supporting players included Joseph Cotten, 73; Melvyn Douglas, 76; and Leif Erickson, 66. The fact was that these still estimable actors were simply appearing together in a badly written and indifferently produced movie.

McGraw was fine as General Crane, displaying equal amounts of authoritarianism while growling orders into a telephone and appropriate gravitas when seated around a conference table.

The company was headquartered in Munich with the studio sequences shot at the Bavaria Film Studios at nearby Grunwald. Charlie received a warm welcoming note from Robert Aldrich concluding, "I hope this letter finds you in good health and good spirits and I look forward to working with you."[213]

McGraw committed an embarrassing gaffe after his arrival in Germany: He invited mem-

A campaign poster for Charlie's character Howard Hendricks from *The Killer Inside Me* (1976) (courtesy Mildred Black).

bers of the cast to a catered ice-breaker in his hotel suite, mistakenly believing that the production company would foot the bill (Aldrich didn't and Charlie had to). But he thoroughly enjoyed Germany and the entire production.

It was unknown whether Aldrich's polite concern about Charlie's well being in his letter was just a pro forma close to a routine business communication or a more direct reference to McGraw's health. Certainly, there were grounds for concern about the latter issue.

29

Last Call

While McGraw might not have believed that his career was winding down, the signs were becoming increasingly evident. His deteriorating health began to impact his work. A letter from an agent addressed an incident that disrupted a commercial job:

I received your nice note, the report from the Doctor and the letter from the advertising agency … Truthfully your word of what happened was enough to convince me that anyone of us can have these things happen. My main concern Charles was your health, and being your friend for many years this was important.[214]

A prolonged sore throat and hacking cough forced McGraw to consult a doctor. According to Millie Black, a diagnosis of throat cancer was made. Charlie was directed to quit smoking immediately with the doctor making arrangements for treatment. McGraw, convinced that he simply had a cold, lit up another Camel, went home and never followed up. When his throat eventually felt better, Charlie was convinced that the doctor was another in the long line of know-it-alls, quacks and con artists that he had clashed with over the years. In truth, his throat cancer was either misdiagnosed or simply went into hiatus. McGraw's philosophy of personal health care for years had been akin to that of a horse: If the actor was able to stand on his feet, he would eventually be all right.

Inevitably, it all came back to the ceaseless consumption of alcohol. A co-worker on a show from the mid–1970s, and requesting anonymity, related that Charlie was really fighting the booze at this point, describing how the company shot around the actor who couldn't remember his lines until he composed himself and returned hours later together to complete a scene. Liquor was now medicine and McGraw could no longer function without it. The ability to taper off of the sauce for extended periods of time in order to work had ended. Millie vividly recalled a day when Charlie was at Warner Brothers to film a show and came down with a case of the DTs that he tried to walk off in a small park adjacent to the sound stages. He couldn't do it. McGraw was in such bad shape that the studio sent him to the doctor. When the actor showed up at home hours later, ashen and wan, he told Millie that he probably experienced an attack of incipient diabetes. Even at this point, Charlie remained in denial. With all of it, he still kept going after work. In 1974, McGraw went to Toronto to make some commercials for General Tire. He passed through Ohio for a brief visit with his father, whom he took out for prime rib at Marcel's Restaurant (owned by an old Central High School chum) in downtown Akron.

McGraw's professional nadir finally occurred when he was on location in Park City, Utah to film a *Life and Times of Grizzly Adams* television episode in late September 1976. Charlie never appeared in front of a camera. In Utah, a state of teetotalers and curious liquor laws, there was no booze available at the remote location. Charlie went into convulsions and was rushed to Wasatch County Hospital in nearby Heber City on September 29. Millie was telephoned from the hospital as the medical people treating Charlie appeared initially clueless. "He needed liquor.

I told them to give him a shot to make him coherent."[215] After receiving emergency treatment, McGraw was flown back to Hollywood.

Millie and a mutual friend met Charlie at Burbank Airport as he was deplaned in a wheel-chair. The long addiction to alcohol finally conquered him. He was hallucinating, delusional, literally out of his head, yet still refusing further hospitalization. McGraw went back home at Millie's, crawled around, had some drinks, slept for a long period and eventually came out of it.

Except for voiceovers, Charles McGraw had worked on his last picture show as the phone gradually stopped ringing. He was frequently not in shape to work. Additionally, the word was out and the actor was now in the untenable position of being perceived as uninsurable. Char-lie had continued to pick up radio work over the years, working on *Hollywood Radio Theatre* in "Deadman's Tale," a suspense show comprised of five half-hour episode spread over a week in January 1974. McGraw's final radio appearance was in an episode of the syndicated sci-fi series *Alien Worlds* in 1979.

His life degenerated into a sad pattern. Charlie continued his early morning routine of going to the bar with whatever money he could cadge. One bartender wrote off a large bar tab run up by McGraw after Millie stepped up to pay it off; the barkeep was a friend and didn't want to take her money. Millie tried everything she could to take care of him while attempting to convince Charlie to quit drinking. She would leave him supportive notes and prose, encouraging him to stop for his own good. Charlie would append his own appreciative comments back to her but nothing would change.

McGraw made sporadic attempts swear off and rally back as he had in 1967, but couldn't make it stick. The actor managed to quit drinking for several months and looked to be on his way back at one point. Then on Thanksgiving Day, Millie had her sister and friends over the house for a buffet dinner. At some point, she noticed that Charlie had disappeared and no one knew where he was. She found McGraw passed out in the back seat of his car with empty cans of ready-mixed cocktails on the floorboards. Charlie was now hiding booze around the house and continued to have health problems. McGraw fractured his left kneecap either falling or get-ting out of his car at the end of 1977 and had to be taken by ambulance to the Motion Picture Home Hospital in Woodland Hills. His subsequent hobbling around on a cane added to a sense of irascible frustration over being unable to earn a living after nearly four decades as a work-ing actor in Hollywood.

At the beginning of 1980, Millie told Charlie he had to get help and quit drinking or move out. McGraw made an initial inquiry about moving in with a friend, but by the early part of the summer, the actor decided that he would try once again to lick his drinking problem though as usual disdaining any outside assistance or help.

The San Fernando Valley was an oven by the afternoon of July 29. The palm trees along Ventura Boulevard drooped like wearied flamingoes in the sweltering heat and people stayed close to their air conditioners either at home or in their cars while sitting in the now-perpetual traffic gridlock.

Charles McGraw had been trying to wean himself off of alcohol for the past month. It was akin to "maintenance drinking." His notion was to get his consumption down to a minimal level and then quit entirely. Millie had been down this road with Charlie more times than she could remember, but retained the faith of the eternal optimist. Maybe, just maybe, this would be the time McGraw would conquer his inner demon.

McGraw's latest physical problem was a long-term arthritic right hip that had become unendurable. By his 66th birthday, the hip joint would intermittently dislocate without warning and the actor would tumble to the ground. Near the end of June, the hip betrayed him and he fell on the sidewalk, striking his forehead badly. After he was X-rayed and sutured up at Riverside Hospital on June 25, McGraw made an appointment for hip replacement surgery in August. Charlie was also on a daily regimen of 100 mg Inderal for an atherosclerotic condition that was starting to embarrass his heart.

After spending the day at the bar, McGraw was at home in the early evening, helping Millie hem the cuffs on a new pair of pants she bought; she tried them on and Charlie pinned them up for her. At around 5:40 p.m., McGraw declared, "I'm going to take a shower."[216] He added that he was going by Riverside Hospital the following day to have the stitches in his forehead removed.

Shortly after the water began running in the shower, Millie Black heard a loud thump and Charlie calling her from the bathroom. She rushed in and encountered a horrifying sight. McGraw was on his back in the tub with the shower running. His left arm had gone through one of the shower glass doors mounted in a sliding track on the rounded edge of the bathtub. The shower door panes, which were extant from when the house was purchased in 1963, were made of regular glass instead of modern safety glass. McGraw's left arm was impaled by huge shard of glass just above his elbow. The shower was cascading water, but it didn't dilute the gouts of blood spurting from Charlie's arm all over the bathtub. Millie tried to stop the bleeding, but couldn't do it. The glass was imbedded in his arm, severing the artery. She also couldn't move McGraw out of the tub that was now slippery with blood. She ran and phoned 911 for the paramedics and then called a neighbor who was a nurse. Millie ran back to Charlie, who was turning white as his life's blood left his body. He said, "Millie, I'm cold, I'm going to die…."[217] McGraw lapsed into semi-consciousness. Millie's neighbor arrived and both women tried to stop the bleeding, but it was too late. He expelled a final sigh and the eyes went blank. It all happened so quickly. Charles McGraw, who had expertly faked death so many times in front of a movie camera, was irretrievably gone.

The firemen and paramedics from Engine Company #89 finally arrived and attempted to revive him without success. Officer Terry Minton from L.A.P.D. received an accidental death radio call and responded to the scene shortly after the paramedics arrived. Recalling his actions over twenty-six years later, Minton knew he had a potentially dicey situation on his hands as he entered the bathroom, viewed McGraw's body, and noted the large amount of blood and massive laceration on the actor's arm:

> Mr. McGraw was already D.O.A. in the bathtub. I recognized him when I arrived. I wanted to make sure that I covered all the bases.[218]

Minton had a more pressing reason before even entering the bathroom to ensure all the rules were followed. "There had been a mix-up on the address. The fire department went to the wrong address. They either were given the wrong address or something happened. They got another call to respond to the correct address."[219]

Asked if the paramedics could have saved McGraw if they initially responded to the correct address, Terry Minton paused and then answered: "I kind of thought, 'Here's a suit against the City of Los Angeles.' It's possible that he wouldn't have bled to death that soon. I remember the paramedics being upset about it, feeling that, 'If I had been there sooner, it wouldn't have occurred.'"[220]

The holdup in the arrival of emergency assistance was confirmed by Millie Black who, in her extreme anxiety, phoned 911 again and then ran out into the street looking for the ambulance while her neighbor remained trying to assist Charlie. "They took forever. When the ambulance pulled up, the paramedic told me that they got lost and couldn't find the street …"221

The duration of the emergency services delay assumed tragic proportions. McGraw fell in the shower at approximately 17:40 hours and was pronounced dead at 18:27, an elapsed time of 47 minutes. Los Angeles City Fire Department, Engine Company #89 is located at 7063 Laurel Canyon Boulevard in North Hollywood, a distance of 3.7 miles from Mildred Black's residence — a drive of less than five minutes, particularly if you don't have to stop at the two traffic lights on the way.

McGraw's body was removed from the tub and placed on the living room floor. Minton remembers Millie Black as being extremely upset and he spent some time with her to provide comfort and help calm her down. Millie composed herself and then phoned Freda to let her know what had happened. Freda went silent for a minute and said she was on her way. Freda added: "Meet me at the door with a glass of water and a tranquilizer."222 Charlie's estranged wife hurried over from her Wilcox Street apartment in Hollywood and Millie met her at the front door as requested. Freda briefly collapsed into hysterics when she saw the body on the floor and embraced her husband. Millie comforted her as Charlie's body was removed to the morgue in the old downtown Hall of Justice where Robert F. Kennedy, Marilyn Monroe and Sharon Tate were autopsied.

Thomas Noguchi, the publicity-loving Los Angeles chief coroner who would eventually be demoted and write a book about his colorful tenure, has his signature rubber-stamped on McGraw's death certificate. The medical investigative report included a requisite amount of detail supporting the determination of the cause of death. McGraw's death was certified to have been caused by an accident. There was no reason to conduct an autopsy.

The decedent was adjudged to be a 66-year-old man who was 69 inches tall and weighed 165 pounds. He had atherosclerotic cardiovascular disease and a chronic dislocated left hip. Charles McGraw died of a massive hemorrhage due to the horrendous cut to his left arm inflicted by the broken glass of the shower door. Quoting from the report:

> Due to the condition of the right hip, the hip would go out and the decedent would fall or collapse to the floor or ground. He never had any warning as to when the hip would go out and he would fall down…. The decedent was in Riverside Hospital 3 weeks ago for head suturing at which time the hip went out and the decedent fell and struck his head. The decedent had made arrangements with his doctor to have a prosthesis inserted in his hip in the near future…. At approximately 17:40 hours, Ms. Black heard a loud noise and the breaking of glass from the bathroom…. He apparently was standing in the shower, possibly washing his hair, his right hip may have gone out and the decedent possibly collapsed or fell and his left arm went through and and shattered the lower part of one pane of the two shower doors. The decedent bled to death in the bathtub and there was much coagulated blood in the tub. He drank several beers during the day, per Ms. Black. I.D. by Miss Black at the scene.223

While a chronic alcoholic has a high metabolism rate for alcohol and McGraw was physiologically to the point where he had a near-constant amount of alcohol in his bloodstream, it is medically improbable that his post mortem BAC of .26 percent was due solely to "several beers" cited in the coroner's report. As an example, a 165 lb. man with an above-average metabolic rate having a BAC of .25 percent would have consumed a minimum of ten beers no more than two hours earlier. It is a certainty that Charlie had considerably more to drink on the day of his death than Millie Black was aware of. It is also likely that McGraw wasn't drunk in the normative sense of the word. While it will never be known with absolute confidence whether McGraw's hip slipped out of joint, making him fall violently in the shower, or he lost his balance and simply slipped in a wet and soapy bathtub, the coroner's conclusion remains the likeliest scenario.

The City of Los Angeles was never requested to provide an official explanation concerning the delay of the paramedics. Aside from Millie Black being told by the driver of the ambulance that they got lost, Terry Minton recalls briefing both Millie and Freda McGraw on the situation regarding the response delay, but cannot recall whether the inaccurate address snafu emanated from the caller, emergency dispatcher or paramedic team. He added, "If you could locate a copy of the death report, all the information I received during the investigation would be in that report. To my knowledge no further investigation was conducted."[224]

A written request from the author to William J. Bratton, police chief of Los Angeles, for a copy of Officer Minton's death report and associated police records about Charles McGraw's death was denied by the Los Angeles Police Department. The stated reason for the denial:

> [I]n order to determine whether hard copy documentation still exists, it would require staff members to hand search through thousands of pages of records. Performing this type of search would place an undue burden on the Department and, as these records are more than 25 years old, the probability of finding any related records in unlikely. Therefore, pursuant to Government Code Section 6255, your request for records is respectfully denied.[225]

Terry Minton retired from the Los Angeles Police Department in 1999. He is enjoying his retirement in the Northwest and seems at peace with himself. And yet, when initially asked whether he remembered Charles McGraw's death, Minton immediately replied, "I recall it all the time." In a macabre coincidence, Minton's own father fell in the shower and grievously cut himself on a glass shower door several years after McGraw died. Fortunately, the paramedics arrived immediately, applied a pressure bandage to stop the bleeding, and the elder Minton fully recovered. When his father had his accident and medical assistance promptly arrived to save him, Terry Minton immediately flashed to the deceased actor he viewed in the North Hollywood bathtub for whom help didn't arrive in time.

Charles McGraw's accidental demise was made all the more tragic due to the delay of emergency assistance that ensured the actor's death. In a final touch of wretched irony, a full-face photo of McGraw remained hanging on the bathroom wall with an inscription in his neat cursive penmanship: "Millie, is this you're considered opinion of where I belong?"

Freda notified Jill, living in Calexico, California, about the death of her father. McGraw had long specified that he did not want to have a funeral, and curiosity seekers will search in vain for a Charles McGraw headstone. He was cremated by the Neptune Society. Freda and Jill scattered his ashes at sea off of the Southern California coast where he used to go on deep sea fishing trips with his pals. In what contemporary counselors would term "closure," Freda returned to Millie's house several weeks after McGraw's death for a visit. The two women chatted easily about Charlie and made small talk for several hours. Millie: "I still don't know why she came by again, but we had a good time talking." They never saw each other again.

The obituaries of McGraw's death repeated a number of the fallacies that Charlie had circulated assiduously to press agents for so long, along with other errors. *Variety* reported that he had been born in the Far East and earned a living as a prizefighter.[226] His hometown paper initially reported that McGraw died of a heart attack and that his last screen appearance was in 1971. Even *The Los Angeles Times*, which managed to get most of their facts right about Charlie by noting, "[H]e never achieved the stardom that is the hallmark of success in the entertainment industry,"[227] incorrectly stated that the actor was born in New York City.

During the first week of August 1980, informal wakes were held for Charlie McGraw in several North Hollywood and Studio City bars, replete with copious toasts, funny stories and long silences. "King Charles" couldn't ever stay at the bar again to have just one more.

30

A Noir-Stained Legacy

Freda McGraw continued living quietly in Los Angeles for ten years after Charlie's death. She never remarried. According to Jill McGraw, her mother, a relentless smoker, was diagnosed with cancer in the summer of 1990 and received treatment in a hospital near Morro Bay, California, where Jill was living. Freda died on August 9, 1990. She was seventy-four years old.

They say a child is never supposed to die before the parents. Charlie outlived his mother Beatrice, who passed away in an Akron nursing home on April 14, 1974, but he died before his father. Frank B. Butters passed away in his hometown of Akron on November 25, 1981. Charlie's father lived to the ripe old age of 95. A lifelong Mason, he was a member of the "United Methodist's men club, Akron Lodge No. 83 F&AM, the Yusef Khan Grotto and the Ancient Accepted Scottish Rite Valley of Cleveland."[228]

Millie Black got on with her life after McGraw's death. She stayed in her house, continued working and renewed a close relationship with an old friend. The succeeding years were cumulatively leavened with sadness caused by the passage of time. She had remained close to her ex-husband, Stan, who now lived in Coeur de Lane, Idaho. When Stan visited her one summer, Millie suddenly found a stranger instead of the genial musician that she loved while both of them toured the country with Barclay Allen's quartet. When she asked what was wrong, Stan told her that he increasingly wasn't aware of where he was going or what he was doing. As Millie remarked later, "This was just before Rita Hayworth and no one knew." Stan, in his early seventies, had Alzheimer's disease. He deteriorated rapidly. Millie went to see him up in Idaho and her husband just sat in a chair, silent. She helped look after him until he passed away.

Her twin sister Marge was next. Marge and her husband had settled comfortably in Burbank years ago and remained a happy and active couple. With sudden swiftness, Marge's husband passed away and soon afterward his widow began acting strangely. One day Millie found her sister crying because she could no longer balance her checkbook. Millie had Marge move in with her. When her sister began watching Asian-language television programs for hours and tried to wash dishes over the gas burners, it was a tragic instance of *déjà vu*. Marge had to be institutionalized with round-the-clock care. Millie faithfully visited every day and animatedly talked with her sister about the old days and current events. The pain of witnessing her twin — the pair literally shared their entire lives together — becoming lost in the eternal fog of Alzheimer's disease was almost too much to bear. She next took care of her older brother as he succumbed to age and illness. Nonetheless, Millie remained resolute and upbeat. She was soldiering on into her eighth decade when Charles McGraw's daughter showed up at the front door one day.

The years had been unkind to Jill. After a series of failed marriages, different households and five children, she returned to where she grew up, totally on her own. Besides the occasional residual check from SAG for her father's films along with Social Security, Jill was broke. She apparently never accepted alimony from her husbands, simply moving on when things didn't work out. One of her ex-husbands was the wealthy horse trainer, Eddie Gregson, who saddled up Gato de Sol to win the Kentucky Derby in 1982. Gregson was a nationally known figure in horse racing who would tragically commit suicide in June 2000.

Jill seldom if ever visited Millie's before her father passed away and the two women didn't know each other at all. McGraw and his daughter had remained in sporadic touch over the years with letters, some phone calls and the occasional visit. Now in her sixties, Jill literally had nowhere else to go. Millie offered Jill a place to stay on a temporary basis. The days turned into weeks and then months. Initially, the two women, linked by their relationship with Charles McGraw, got on quite well, but the relationship eventually soured.

Although a natural caregiver and generous to a fault, Millie was the last of the independents and possessed a low threshold for being bossed around in her own house. Jill had her father's bullheadedness absent his sense of humor while toting around a veritable baggage train of regrets and troubles.

When it seemed that no further grief could be stacked onto McGraw's noir-stained legacy, a senseless tragedy occurred. Late in 2004, Jill returned to her former residence of Santa Fe, New Mexico to search for her 24-year-old son after filing a missing persons report. She had been unable to reach her child on the telephone and was deeply concerned. Charlie's grandson was eventually located after dying in an Albuquerque hospital on November 12 from severe head-trauma complications and pneumonia. The young man was brought to the hospital in a coma by the police on Halloween night after being viciously beaten at a local hotel. Heaping rancor onto tragedy, the hospital staff repeatedly informed the grandson's frantic girlfriend, who called several times looking for him, that no one by that name was registered as a patient. This horrific omission that caused Jill's son to die alone was attributed to a "computer glitch."[229] A stranger was subsequently arrested in Albuquerque and charged with the murder of Charlie's grandson. Jill became severely traumatized by grief. Millie let Jill stay on at her house until the summer of 2006 when she departed to somewhere else on her lifelong search for contentment.

Hollywood quickly forgot about Charles McGraw as the movie business continued to evolve as an elemental cultural imperative. After a couple of decades passed, the entire town and its culture became increasingly geared to an ever-younger, more informal milieu. While Charlie lived long enough to own a Nehru jacket, it was difficult to compare the conventional thirty-four-year-old Angelino male on a weekend, perhaps wearing sandals, in a T-shirt, eating a vegetarian entree in a Studio City bistro, with the Charles McGraw of the same age tucking himself into a thick Porterhouse at Jack LaRue's restaurant on a Saturday night, wearing the suit and tie of nearly a half a century earlier.

"I hate to sound like an old fart, but the town started losing its class when people stopped getting dressed up to go out," groused Bobby Hoy. The city had indeed changed many times since McGraw arrived, had his career, lived and died. There was still terrific energy and excitement in Hollywood and down in the Valley and certainly much more money. But the glamour and disarming, fun-loving excess seemed to be gone.

Hollywood proper was beginning to rehabilitate itself after a long decline, but it is challenging to find some of the old landmarks. So much had been demolished. What used to be RKO Studios is now part of the Paramount lot which eventually extended far enough to swallow the famous ornate old gate inside the studio grounds. Lucy's El Adobe Café, where McGraw and Mitchum drank beer and planned for their impromptu Mardi Gras, remains open on Melrose, but it now costs over $15 for a taco combination plate, and the margaritas are lousy. Charles McGraw's Walk of Fame star is resolutely embedded in the Hollywood Boulevard sidewalk front of Grauman's Chinese Theatre, trod over by a horde of tourists going to the new Hollywood & Highland mall or entering the Kodak Theatre where the Oscars are now held.

Although Charles McGraw never became a bona fide movie star, his name adorns a theatre marquee in this shot of San Francisco's Castro Theatre, which screened a double feature of his RKO pictures during the "Noir City 5" film festival in January 2007.

The San Fernando Valley unsuccessfully tried to secede from the City of Los Angeles several years ago. It would have been the fifth largest U.S. city with 49 percent of the current residents born in a foreign country. The Valley was crammed to overflowing with houses, strip malls and pavement several decades ago. RKO's old Encino Ranch facilities became parkland and the Warner Ranch, where Elizabeth Taylor rode *National Velvet*, is now called Warner Center, a steel and mortar collage of stores, businesses and condominiums. The last open land in the traditional Valley, the Universal Studios back lot, is being considered for subdivision into a luxury housing community that will add another 20,000 souls to the choked freeways and pot-holed surface roads that resolutely lack left-hand turn signal lights.

By any way of reckoning, Studio City lost its small town ambience. Ventura Boulevard is now an alternative freeway. If the Van Sickels were still around, they could literally walk across the Boulevard on top of cars during rush hour if they chose to. Even though CBS Studio Center at the old Republic site remains busy with television production, the area had been culturally cleansed of its plethora of stuntmen, cowboys, and local characters like Peter the Hermit who formerly populated the working class barrooms and drive-ins. None of the studios makes film noirs or Westerns any more. The old-time joints and proletarian businesses were replaced by boutiques, latte klatches and trendy nightclubs cordoned off by sash ropes and guarded by bouncers for well-heeled patrons of both sexes who frequently sport tattoos and body jewelry. The Studio City Camera Exchange that opened in 1944, where Charlie and Freda always had the slides and home movies developed from their movie location trips, recently closed. The sole landmark from the old days that endures inviolate is Dupars Restaurant, near the corner of Laurel Canyon and Ventura since 1938. One now has to be a millionaire in order to buy a house on the crowded hillside. A case in point was Charles

McGraw's former dream house at 3751 Reklaw Drive which was sold on October 3, 2005 for a reported $2,225,022.

Due to the resurgent popularity of film noir, a new generation of filmgoers is rediscovering Charles McGraw. The actor has become a pop culture figure to many fans of vintage movies. Film noir chronicler and novelist Eddie Muller wrote:

> ... McGraw's broad blocky presence lent any scene additional heft. As villains, not many players were as physically threatening. As heroes, few conveyed juggernaut determination so offhandedly or believably. McGraw was simply a natural on screen.[230]

While his films and TV shows still show up on television, McGraw's film noir pictures including *The Narrow Margin, T-Men, Armored Car Robbery, and Border Incident* are back on big theatre screens at film festivals and revival houses all over the country. Several of these pictures have recently been released as part of DVD box sets. No doubt that McGraw would have loved it; he would have been a hell of a post-screening Q&A guest at one of his pictures. Except he would have expected a check along with a few drinks at the bar afterward.

While the celluloid McGraw remains authentically compelling, it is left to a dwindling few to provide a more personal summation. Charlie wasn't an easy person to quantify. Although his daughter remembers the soft side of her father from childhood, McGraw resolutely kept his inner self walled off behind the liquor, stories, bluster and folklore even from those closest to him. As a young man, Charlie discovered that peace of mind, of a rather debilitating variety, existed in bottles. The booze provided a calmative effect on his anxieties until it overwhelmed him and brought nothing but tragedy. Millie Black believed that Charlie was unable to simply relax and be content with the person he actually was. The burgeoning love she had for him became cauterized after bearing witness to his lengthy self-destruction that occurred long before that final tragic day in the shower. Millie provided a poem she wrote in 1977 that was a disastrous cry from her soul, a literal dirge about the tragedy that Charlie's life became.

"The Bottle of Life"

To the bar he must go, to join all the drunks
They wouldn't care if it were littered with skunks
The zoo opens up at six in the morn
To go, or to not is the way he is torn

The answer of course, is always a "Yes"
The urge to be there as their favorite guest
He rants and he raves in the guise of debate
As he feeds his ego in chaos and hate

On his box he does stand, against gambling and such
It's his only way of keeping in touch
He drinks just a little, maybe a bottle or two
But gamblings a no-no, a great big taboo

When he drinks his fill of that poisonous flit
He comes home to me in a terrible snit
He recaps the day a few times or more
And demands my attention while he still has the floor

Another drink or a promise or two
He drinks some more, but never too few
His legs both give out as he heads for the bed
To sleep it off like a barrel of lead

A few hours later he's ready for more
But he says he's only going to the store
On goes his hat, with his keys in his hand
"I'll be right back," he says with a stand
He knows he is lying, that the drunks do await
For their favorite drinker who can never be late
Today as always is his last day of drink
Too much to do, with no time to think

He hurts me, he knows, so out with the booze
But the next day is here, with the same old sad news
Next morning at six, he gets in the car
And wends his way to the neighborhood bar
They greet him as though it's been over a year
As they burp, and they smoke and they slurp up their beer
Their clothes are disheveled and their hair all askew
But none of them have had more than a few

To home he does come, to blow off some steam
The nightmare is here, what should be a dream
The bottle is winning in his game of life
Destroying all, but mostly his wife

He's gaunt and he's thin and he eats ne'er a bite
But he has enough strength to continue to fight
His clothes need a change and his face needs a shaving
It makes no difference while he still had that craving

To seek outside help for drinkers you see
Applies to all, "But never to me."
The hours drag on by, from morning 'til night
Never escaping that serious fight

Who once was a bright and brilliant man
Is a pitiful sight with a drink in his hand
Oh God, save this man, from the fate he must face
If he continues to drink at this furious pace

No one knows the anguish and pain
To watch this life go slowly down the drain
God knows what he spends in that sleazy old den
But who gives a damn, as he still has that yen

His work goes to hell, His kids and his wife
As long as he struggles with his bottle of life
Examples of friends who drank to their grave
Makes him much stronger and even more brave

His battle goes on as he hollers for more
In his sick mind, he had evened the score
He is haunted by fears away in the past
But, oh my God, how long can this last?

I no longer have the pity, interest or trust
As long as he has this horrible lust
Such a waste of a human I really can't see
But the Dear Lord above hasn't left it to me

Nearly all of Charlie's roistering buddies from the old days are gone. Charlie Horvath, who loved to tease him, died young at age 58. One of Charlie's closest buddies, Johnny Daheim, who retired to San Diego after graduating to being a stunt coordinator on films through the 1970s, died in 1991. McGraw's *Golden Boy* pal from the beginning of his career, Bert Conway, passed away in 2002 at 86. Nearly all of his co-workers, friends, local characters from the bars and sound stages of yesteryear have slipped away.

Bobby Hoy nursed his cup of coffee and wore a warm jacket that displayed his Stuntman's Association patch while chatting in a coffee shop on a rainy day. Still active and animatedly discussing a future European vacation with his wife, Hoy paused when asked about McGraw. His eyes got cloudy as the rain misted outside with the passing traffic. Finally he said, "I loved old Charlie, I really did. I still miss him."

Charles McGraw led a life that descended into a noir-stained tragedy. From *In Cold Blood* (1967).

For Bobby and all the others who lived during a bygone era of steady work at the studios, suits and fedoras on Saturday night and the insular camaraderie of a small town of actors, stuntmen and blue-collar guys that manufactured entertainment for the rest of the world, Ventura Boulevard in the spring was never the same again without Charlie McGraw.

Critical Filmography

The first four credited players are listed for every movie. Film noir titles are in **_bold italic_**.

1. *The Undying Monster* (20th Century–Fox, 1942) Producer: Bryan Foy, Director: John Brahm, Writers: L. Hayward, M. Jacoby, Photography: Lucien Ballard. James Ellison, Heather Angel, John Howard, Bramwell Fletcher. Under his stage name Charles Crisp, McGraw made his screen debut in this second-billed horror programmer as a Scottish groomsman. A substantial part with a nice accent.

2. *The Moon Is Down* (20th Century–Fox, 1943) Producer: Nunnally Johnson, Director: Irving Pichel, Writers: Johnson, J. Steinbeck. Photography: Arthur C. Miller. Cedric Hardwicke, Henry Travers, Lee J. Cobb, Doris Bowden. Literate, stylishly played war drama from Steinbeck. McGraw has a bit as a Norwegian soldier.

3. *Tonight We Raid Calais* (20th Century–Fox, 1943) Producer: Andre Daven, Director: John Brahm, Writers: R. Lee, W. Salt, L. Willinger, Photography: Lucien Ballard. Annabella, John Sutton, Lee J. Cobb, Beulah Bondi. Okay war drama. McGraw is briefly seen as a corporal.

4. *They Came to Blow Up America* (20th Century–Fox, 1943) Producer: Lee S. Marcus, Director: Edward Ludwig, Writers: M. Jacoby, A. Wisberg, Photography: Lucien Ballard. George Sanders, Anna Sten, Ward Bond, Dennis Hoey. Jingoistic with a capital J. McGraw plays a Nazi who exchanges dialogue with Kurt Katch and has a couple of close-ups opposite Sanders.

5. *Two Tickets to London* (Universal, 1943) Producer: Edwin L. Marin, Director: Roy William Neill, Writers: Neill, Tom Reed, Photography: Milton Krasner. Michele Morgan, Alan Curtis, C. Aubrey Smith, Barry Fitzgerald. McGraw has an uncredited bit as Hendrik.

6. *Mechanized Patrolling* (WB, 1943) Producer: Gordon Hollingshead, Director: B. Reeves Easton, Writer: L. Rosten, Photography: James Van Trees. Walter Sande, Phil Warren, Gary Bruce, Brent Richards. This half-hour short made under the auspices of the U.S. Army Signal Corps features "Corp. McGraw."

7. *Destroyer* (Columbia, 1943) Producer: Louis Edelman, Director: William A. Seiter, Writers: B. Chase, L. Meltzer, F. Mead, Photography: Franz Planer. Edward G. Robinson, Glenn Ford, Marguerite Chapman, Edgar Buchanan. Top-notch human drama at sea with McGraw briefly visible in a flooding engine room as an assistant engineer.

8. *Corvette K-225* (Universal, 1943) Producer: Howard Hawks, Director: Robert Rossen, Hawks (uncredited), Writer: J.R. Sturdy, Photography: Tony Gaudio, H. Perry. Randolph Scott, James Brown, Ella Raines, Barry Fitzgerald. Wartime tribute to the Canadian destroyer escorts of the Merchant Marine in the North Atlantic. Top cast and Hawksian quality shine through. Watch for a young Robert Mitchum as a sailor. McGraw plays the chief engineer who breaks up fights between brain-dead duo of Andy Devine and Fuzzy Knight.

9. *The Mad Ghoul* (Universal 1943) Producer: Ben Pivar, Director: James Hogan, W: P. Gangelin, H. Kraly, B. Weisberg, Photography: Milton Krasner. David Bruce, Evelyn Ankers, George Zucco, Robert Armstrong. Better-than-average Universal horror programmer. Playing Detective Garrity, McGraw has a substantial role working with fellow copper Milburn Stone.

10. *The Imposter* (Universal, 1944) Producer: Julian Duvivier, Director: Duvivier, Writers: M. Connelly, Duvivier, S. Longstreet, L. Starling, Photography: Paul Ivano. Jean Gabin, Richard Whorf,

191

Allen Joslyn, Ellen Drew. Intriguing war story contrasts effective performances with excessive dialogue. Gabin is a French soldier who escapes death, assuming another man's identity to fight again in Africa. McGraw appears briefly as a soldier who is killed.

11. *The Seventh Cross* (MGM, 1944) Producer: Pandro S. Berman, Director: Fred Zinnemann, Writers: H. Deutsch, A. Seghers, Photography: Karl Freund. Spencer Tracy, Signe Hasso, Hume Cronyn, Jessica Tandy. In this exceptional movie about a concentration camp escapee, McGraw has an uncredited bit as a member of the Underground who gets killed by the Nazis.

12. **The Killers** (U-I, 1946) Producer: Mark Hellinger, Director: Robert Siodmak, Writers: A. Veiller, J. Huston (uncredited), R. Brooks (uncredited), E. Hemingway, Photography: Woody Bredell. Burt Lancaster, Ava Gardner, Edmond O'Brien, Albert Dekker. The *Citizen Kane* of film noir gets better with age. McGraw's titular role (that he shared with William Conrad) established him as a film actor of consequence.

13. *The Farmer's Daughter* (RKO, 1947) Producer: Dore Schary, Director: H.C. Potter, Writers: H. Wuolijoki, A. Rivkin, L. Kerr, Photography: Milton Krasner. Loretta Young, Joseph Cotten, Ethel Barrymore, Charles Bickford. Classic sentimental comedy has McGraw in a bit part as a thug brawling with Young's brothers (Keith Andes, Lex Barker, James Arness).

14. **The Big Fix** (PRC, 1947) Producer: Benjamin Stoloff, Director: James Flood, Writers: G. Bricker, S. Chernus, J. Malone, G. Ross, A. Wisberg, Photography: Virgil Miller. James Brown, Sheila Ryan, Noreen Nash, Regis Toomey. A "lost" film about crooks fixing college basketball games, this picture has the dubious distinction of one of the final PRC releases before the company was absorbed by Eagle-Lion. McGraw is seventh-billed as Armiston.

15. **The Long Night** (RKO, 1947) Producers: Raymond Hakim, Robert Hakim, Anatole Litvak, Director: Litvak, Writers: J. Viot, J. Wesley, Photography: Sol Polito. Henry Fonda, Barbara Bel Geddes, Vincent Price, Ann Dvorak. Very long indeed. Noir remake of *Le jour se lève* (1939) is excessively flashbacked and flaccid. McGraw is a cop who closes in on Fonda.

16. **Brute Force** (U-I, 1947) Producer: Mark Hellinger, Director: Jules Dassin, Writers: R. Brooks, R. Patterson, Photography: William Daniels. Burt Lancaster, Hume Cronyn, Charles Bickford, Yvonne De Carlo. The grimmest and the best men-in-prison picture ever made. McGraw works in the prison garage, makes and chucks Molotov cocktails during the big breakout.

17. *On the Old Spanish Trail* (Republic, 1947) Producer: Edward J. White, Director: William Witney, Writers: S. Nibley, J. Geraghty, Photography: Jack Marta. Roy Rogers, Tito Guizar, Jane Frazee, Andy Devine. Hackneyed, cheap-looking Rogers oater. How do you know Harry Blaisdell (McGraw) is the bad guy? He's the only actor completely outfitted in black.

18. **Roses Are Red** (20th Century–Fox, 1947) Producer: Sol Wurtzel, Director: James Tinling, Writer: I. Elman, Photography: Benjamin Kline. Don Castle, Peggy Knudsen, Patricia Knight, Joe Sawyer. Entertaining programmer features Castle in a dual role as D.A.-crook. McGraw plays the lead thug to Edward Keane's criminal kingpin.

19. **The Gangster** (King Bros./Allied Artists, 1947) Producers: The King Bros., Director: Gordon Wiles, Writer: D. Fuchs, Photography: Paul Ivano. Barry Sullivan, Belita, Akim Tamiroff, Harry Morgan. Well-staged and nicely written noir about a doomed small-time crook. McGraw plays Dugas, a threatening acolyte of Sheldon Leonard.

20. **T-Men** (Eagle-Lion, 1947) Producers: Edward Small, Aubrey Schenck, Director: Anthony Mann, Writers: J.C. Higgins, V. Kellogg, Photography: John Alton. Dennis O'Keefe, Mary Meade, Alfred Ryder, Wallace Ford. The best of the post-war "docu-noirs" is a visually evocative, suspenseful picture. McGraw is unforgettably brutal as Moxie.

21. **The Hunted** (Allied Artists, 1947) Producer: Scott Dunlap, Director: Jack Bernhard, Writer: S. Fisher, Photography: Harry Neumann. Preston Foster, Belita, Russell Hicks, Frank Ferguson. A well-written yarn becomes an austere programmer with McGraw showing up as a hard-edged cop.

22. *Berlin Express* (RKO, 1948) Producer: Dore Schary, Bert Granet, Director: Jacques Tourneur, Writers: C. Siodmak, H. Medford, Photography: Lucien Ballard. Merle Oberon, Robert Ryan, Charles

Korvin, Paul Lukas. Well-crafted, stylish post–World War II suspenser on a train with McGraw as a nicely turned out Army colonel.

23. *Hazard* (Paramount, 1948) Producer: Mel Epstein, Director: George Marshall, W: R. Chanslor, A. Sheekman, Photography: Daniel L. Fapp. Paulette Goddard, Macdonald Carey, Fred Clark, Percy Helton. A seldom viewed comedy that showcases the considerable assets of Goddard. McGraw is a henchman to gambler-heavy Fred Clark.

24. **Blood on the Moon** (RKO, 1948) Producer: Sid Rogell, Director: Robert Wise, Writers: L. Hayward, L. Short, H. Shumate, Photography: Nicholas Musuraca. Robert Mitchum, Barbara Bel Geddes, Robert Preston, Walter Brennan. Film noir as "Home on the Range." One of the top Westerns. McGraw is notably scruffy as Milo Sweet.

25. *Once More My Darling* (Neptune, U-I, 1948) Producer: Joan Harrison, Director: Robert Montgomery, Writers: R. Carson, O. Saul, Photography: Franz Planer. Robert Montgomery, Ann Blyth, Jane Cowl, Charles McGraw. McGraw scores big-time as comedic boxer-chauffeur of Blyth in a Hollywood-insider comedy that doesn't work well.

26. **Reign of Terror** (W. Wanger/Eagle-Lion, 1949) Producer: Walter Wanger, Director: Anthony Mann, Writers: A. McKenzie, P. Yordan, Photography: John Alton. Robert Cummings, Richard Basehart, Richard Hart, Arlene Dahl. Brilliant visual composition and suspenseful "histo-noir" set in bloody post–French Revolution. McGraw is striking as a brutal sergeant serving Robespierre.

27. **Border Incident** (MGM, 1949) Producer: Nicholas Nayfack, Director: Anthony Mann, Writers: J.C. Higgins, G. Zuckerman, Photography: John Alton. Ricardo Montalban, George Murphy, Howard Da Silva, James Mitchell. Magnificently lensed and compellingly brutal saga of undercover police from both sides of the border after alien smugglers. Top performances all around with one of McGraw's most amorally memorable turns.

28. **The Story of Molly X** (U-I, 1949) Producer: Aaron Rosenberg, Writer-Director: Crane Wilbur, Photography: Irving Glassberg. June Havoc, John Russell, Dorothy Hart, Elliott Lewis. Interesting, obscure film about crime boss Havoc's fall and redemption in prison. McGraw's role as a tough copper was significantly reduced to a supporting part. Universal is reportedly striking a new 35mm print of this seldom seen film.

29. **The Threat** (RKO, 1949) Producer: Hugh King, Director: Felix Feist, Writers: D. Hyland, King, Photography: Harry J. Wild. Michael O'Shea, Virginia Grey, Charles McGraw, Julie Bishop. McGraw's starring *tour de force*, as an escaped con on a revenge spree, cemented his reputation as a rising actor in Hollywood and earned him an RKO contract.

30. **Side Street** (MGM, 1950) Producer: Sam Zimbalist, Director: Anthony Mann, Writer: Sydney Boehm, Photography: Joseph Ruttenberg. Farley Granger, Cathy O'Donnell, James Craig, Paul Kelly. Top-flight, suspenseful and beautifully filmed New York film noir with McGraw as a stylishly tough John Law.

31. *Ma and Pa Kettle Go to Town* (U-I, 1950) Producer: Leonard Goldstein, Director: Charles Lamont, Writers: M. Ragaway, L. Stern, Photography: Charles Van Enger. Marjorie Main, Percy Kilbride, Richard Long, Meg Randall. Amusing series entry with McGraw as Shotgun Mike Munger, being overwhelmed by the Kettle clan of rug rats.

32. *I Was a Shoplifter* (U-I, 1950) Producer: Leonard Goldstein, Director: Charles Lamont, Writer: I. Gielgud, Photography: Irving Glassberg. Scott Brady, Mona Freeman, Andrea King, Tony Curtis. Interesting primarily for a young Curtis and other actors who have uncredited bit parts. McGraw is barely noticeable.

33. **Armored Car Robbery** (RKO, 1950) Producer: Herbert Schlom, Director: Richard Fleischer, Writers: E. Felton, G.D. Adams, R. Angus, R. Leeds, Photography: Guy Roe. Charles McGraw, Adele Jergens, William Talman, Douglas Fowley. The prototype noir-caper movie beautifully paced, well written and excellently acted. McGraw's Lt. Cordell is the template cinematic tough copper.

34. *Double Crossbones* (U-I, 1950) Producer: Leonard Goldstein, Director: Charles T. Barton, Writers: O. Brodney, J. Grant, Photography: Maury Gertsman. Donald O'Connor, Helena Carter,

Will Geer, John Emery. Oddball, rarely seen pirate musical with McGraw playing a one-eyed, cut-lass-waving pirate captain. Recently released on DVD.

35. *His Kind of Woman* (RKO, 1951) Producers: Robert Sparks, Howard Hughes (uncredited), Directors: John Farrow, Richard Fleischer (uncredited), Writers: G.D. Adams, F. Fenton, J. Leonard, E. Felton (uncredited), Photography: Harry J. Wild. Robert Mitchum, Jane Russell, Vincent Price, Tim Holt. An emblematic "movie-movie" with an even better back story. McGraw plays a sinister heavy and narrates the film's opening.

36. *Roadblock* (RKO, 1951) Producer: Lewis Rachmil, Director: Harold Daniels, Writers: G. Bricker, S. Fisher, R. Landau, D. Mainwaring, Photography: Nicholas Musuraca. Charles McGraw, Joan Dixon, Lowell Gilmore, Louis Jean Heydt. Cut-rate but compelling film noir with McGraw at his most morally conflicted as star-crossed insurance agent Joe Peters.

37. *The Narrow Margin* (RKO, 1952) Producer: Stanley Rubin, Director: Richard Fleischer, Writers: E. Felton, M. Goldsmith, J. Leonard, Photography: George Diskant. Charles McGraw, Jacqueline White, Marie Windsor, Gordon Gebert. A genuine classic. Superbly directed, acted and produced. McGraw and Windsor make an unforgettably vitriolic and appealing tandem. Perhaps McGraw's finest screen performance.

38. *One Minute to Zero* (RKO, 1952) Producer: Edmund Grainger, Director: Tay Garnett, Writers: W. Haines, M. Krims, A. Solt, Photography: Sherman Todd. Robert Mitchum, Ann Blyth, William Talman, Charles McGraw. Turgid war drama with McGraw providing needed relief to a distracted Mitchum as a tough, heart-of-gold sergeant.

39. *War Paint* (Bel-Air/United Artists, 1953) Producers: Howard W. Koch, Aubrey Schenck, Director: Lesley Selander, Writers: F. Freiberger, W. Tunberg, R. Simmons, M. Berkeley, Photography: Gordon Avil. Robert Stack, Joan Taylor, Charles McGraw, Keith Larsen. Suspenseful, well-crafted Western with McGraw in top form as a cavalry sergeant.

40. *Thunder Over the Plains* (WB, 1953) Producer: David Weisbart, Director: Andre de Toth, Writer: R. Hughes, Photography: Bert Glennon. Randolph Scott, Lex Barker, Phyllis Kirk, Charles McGraw. Nice De Toth oater. McGraw's Ben Westman is a roguish "Robin Hood" in post–Civil War Texas.

41. *Loophole* (Allied Artists, 1954) Producer: Lindsley Parsons, Director: Harold Schuster, Writers: D. Babcock, G. Bricker, W. Douglas, Photography: William A. Sickner. Barry Sullivan, Dorothy Malone, Charles McGraw, Don Haggerty. An interesting "blind alley" noir with McGraw as a nightmarish insurance investigator plaguing an innocent Sullivan. A "lost" film with no 35mm print currently available.

42. *The Bridges at Toko-Ri* (Paramount, 1955) Producers: William Perlberg, George Seaton, Director: Mark Robson, Writers: J. Michener, V. Davies, Photography: Loyal Griggs. William Holden, Grace Kelly, Fredric March, Mickey Rooney. Grandly conceived, all-star war movie that holds up magnificently. One of McGraw's best performances as a dedicated carrier air group commander.

43. *Away All Boats* (U-I, 1956) Producer: Howard Christie, Director: Joseph Pevney, Writers: K. Dodson, T. Sherdeman, Photography: William Daniels. Jeff Chandler, George Nader, Lex Barker, Julie Adams. Underrated, robust, masculine war-drama with McGraw as a small boat lieutenant.

44. *Toward the Unknown* (WB, 1956) Producer-Director: Mervyn LeRoy, Writer: Beirne Lay Jr. Photography: Harold Rosson. William Holden, Virginia Leith, Lloyd Nolan, Charles McGraw. Seldom-remembered, effective drama of Air Force test pilots. McGraw is stolid as Nolan's adjutant and Holden's buddy. James Garner's film debut.

45. *The Cruel Tower* (Allied Artists, 1956) Producer: Lindsley Parsons Jr., Director: Lew Landers, Writers: W. Douglas, W. Hartley, Photography: Ernest Haller. John Ericson, Mari Blanchard, Charles McGraw, Steve Brodie. Riotous low-tier, noir soap opera with McGraw chewing scenery throughout.

46. *Joe Butterfly* (U-I, 1957) Producer: Aaron Rosenberg, Director: Jesse Hibbs, Writers: S. Gomberg, M. Hargrove, J. Ruge, J. Sher, E. Wylie, Photography: Irving Glassberg. Audie Murphy, George Nader, Keenan Wynn, Keiko Shima. Inventive, fresh, postwar comedy with McGraw as a Yank magazine staffer in Tokyo.

47. **_Slaughter on Tenth Avenue_** (U-I, 1957) Producer: Albert Zugsmith, Director: Arnold Laven, Writers: R. Carter, W. Keating, L. Roman, Photography: Fred Jackman Jr. Richard Egan, Jan Sterling, Dan Duryea, Julie Adams. Social commentary as crime drama. McGraw is rock-solid as Lt. Anthony Vosnick opposite sleazy Duryea and Walter Matthau.

48. *Joe Dakota* (U-I, 1957) Producer: Howard Christie, Director: Richard Bartlett, Writers: N. Jolley, W. Talman. Photography: George Robinson. Jock Mahoney, Luana Patten, Charles McGraw, Barbara Lawrence. Neat Western with mystery plot has McGraw in top form. Yes, the picture was co-written by actor William Talman.

49. *Saddle the Wind* (MGM, 1958) Producer: Armand Deutsch, Director: Robert Parrish, Writers: R. Serling, D. Fuchs (uncredited), T. Thompson. Photography: George J. Folsey. Robert Taylor, Julie London, John Cassavetes, Donald Crisp. Fatalistic oater includes one of McGraw's most memorable Western heavies.

50. *The Defiant Ones* (Stanley Kramer/United Artists, 1958) Producer-Director: Stanley Kramer, Writers: N. Young, H.J. Smith, Photography: Sam Leavitt. Tony Curtis, Sidney Poitier, Theodore Bikel, Charles McGraw. One of the all-time groundbreaking films has become somewhat dated, but no matter. Rousing entertainment is due in no small part to McGraw's memorable turn as a hardline state police captain jousting with Bikel.

51. *Twilight for the Gods* (U-I, 1958) Producer: Gordon Kay, Director: Joseph Pevney, Writer: Ernest Gann, Photography: Irving Glassberg. Rock Hudson, Cyd Charisse, Arthur Kennedy, Leif Erickson. A great supporting cast and photography is wasted in a leaden soaper filmed in Hawaii.

52. *The Man in the Net* (Mirisch/United Artists, 1958) Producer: Walter Mirisch, Director: Michael Curtiz, Writers: R. Rose, H. Wheeler, Photography: John Seitz. Alan Ladd, Carolyn Jones, Diane Brewster, John Lupton. McGraw and the child actors are the only energetic aspects of this dud mystery.

53. *The Wonderful Country* (D.R.M./United Artists, 1959) Producer: Robert Mitchum, Director: Robert Parrish, Writers: T. Lea, R. Audrey, W. Bernstein (uncredited), Photography: Floyd Crosby, Alex Philips. Robert Mitchum, Julie London, Albert Dekker, Jack Oakie. Terrifically conceived Western with McGraw at his best as a rough-hewn country sawbones.

54. *Spartacus* (Bryan, U-I, 1960) Producer: Kirk Douglas, Director: Stanley Kubrick, Writers: D. Trumbo, H. Fast, C. Willingham (uncredited), P. Ustinov (uncredited). Photography: Russell Metty. Kirk Douglas, Laurence Olivier, Jean Simmons, Charles Laughton. Stupendous spectacle is the best of its type highlighted by ultimate McGraw villainous turn as Marcellus.

55. *Cimarron* (MGM, 1960) Producer: Edmund Grainger, Directors: Anthony Mann, Charles Walters, Writers: E. Ferber, A. Schulman, Photography: Robert Surtees. Glenn Ford, Maria Schell, Anne Baxter, Arthur O'Connell. Sprawling Edna Ferber saga with solid Ford and miscast Schell in lead roles. McGraw is fine as a malevolent saddle tramp.

56. *The Horizontal Lieutenant* (MGM, 1962) Producer: Joe Pasternak, Director: Richard Thorpe, Writers: G. Cutler, G. Wells, Photography: Robert J. Bronner. Jim Hutton, Paula Prentiss, Jack Carter, Jim Backus. One of the final pictures for the veteran producer-director duo of Pasternak and Thorpe. McGraw plays a grumpy colonel providing needed comedy relief to a movie that is only moderately amusing.

57. *The Birds* (Hitchcock/Universal, 1963) Producer-Director: Alfred Hitchcock, Writers: D. Du Maurier, E. Hunter, Photography: Robert Burks. Rod Taylor, Jessica Tandy, Suzanne Pleshette, Tippi Hedren. One-of-a-kind Hitchcock film about avian invasion still enthralls. McGraw scores as weathered skeptic Sebastian Sholes.

58. *It's a Mad Mad Mad Mad World* (Casey/United Artists, 1963) Producer-Director: Stanley Kramer, Writers: W. Rose, T. Rose, Photography: Ernest Laszlo. Spencer Tracy, Milton Berle, Sid Caesar, Buddy Hackett. Elephantine, all-star laughfest with huge ensemble cast. McGraw plays a police lieutenant who works for Tracy.

59. *The Busy Body* (Castle Productions/Paramount, 1967) Producer-Director: William Castle, Writers: B. Starr, D. Westlake, Photography: Hal Stine. Sid Caesar, Robert Ryan, Anne Baxter, Kay

Medford. A mostly unfunny comedy notable for screen debut of Richard Pryor. McGraw plays a henchman to crime boss Robert Ryan.

60. *In Cold Blood* (Pax/Columbia, 1967) Producer-Director: Richard Brooks, Writers: T. Capote, R. Brooks, Photography: Conrad Hall. Robert Blake, Scott Wilson, John Forsythe, Paul Stewart. Epochal, beautiful dark rendering of Capote's book. McGraw is unforgettable as Blake's father. Filmmaking at its best.

61. *Hang 'Em High* (Eastwood-Freeman/United Artists, 1968) Producer: Leonard Freeman, Director: Ted Post, Writers: Freeman, M. Goldberg, Photography: Richard Kline, Leonard South. Clint Eastwood, Inger Stevens, Ed Begley, Pat Hingle. Early Eastwood revenge tale with strong cast. McGraw portrays a spineless, burned-out sheriff.

62. *Pendulum* (Columbia, 1969) Writer-Producer: Stanley Niss, Director: George Schaefer, Photography: Lionel Lindon. George Peppard, Jean Seberg, Richard Kiley, Charles McGraw. Effective, frequently overlooked detective mystery with McGraw as a conflicted police chief.

63. *Tell Them Willie Boy is Here* (Universal, 1969) Producer: Jennings Lang, Director: Abraham Polonsky, Writers: H. Lawton, Polonsky, Photography: Conrad Hall. Robert Redford, Katharine Ross, Robert Blake, Susan Clark. Terrific fact-based Western artfully filmed, paced and beautifully written. McGraw essays yet another sheriff— this time a political creature.

64. *Johnny Got His Gun* (World Entertainment/Cinemation, 1971) Producer: Bruce Campbell, Writer-Director: Dalton Trumbo, Photography: Jules Brenner. Timothy Bottoms, Kathy Fields, Marsha Hunt, Jason Robards. Trumbo's haunting anti-war polemic, adapted from his novel, is unevenly edited and produced, but still powerful. McGraw plays Bottoms' father-in-law in flashback.

65. *Chandler* (MGM, 1971), Producer: Michael Laughlin, Director: Paul Magwood, Writers: Magwood, J.S. Young, Photography: Alan Stensvold. Warren Oates, Leslie Caron, Alex Dreier, Mitchell Ryan. Despite Oates and a veteran cast, a confused mishmash. McGraw appears distracted and disheveled.

66. *A Boy and His Dog* (LQ/JAF, 1975) Producer-Director: L.Q Jones, Writers: H. Ellison, Jones, W. Cruseturner (uncredited), Photography: John Arthur Morrill. Don Johnson, Susanne Benton, Jason Robards, Tim McIntire. Apocalyptic sci-fi picture that is like no other. McGraw is a bizarre, white-faced preacher in this independent feature.

67. *The Killer Inside Me* (Devi/WB, 1976) Producer: Michael Leighton, Director: Burt Kennedy, Writers: J. Thompson, R. Chamblee, E. Mann, Photography: William Fraker. Stacy Keach, Susan Tyrrell, Tisha Sterling, Keenan Wynn. Thompson's haunting serial killer novel gets an interesting, but ultimately unfulfilling send-up. McGraw plays a doomed D.A. with mayoral ambitions.

68. *Twilight's Last Gleaming* (Bavaria A.G.H./Geria/Lorimar/Allied Artists, 1976) Producer: Helmut Jedele, Director: Robert Aldrich, Writers: R. Cohen, E. Huebsch, W. Wager, Photography: Robert Hauser. Burt Lancaster, Richard Widmark, Charles Durning, Melvyn Douglas. Cast of old-timers can't save poorly written and indifferently produced suspenser. McGraw is an Army general in his final feature film.

Television Credits

Leading or Recurring Roles in Episodic Series

1952: *Foreign Legion* "Sergeant Flint" pilot episode
1954: *The Adventures of Falcon* "Mike Waring," 39 episodes
1955: *Casablanca*, "Rick Blaine," 8 episodes
1971–72 *The Smith Family*, "Captain Hughes," 39 episodes*

Television Movies

1964: *Nightmare in Chicago* aka *Once Upon a Savage Night*
1970: *The Andersonville Trial*
1971: *O'Hara, U.S. Treasury*
1971: *The Devil and Miss Sarah*
1972: *The Night Stalker*
1972: *The Longest Night*
1973: *Money to Burn*
1973: *Hawkins on Murder*
1976: *Perilous Voyage* (filmed in 1968)

Episodic Series Guest Appearances

1953: *Mr. and Mrs. North, Cavalcade of America, G.E. Theatre*
1954: *The Whistler* (2), *Cavalcade of America*
1956: *TV's Reader's Digest*
1957: *Conflict, Crossroads* (2)
1959: *Johnny Staccato, Hotel de Paree, The Untouchables, Troubleshooters*
1960: *The Man from Blackhawk, The Life and Legend of Jesse James, The Detectives, The Deputy, Route 66, Thriller, The Untouchables*
1961: *Shirley Temple's Storybook, Laramie, The Dick Powell Theatre, G.E. Theatre, Follow the Sun, The New Breed, Dr. Kildare*
1962: *Bonanza, Cain's Hundred, 87th Precinct, Wagon Train, The Untouchables*
1963: *The Virginian, The Alfred Hitchcock Hour, The Untouchables, Dr. Kildare, The Lieutenant*
1964: *77 Sunset Strip, The Travels of Jamie McPheeters, Grindl, Gunsmoke, Destry, Voyage to the Bottom of the Sea, Kraft Suspense Theatre*
1965: *Ben Casey, Kraft Suspense Theatre, Bob Hope Presents the Chrysler Theatre, A Man Called Shenandoah*
1966: *Run for Your Life*
1967: *Hondo, The Man from U.N.C.L.E, Judd for the Defense, Gunsmoke*
1968: *The Outcasts, The Wild Wild West, Judd for the Defense*
1969: *Bonanza*

*The exact number of Smith Family episodes McGraw appeared in could not be determined.

1970: *The Mod Squad, The Name of the Game* (2), *Matt Lincoln*
1971: *Adam-12, Gunsmoke, Monty Nash* (2), *Nichols, The Man and the City*
1972: *O'Hara, U.S. Treasury; Nichols, Ironside*
1973: *Banyon, Emergency!, Mission: Impossible, Adam-12*
1974: *Police Story* (2)

Chapter Notes

Chapter 1

1. Letter from F. Butters to parents, November 10, 1907.
2. Charles McGraw diary entry, February 22, 1932.
3. Charles McGraw diary entry, February 26, 1932.
4. Charles McGraw letter, February 3, 1953.
5. "Akronites Back After Long Trip," *Akron Beacon Journal*, July 12, 1932.
6. Email from John V. Miller, Director of Archival Services, University of Akron, November 8, 2006.
7. Dialogue from *The Asphalt Jungle* (1950).
8. "Akron's 'Killer' Makes Good" by Jerry Ross, *Akron Beacon Journal*, April 13, 1947.

Chapter 2

9. Lee Server, *Robert Mitchum: Baby, I Don't Care*, p. 22.
10. Charles McGraw biography (co-starring in Universal-International's *Joe Butterfly*), June 28, 1956.
11. Joseph Pevney interview with author.
12. Bobby Hoy interview with author.
13. "*The Jazz Age*," *Variety*, July 20, 1937.
14. Patrick McGilligan and Paul Buhle, *Tender Comrades*, p. 187.
15. Tom Weaver, *Monsters, Mutants and Heavenly Creatures*, p. 241–42.
16. *The Hollywood Reporter*, November 5, 1937.
17. "Tobacconist and actor 'save' play" by John Grime, *The Daily Express*, London, October 15, 1938.
18. Charles McGraw biography (co-starring in Universal-International's *Joe Butterfly*), June 28, 1956.
19. "Courtroom drama presented at Shubert," *Brooklyn Eagle*, 1939.
20. *Railroads on Parade* program from the New York World's Fair, 1940.
21. Betty Garrett interview with author.

Chapter 4

22. Biography of Charles McGraw, Paramount Studios, November 1966.
23. Millie Black interview with author.
24. National Personnel Records Center FOIA response: Butters, Charles C., of December 26, 2005.
25. Jill McGraw interview with author.
26. Darr Smith column, *L.A. Daily News*, November 1, 1949.
27. Marc Lawrence, *Long Time No See*, p. 121.

Chapter 5

28. Bishop, Jim, *The Mark Hellinger Story*, p. 231.
29. Biography of Charles McGraw, Paramount, 1966.
30. "Akron's 'Killer' Makes Good" by Jerry Ross, *Akron Beacon Journal*, April 13, 1947.
31. U-I financial report on *The Killers*, November 16, 1947.
32. Anthony Veiller letter to Mark Hellinger, December 2, 1945.
33. Mark Hellinger telegram to John Huston, January 2, 1946.
34. Mark Hellinger, *Photoplay Magazine*, December 9, 1946.
35. Kate Buford, *Burt Lancaster: An American Life*, p. 118.
36. *Newsweek*, September 9, 1946.
37. Universal-International publicity release, October 17, 1949.

Chapter 6

38. Charles McGraw letter to Freda McGraw, January 6, 1947.
39. Jules Dassin letter to author of January 15, 2006.
40. Joseph I. Breen letter, December 20, 1946.
41. Mark Hellinger telegram to Joseph I. Breen, May 7, 1947.
42. Joseph I. Breen letter to Mark Hellinger, May 9, 1947.
43. "*The Big Fix*," *Hollywood Reporter*, May 5, 1947.
44. McGulligan and Buhle, *Tender Comrades*, p. 88.
45. Daniel Fuchs, *Low Company*, 1937, as excerpted in *Los Angeles Times*, November 26, 2006.
46. Pressbook, *T-Men*, "John Alton, Production Stories," p. 29.
47. Max E. Youngstein telegram to Ed Small, November 25, 1947.
48. Eddie Muller, *Dark City*, p. 41.
49. Mickey Knox interview with author.
50. Mickey Knox interview with author.
51. Kenneth Nichols, *Akron Beacon Journal*, October 11, 1948.
52. Charles McGraw letter to Freda McGraw, January 6, 1947.

Chapter 7

53. Scott Eyman, *Lion of Hollywood*, p. 427.

54. John C. Higgins, *Border Patrol* script, September 3, 1948.

55. Bobby Hoy interview with author.

Chapter 8

56. Universal-International publicity release, October 17, 1949.

57. Dialogue from *Once More My Darling* (1949).

58. Robert Montgomery, Universal-International publicity release, August 18, 1949.

59. *Newsweek*, August 15, 1949.

60. Dialogue from *Side Street* (1950).

61. MGM pressbook, *Side Street*, p. 2.

62. Dialogue from *Side Street* (1950).

63. *Daily Variety*, November 20, 1950.

64. *The Hollywood Reporter*, November 20, 1950.

65. Universal-International publicity release, October 25, 1949.

66. Universal-International publicity release, September 30, 1949.

67. Universal-International publicity release, September 30, 1949.

68. Tino Balio, *United Artists: The Company That Changed the Film Industry*, p. 27.

Chapter 9

69. Frank, Nino, *A New Kind of Police Drama: The Criminal Adventure*, p. 3.

70. Jacobellis v. Ohio, 378 U.S. 184 (1964).

71. Hirsch, Foster, *Detours and Highways: A Map of Neo-Noir*, back cover.

72. Lawrence Basoff, *Crime Scenes — Movie Poster Art of the Film Noir*, p. 11.

73. Lawrence Basoff, *Crime Scenes — Movie Poster Art of the Film Noir*, p. 11.

74. Barbara Hale interview with author.

75. TCM interview with Edward Dmytryk.

76. *A Personal Journey with Martin Scorsese Through American Movies*: "The Director as Smuggler".

77. Richard Fleischer, *Just Tell Me When to Cry*, p. 31.

78. Edith Kermit Roosevelt, "Fans want more love, actor says," *L.A. Daily News*, June 7, 1952.

79. *Hollywood Reporter*, October 26, 1949.

80. *Daily Variety*, October 26, 1949.

81. *Today's Cinema*, October 1949.

82. *Variety*, October 24, 1949.

83. *Showmen's Trade Review*, 1949.

84. Jon Tuska, *The Detective in Hollywood*, p. 152.

Chapter 10

85. Jill McGraw interview with author.

86. Web blog, sickcandy.com, March 23, 2005.

87. Kevin Roderick, *The San Fernando Valley: America's Suburb*, p. 7.

88. The Valley Observed, www.americassuburb.com /quotes.

90. Stevens, George Jr., *Conversations with the Great Moviemakers of Hollywood's Golden Age*, p. 29.

91. Bobby Hoy interview with author.

92. Millie Black interview with author.

93. Millie Black interview with author.

Chapter 11

94. Edwin Schallert, *Los Angeles Times*, December 23, 1949.

95. *The RKO Flash*, January 21, 1950.

96. Dialogue from *Armored Car Robbery* (1950).

97. Joseph I. Breen letter to RKO, January 6, 1950.

Chapter 12

98. Gus Russo, *Supermob*, p.128.

99. Paul Boller, *Hollywood Anecdotes*, p. 97.

100. Richard Fleischer, *Just Tell Me When to Cry*, p. 39.

101. Lee Server, *Robert Mitchum: Baby, I Don't Care*, p. 193.

102. John Mitchum, *Them Ornery Mitchum Boys*, p. 142.

103. Bobby Hoy interview with author.

104. Quotes from RKO daily production notes of *His Kind of Woman* (1951).

Chapter 13

105. Stanley Rubin interview with author.

106. Richard Fleischer interview with author.

107. Stanley Rubin interview with author.

108. Dialogue from *The Narrow Margin* (1952).

109. Dialogue from *The Narrow Margin* (1952).

110. Jacqueline White interview with author.

111. Gordon Gebert interview with author.

112. Jacqueline White interview with author.

113. Jerry Renshaw, *Tales of Noir and B Movies*, interview with Marie Windsor, *The Austin Chronicle*, October 31–November 6, 1997.

114. Howard Hughes to Jim Wilkinson, *Cutting Instructions — Target*, November 29, 1950.

115. Howard Hughes to Jim Wilkinson, *Cutting Instructions — Target*, November 29, 1950.

116. Howard Hughes to Jim Wilkinson, *Cutting Instructions — Target*, November 29, 1950.

117. Added scenes 125–26 for *Target*, RKO Production file, December 18, 1951.

118. Added scene 155 for *Target*, RKO Production file, December 20, 1951.

119. Jerry Renshaw, *Tales of Noir and B Movies*, interview with Marie Windsor, *Austin Chronicle*, October 31–November 6, 1997.

120. Erskine Johnson, *Erskine in Hollywood*, syndicated, *Harrisburg Daily Register*, September 4, 1952.

Chapter 14

121. Mickey Knox interview with author.

122. Richard Fleischer interview with author.

123. Lana Turner, *Lana: the Lady, the Legend, the Truth*, p. 86.

124. Tay Garnett, *Light Your Torches and Pull Up Your Tights*, p. 283.

125. Tay Garnett, *Light Your Torches and Pull Up Your Tights*, p. 282.

126. Dick Martin interview with author.

127. "Mitchum and GI in fight in saloon," AP, November 7, 1951.

128. "Mitchum and GI in fight in saloon," AP, November 7, 1951.

129. Lee Server, *Robert Mitchum: Baby, I Don't Care*, p. 225.

130. "Robert Mitchum 'Aggressor' in Barroom Brawl," UPI, November 8, 1951.

131. Frances B. Murphey, "War Film, Audience Make Noise," *Akron Beacon Journal*, October 6, 1952.

132. Bosley Crowther, *"One Minute to Zero,"* *New York Times*, September 20, 1952.

Chapter 15

133. Richard Fleischer interview with author.

134. Jean Simmons interview with author.

135. Jean Simmons interview with author.

136. Jean Simmons interview with author.

137. Stanley Rubin interview with author.

138. Gus Russo, *Supermob*, p. 130.

139. Betty Lasky, *RKO— The Biggest Little Major of Them All*, p. 1.

Chapter 16

140. Tom Weaver, *Return of the B Science Fiction and Horror Heroes*, p. 220.

141. Lindsley Parsons Jr. interview with author.

Chapter 17

142. Dialogue from *The Adventures of Falcon*, "Kiss Me Not," 1954.

143. L.Q. Jones interview with author.

144. L.Q. Jones interview with author.

145. Millie Black interview with author.

Chapter 18

146. Dialogue from *The Bridges at Toko-Ri* (1955).

147. Jimmie Fidler, *Fidler in Hollywood*, December 15, 1954.

148. Joseph Pevney interview with author.

149. Jill McGraw interview with author.

150. Michael Barnum, "William Reynolds, A Classic Son," *Classic Images*, #356–61.

151. Bobby Hoy interview with author.

152. Joseph Pevney interview with author.

153. Joseph Pevney interview with author.

154. L.Q. Jones interview with author.

155. Lindsley Parsons Jr. interview with author.

156. Lindsley Parsons Jr. interview with author.

157. John Ericson interview with author.

Chapter 19

158. Bobby Hoy interview with author.

159. Jill McGraw interview with author.

160. Jill McGraw interview with author.

161. "Ventura Boulevard in the Spring" was on a couple of aged typewritten sheets that I found in the bottom of a box of McGraw's stuff in Millie Black's garage.

162. Earl Wilson, "Gravel-voiced Charles McGraw: Akron Actor No Hero to Daughter," February 14, 1955.

Chapter 20

162. *Slaughter on Tenth Avenue* (1957) opening credits extract.

163. Julie Adams interview with author.

164. Richard Erdman interview with author.

165. Richard Erdman interview with author.

166. Theodore Bikel email of July 16 2006.

167. Bernard J. Dusseault, "Acting, to Charles McGraw, More Fun Than Hard Work," *Worcester Sunday Telegram*, June 29, 1958.

168. Michael McGreevey interview with author.

169. Michael McGreevey interview with author.

170. Michael McGreevey interview with author.

171. Michael McGreevey interview with author.

172. Lee Server, *Robert Mitchum: Baby, I Don't Care*, p. 338.

Chapter 21

173. Richard Fleischer, *Just Tell Me When to Cry*, p. 159.

174. Peter Ustinov video interview, *Spartacus*, Criterion Collection, 2001.

175. Dialogue from *Spartacus* (1960).

176. Jean Simmons interview with author.

177. Millie Black interview with author.

178. Kirk Douglas audio commentary, *Spartacus*, Criterion Collection, 2001.

179. Jean Simmons interview with author.

Chapter 22

180. L.Q. Jones interview with author.

181. Dialogue from *The Horizontal Lieutenant* (1962).

182. Stevens, George, Jr., *Conversations with the Great Movie Makers of Hollywood's Golden Age*, p. 166.

183. Farley Granger interview with author.

184. Millie Black interview with author.

Chapter 23

185. Jill McGraw interview with author.

186. Scott Eyman, *The Lion of Hollywood*, p. 490.

187. Johnny Grant interview with author.

188. Bobby Hoy interview with author.

Chapter 24

189. Gene Fernett, *Hollywood's Poverty Row, 1930–1950*, p. 81.
190. Gene Fernett, *Hollywood's Poverty Row, 1930–1950*, p. 88.

Chapter 25

191. Gerald Nachman, "*The Busybody*," *Oakland Tribune*, February 9, 1967.

Chapter 26

192. Email from Jim Steranko, October 10, 2006.
193. Jean Simmons interview with author.
194. Jean Simmons interview with author.
195. Letter from Mrs. John Forsythe, October 25, 2006.

Chapter 27

196. Andrew J. Fenady letter to Charles McGraw, October 2, 1967.
197. L.Q. Jones interview with author.
198. L.Q. Jones interview with author.
199. Abraham Polonsky Archive of American Television Interview, Part 6 of 6, July 6, 1999.
200. Dialogue from *Tell Them Willie Boy Is Here* (1969).
201. Jeff Jensen, *Entertainment Weekly*, February 5, 1999.
202. Warren Stevens interview with author.
203. Michael J. Hayde, *My Name's Friday*, p. 218.
204. Rasosh, Ronald and Allis, Red, *Star over Hollywood*, p. 229.

Chapter 28

205. Millie Black interview with author.
206. Millie Black interview with author.
207. Millie Black interview with author.
208. Bobby Hoy interview with author.
209. Mike Mazurki letter to Charles McGraw, January 27, 1975.
210. Millie Black interview with author.
211. "*Twilight's Last Gleaming* — No Star," *New York Times*, February 10, 1977.
212. Robert Aldrich letter to Charles McGraw, February 21, 1976.

Chapter 29

213. Lew Sherrell letter to Charles McGraw, October 30, 1975.
214. Millie Black interview with author.
215. Millie Black interview with author.
216. Millie Black interview with author.
217. Terry Minton interview with author.
218. Terry Minton interview with author.
219. Terry Minton interview with author.
220. Millie Black interview with author.
221. Millie Black interview with author.
222. County of Los Angeles, Coroner Report, Case No. 80–9706, Death of Charles McGraw.
223. Terry Minton email of December 4, 2006.
224. William J. Bratton letter to Alan K. Rode, November 9, 2006.
225. Charles McGraw obituary, *Variety*, August 1, 1980.
226. Eric Malnic, Charles McGraw obituary, *Los Angeles Times*, August 4, 1980.

Chapter 30

227. Frank P. Butters obituary, *Akron Beacon Journal*, November 28, 1981.
228. Jason Auslander, "Man Charged in Deadly Halloween Brawl," *Santa Fe New Mexican*, November 17, 2004.
229. Eddie Muller, *Dark City*, p. 154.

Sources

Interviews, Discussions and Communications

Julie Adams
Theodore Bikel
Mildred Black
Jules Dassin
Richard Erdman
John Ericson
Richard Fleischer
Mr. & Mrs. John
    Forsythe
Betty Garrett
Gordon Gebert
Susan Gordon
Farley Granger
Johnny Grant
Barbara Hale
Earl Holliman
Bobby Hoy

L.Q. Jones
Mickey Knox
Jill Julia McGraw
Michael McGreevey
Dick Martin
Terry Minton
Lindsley Parsons Jr.
Joseph Pevney
Paul Picerni
Stanley Rubin
Mark Schucart
Jean Simmons
Jim Steranko
Warren Stevens
Joan Taylor
Peggy Webber
Jacqueline White

Books

Alton, John. *Painting with Light*. University of California Press, 1995.

Balio, Tino. *United Artists: the Company That Changed the Film Industry*. University of Wisconsin Press, 1987.

Bartlett, Howard, and James Steele. *Howard Hughes: His Life and Madness*. W.W. Norton, 1984.

Basinger, Janine. *Anthony Mann*. Twayne Publishers, 1979.

Bassoff, Lawrence. *Crime Scenes: Movie Poster Art of the Film Noir*. Lawrence Bassoff Collections, 1997.

Bishop, Jim, *The Mark Hellinger Story: A Biography of Broadway and Hollywood*. Appleton Century Crofts, 1952.

Bogdanovich, Peter. *Who the Devil Made It*. Ballantine, 1997.

Borde, Raymond, and Etienne Chaumeton. *A Panorama of American Film Noir 1941–1953*. City Lights Books, 2002.

Brode, Douglas. *Lost Films of the Fifties*. Carol Publishing Group, 1991.

Bruck, Connie. *When Hollywood Had a King*. Random House, 2003.

Buford, Kate. *Burt Lancaster: An American Life*. DaCapo Press, 2000.

Buhle, Paul, and Dave Wagner. *Radical Hollywood*. New Press, 2002.

Callow, Simon. *The Night of the Hunter*. British Film Institute, 2000.

Clarens, Carlos. *Crime Movies: An Illustrated History*. W.W. Norton, 1979.

Clarke, Robert, and Tom Weaver. *To "B" or Not to "B": A Film Actor's Odyssey*. MidMar Press, 1996.

Cross, Robin. *The Big Book of "B" Movies or How Low Was My Budget*. St. Martin's Press, 1984.

De Carlo, Yvonne, with Doug Warren. *An Autobiography: Yvonne*. St. Martin's Press, 1987.

Dick, Bernard F. The *Merchant Prince of Poverty Row: Harry Cohn of Columbia Pictures*. University Press of Kentucky, 1993.

Dickos, Andrew. *Street with No Name: A History of the Classic American Film Noir*. University Press of Kentucky, 2002.

Dietrich, Noah. *Howard: The Amazing Mr. Hughes*. Fawcett, 1972.

Dixon, Wheeler Winston. *The Films of Reginald Le Borg*. Scarecrow Press, 1992.

Dmytryk, Edward. *Hollywood's Golden Age*. Bear-Manor Media, 2003.

Eyman, Scott. *Lion of Hollywood: The Life and Legend of Louis B. Mayer*. Simon & Schuster, 2005.

Fernett, Gene. *Hollywood's Poverty Row, 1930–1950*. Coral Reef Publications, 1973.

Finler, Joel W. *The Hollywood Story*. Crown Publisher, 1988.

Fitzgerald, Michael. *Universal Pictures*. Arlington House, 1977.

Fleischer, Richard. *Just Tell Me When to Cry*. Carroll and Graf, 1993.

_____, and Earl Felton. *The Narrow Margin* (Screenplay). RKO Classic Screenplays, 1952, 1980.

Friedrich, Otto. *City of Nets*. Harper & Row, 1986.

Gabler, Neal. *An Empire of Their Own*. Doubleday, 1988.

Garnett, Tay, with Fredda Dudley Balling. *Light Your Torches and Pull Up Your Tights*. Arlington House, 1973.

Granger, Stewart. *Sparks Fly Upward*. G.P. Putnam, 1981.

Greco, Joseph. *The File on Robert Siodmak in Hollywood 1941–1951*. Dissertation.com, 1991.

Hannsberry, Karen. *Bad Boys: The Actors of Film Noir*, McFarland, 2003.

_____. *Femme Noir: Bad Girls of Film*. McFarland, 1998.

Harmetz, Alijean. *The Making of* Casablanca. Hyperion Books, 2002.

Hayde, Michael J. *My Name's Friday.* Cumberland House, 2001.

Heimann, Jim. *Sins of the City: The Real Los Angeles Noir.*Chronicle Books, 1999.

Hemingway, Ernest. *The Killer.* (Screenplay.) Property of Mark Hellinger Productions Inc., not dated.

Higham, Charles. *Howard Hughes: The Secret Life.* St. Martin's Griffin, 2004.

Hirsch, Foster. *Detours and Highways: A Map of Neo-Noir.* Limelight Editions, 1999.

_____. *Film Noir: The Dark Side of the Screen.* De Capo Press, 1981.

Humphreys, Justin. *Names You Never Remember, With Faces You Never Forget.* BearManor Media, 2006.

Jarlett, Franklin. *Robert Ryan: A Biography and Critical Filmography.* McFarland, 1990.

Jewell, Richard B., with Vernon Harbin. *The RKO Story.* Arlington House, 1982.

Kashner, Sam, and Jennifer MacNair. *The Bad and the Beautiful.* W.W. Norton, 2002.

Kellow, Brian. *The Bennetts: An Acting Family.* University Press of Kentucky, 2004.

Kitses, Jim. *Gun Crazy.* British Film Institute, 1996.

Knox, Mickey. *The Good, the Bad and the Dolce Vita.* Nation Books, 2004.

Kramer, Stanley. *A Mad, Mad, Mad, Mad World: A Life in Hollywood.* Harcourt Brace, 1997.

Lasky, Betty. *RKO: The Biggest Little Major of Them All.* Prentice Hall, 1984.

Lawrence, Marc. *Long Time No See: Confessions of a Hollywood Gangster.* Ursus Press, 1991.

Lucas, John Meredyth. *Eighty Odd Years in Hollywood.* McFarland, 2004.

Lyons, Arthur. *Death on the Cheap.* DeCapo Press, 2000.

MacAdams, William. *Ben Hecht.* Barricade Books, 1990.

Maltin, Leonard. *Leonard Maltin's Classic Movie Guide.* Plume, 2005.

Manush, Barry. *The Encyclopedia of Hollywood Film Actors.* Applause Books, 2003.

Margulies, Stan. *Spartacus: The Illustrated History of the Motion Picture Production.* Bryna Productions and Universal Studios, Inc., 1960.

McClelland, Doug. *Forties Film Talk.* McFarland, 1992.

McDougal, Dennis. *The Last Mogul: Lew Wasserman, MCA and the Hidden History of Hollywood.* De Capo Press, 2001.

McGilligan, Patrick, and Paul Buhle. *Tender Comrades.* St. Martin's Griffin, 1997.

McWilliams, Carey. *Southern California: An Island on the Land.* Peregrine Smith Books, 1946, 1973.

Miller, Don. *"B" Movies.* Curtis Books, 1973.

Mitchum, John. *Them Ornery Mitchum Boys.* Creatures at Large Press, 1989.

Montalban, Ricardo, with Bob Thomas. *Reflections: A Life in Two Worlds.* Doubleday, 1980.

Mosley, Leonard. *Zanuck: The Rise and Fall of Hollywood's Last Tycoon.* Little, Brown and Company, 1984.

Muller, Eddie. *The Art of Noir.* Overlook Press, 2002.

_____. *Dark City: The Lost World of Film Noir.* St. Martin's Press, 1998.

Neibaur, James L. *The RKO Features.* McFarland, 1994.

Parish, James Robert. *Prison Pictures from Hollywood.* McFarland, 1991.

_____. *The RKO Girls.* Rainbow Books, 1974.

Parrish, Robert. *Growing Up in Hollywood.* Harcourt Brace Jovanovich, 1976.

Polito, Robert. *Savage Art: A Biography of Jim Thompson.* Vantage Books, 1996.

Radosh, Ronald, and Allis Radosh. *Red Star Over Hollywood.* Encounter Books, 2005.

Rappleye, Charles and Ed Becker. *All American Mafioso: The Johnny Rosselli Story.* Doubleday, 1991.

Roberson, Chuck. *The Fall Guy.* Hancock House, 1980.

Russell, Jane. *Jane Russell: An Autobiography,* J&J Peoples, 1985.

Russo, Gus. *The Outfit.* Bloomsbury, 2001.

_____. *Supermob.* Bloomsbury, 2006.

Schatz, Thomas. *The Genius of the System.* Henry Holt, 1996.

Schwartz, Nancy Lynn. *The Hollywood Writers' War.* Alfred A. Knopf, 1982.

Selby, Spencer. *Dark City: The Film Noir.* McFarland, 1984.

Server, Lee. *Ava Gardner: Love is Nothing.* St. Martin's Press, 2006.

_____. *Robert Mitchum: Baby, I Don't Care.* St. Martin's Press, 2001.

_____, Ed Gorman and Martin Greenberg. *The Big Book of Noir.* Carroll and Graf, 1998.

Silver, Alain and Elizabeth Ward. *Film Noir: An Encyclopedic Reference to the American Style.* The Overlook Press, 1992.

Slide, Anthony. *Actors on Red Alert.* Scarecrow Press, 1999.

Smith, Mona Z. *Becoming Something: The Story of Canada Lee,* Faber & Faber, 2004.

Sperling, Cass Warner and Cork Millner with Jack Warner Jr. *Hollywood Be Thy Name.* Prima Publishing, 1994.

Stevens, George Jr. *Conversations with the Great Moviemakers of Hollywood's Golden Age.* Alfred A. Knopf, 2006.

Thompson, Jim. *The Killer Inside Me.* William Morrow, 1952, 1983.

Thomson, David. *Rosebud: The Story of Orson Welles.* Alfred A. Knopf, 1996.

_____. *The Whole Equation: A History of Hollywood,* Alfred A. Knopf, 2005.

Turner, Lana. *Lana: The Lady, The Legend and The Truth.* Pocket Books, 1982.

Tuska, Jon. *The Detective in Hollywood.* Doubleday, 1978.

Twomey, Alfred E. and Arthur F. McClure. *The Versatiles.* Castle Books, 1969.

Weaver, Tom. *Earth vs. the Sci-Fi Filmmakers.* McFarland, 2005.

_____. *Interviews with B Science Fiction and Horror Movie Makers.* McFarland, 1988.

_____. *It Came from Weaver Five.* McFarland, 1996.

_____. *John Carradine: The Films.* McFarland, 1999.

_____. *Monsters, Mutants and Heavenly Creatures.* MidMar Press, 1996.

_____. *Science Fiction and Fantasy Film Flashbacks.* McFarland, 2004.

Wilk, Max. *Schmucks with Underwoods: Conversations with Hollywood's Classic Screenwriters.* Applause Books, 2004.

Williams, Gregory Paul. *The Story of Hollywood.* BL Press LLC, 2006.

Zollo, Paul. *Hollywood Remembered.* Cooper Square Press, 2002.

Newspaper and Periodical Articles

"Across Many Bridges," John Watson, *New York Journal American*, February 3, 1955.

"Actor Charles McGraw Obtained His Release Over the Weekend...," *Hollywood Citizen News*, January 7, 1952.

"Actor's Vagabond Past Out Dazzles Real Life," Sam Hood, *Pittsburgh Press*, February 1, 1955.

Agreement dated January 11, 1950, between RKO Radio Pictures Inc. and Charles McGraw.

"Aircraft Carrier Life Amazes Charles McGraw," Sherwood Kohn, *Cincinnati Times Star*, February 5, 1955.

"Akronites Back After Long Trip." *Akron Beacon Journal*, July 12, 1932.

"Another for McGraw." *Hollywood Reporter*, undated.

"Another Hit from Marge and Percy; *Ma and Pa Kettle Go to Town*." *Hollywood Reporter*, March 29, 1950.

"Apprehension over Shoplifting." *Hollywood Reporter*, October 24, 1949

Auslander, Jason. "Man Charged in Deadly Halloween Brawl." *Santa Fe New Mexican*, November 17, 2004.

Barnum, Michael. "William Reynolds, A Classic Son." Classic Images, # 356–61.

"Bartley, McDonald, Map More Telepix," *Variety*, May 16, 1952.

"Behind the Make-up," Harry Crocker, *Los Angeles Examiner*, May 14, 1951.

"*The Big Fix*." Review. *Hollywood Reporter*, May 5, 1947.

"*The Big Fix*." Review. *Daily Variety*, May 5, 1947.

"*The Black Book*." Review. *New York Times*, October 17, 1949.

"*Border Incident*." Review. *New York Times*, November 21, 1949.

"*Border Incident*." Review. *Hollywood Reporter*, August 26, 1949.

"'The Bridges of Toko-Ri' at Radio City," *New York Herald Tribune*, January 21, 1955.

Brierly, Dean. "A Tribute to the Tough Guys." *Filmfax*, June-July 1999.

"*The Brooklyn Novels*." *Los Angeles Times* Book Review, November 26, 2006.

"Buster Collier and Charles McGraw from Collier-McGraw Radio Enterprises...," *Hollywood Reporter*, March 17, 1950.

Butters, Frank. Obituary. *Akron Beacon Journal*, November 28, 1981.

"Central High School's Graduating Class of January '31 Waited Expectantly..." *Akron Beacon Journal*, 1959.

"Charles McGraw Becomes a Star," Ann St. John, *Hollywood Citizen-News*, May 5, 1952.

"Charles McGraw No Crisp." *Hollywood Reporter*, undated.

"Charles McGraw Obituary." *Variety*, August 1, 1980.

"Charles McGraw, the Most Vindictive Killer..." Edwin Schallert, *Los Angeles Times*, January 4, 1947.

"Charles *The Threat* McGraw Emerges as a New Star..." *Hollywood Life*, December 16, 1949.

"Chas. McGraw Signed as Star of *Code 3*." *Hollywood Reporter*, December 23, 1949.

"Courtroom Drama Presented at Shubert." *Brooklyn Eagle*, 1939.

"Collier-McGraw Enterprises have Been Formed..." *Hollywood Life*, March 24, 1950.

Crowther, Bosley. "One Minute to Zero." *New York Times*, September 20, 1952.

Dolven, Frank. "The Saga of Tough Guy Charles McGraw." *Classic Images* #206, August 1992.

"*Double Crossbones*." Review. *Hollywood Reporter*, November 20, 1950.

"*Double Crossbones*." Review. *Daily Variety*, November 20, 1950.

Dusseault, Bernard J. "Acting, to Charles McGraw, More Fun Than Hard Work." *Worcester Sunday Telegram*, June 29, 1958.

"Fairbanks Pacts McGraw" *The Hollywood Reporter*, May 23, 1952.

"Falcon Is Here in Person," *Detroit Times*, February 2, 1955.

Fidler, Jimmie. *Fidler in Hollywood*. December 15, 1954.

Fisher, George. "... I'm Afraid the Picture Is Quite Stolen by Charles McGraw..." *In Hollywood*, Broadcast copy, KNX-CBS.

"Glenn Ford at Best." *Hollywood Reporter*, August 11, 1943.

"*Golden Boy*." *Hollywood Reporter*, November 5, 1937.

"*Golden Boy*." Review posted at St. James Theatre in London, England, 1938. No source available.

Goodman, Ezra. "Charles McGraw Mentioned as a Golden Glover..." *L.A. Daily News*, October 13, 1949.

Grime, John. "Tobacconist and Actor 'Save' Play." *Daily Express*, London, October 15, 1938.

"Group Theatre Now Banded in Films." *Hollywood Reporter*, undated.

Handsaker, Gene. "Charles McGraw ... Was Scared to Death of the Microphone When He First Went on Radio..." *The Progress*, July 6, 1950.

Haynes, Lincoln. "Playhouse Vet McGraw Ends up as TV Bartender." *Pasadena Independent*, December 23, 1955.

Hedda Hopper column, *Los Angeles Times*, March 24, 1952.

Hedda Hopper column, *Los Angeles Times*, May 23, 1952.

Hedda Hopper column, *Los Angeles Times*, June 21, 1949.

"Hellinger Gets 2 Gunmen from East," *Variety*, June 13, 1946.

Hellinger, Mark. *Photoplay Magazine*, December 9, 1946.

Heymann, Curt L. "*T-Men*—Film Dramatizes Work of Treasury Police Force." *New York Times*, October 26, 1947.

"Hollywood Getting Rid of Its Deadwood," Louis R. Guzzo, *The Seattle Times*, February 11, 1955.

Hollywood-Vine Yard, Milton Epstein, *The Film Daily*, May 15, 1950.

"*The Jazz Age*." Review. *Variety*, July 20, 1937.

Jensen, Jeff. *Entertainment Weekly*, February 5, 1999.

Johnson, Erskine. "Erskine Johnson in Hollywood." (syndicated.) *Harrisburg Daily Register*, September 4, 1952.

"*The Killers*." Review. *Daily Variety*, August 7, 1946.

"*The Killers*." Review. *Newsweek*, September 9, 1946.

"*The Killers*." Review. *Hollywood Reporter*, August 7, 1946.

"*The Mad Ghoul*." Review. *Daily Variety*, October 29, 1943.

"*The Mad Ghoul*." Review. *Hollywood Reporter*, October 29, 1943.

Malnic, Eric. "Charles McGraw Obituary," *Los Angeles Times*, August 4, 1980.

"The Man Who Went from Running Messages to Mugging…" *Akron Beacon Journal*, October 11, 1948.

"McGraw, *Code 3* Star." *Los Angeles Times*, December 23, 1949.

"McGraw Drops His Contract," *Los Angeles Daily News*, Thursday January 17, 1952.

"McGraw Inked…," Edwin Schallert, *Los Angeles Times*, May 10, 1952.

"McGraw Moved from Paul Wilkins to the Jaffe Agency," *Hollywood Reporter*, May 12, 1952.

"McGraw Scores…" *Los Angeles Evening Herald and Express*, January 17, 1950.

"McGraw Signs Term Contract with RKO." *Daily Variety*, December 23, 1949.

Matt Weinstock column, *Los Angeles Daily News*, June 2, 1952.

"MGM Is Talking Turkey with Charles McGraw Who Just Finished Two Pictures…" *Hollywood Reporter*, October 11, 1949.

"M'Graw Candidate for RKO Buildup," Edwin Schallert, *Los Angeles Times*, June 3, 1949.

"Mitchum and GI in Fight in Saloon." AP, November 7, 1951.

Muir, Florabel. "Charles McGraw Promises to Become a Triple Threat…" *Daily Variety*, October 27, 1949.

Murphey, Frances B. "War Film, Audience Make Noise." *Akron Beacon Journal*, October 6, 1952.

Nachman, Gerald. "*The Busy Body*." *Oakland Tribune*, February 9, 1967.

Nichols, Ken. *Akron Beacon Journal*, October 11, 1948.

Nichols, Ken. "Akron Native, Charles McGraw was Film Tough Guy." *Akron Beacon Journal*, August 1, 1980.

Nichols, Ken. "*The Killers* Was Also the Film That Launched the Career of Charles McGraw…" *Akron Beacon Journal*, April 11, 1977.

Oliver, Wayne. "He Lived the Title Role." Associated Press, February 8, 1955.

"On the Air," *The Hollywood Reporter*, September 12, 1950.

"*Once More My Darling*." *Newsweek*, August 15, 1949.

Rasmussen, Cecelia. "Sharing a Colorful Past with the Old Hall of Justice." *Los Angeles Times*, October 29, 2006.

Renshaw, Jerry. "Tales of Noir and B Movies, Interview with Marie Windsor." *Austin Chronicle*, October 31–November 6, 1997.

Ross, Jerry. "Akron's 'Killer' Makes Good." *Akron Beacon Journal*, April 13, 1947.

"RKO Exercises Option, Holds McGraw on Pact." *Los Angeles Evening Herald and Express*, January 11, 1950.

"RKO gets *Target* for Rubin…" *Hollywood Reporter*, February 2, 1950.

"Robert Mitchum 'Aggressor' in Barroom Brawl." UPI, November 8, 1951.

Roosevelt, Edith Kermit. "Fans Want More Love, Actor Says," *L.A. Daily News*, June 7, 1952.

"Roving Reporter," Norman Winter, *Hollywood Life*, May 5, 1950.

Schallert, Edwin. "Adele Jergens Will Brighten Cast of *Code 3*…" *Daily Variety*, December 26, 1949.

Schallert, Edwin. "Charles McGraw Plays *Toko-Ri* Commander." *Los Angeles Times*, December 14, 1953.

Schallert, Edwin. "Charles McGraw … Has Signed a Seven-year Contract…" *Los Angeles Times*, January 7, 1950.

Schallert, Edwin. "McGraw on Other Side…" *Los Angeles Times*, December 23, 1949.

Scott, Vernon. "Comeback Rare in 'Show Biz.'" UPI, October 4, 1967.

Scott, Vernon, "Costly *Spartacus* Finally on Film." UPI, August 7, 1960.

"*Side Street*." *New York Times*, March 24, 1950.

Smith, Darr. Column. *L.A. Daily News*, November 1, 1949.

"Society as I Find It," Cobina Wright, *Los Angeles Herald & Express*, June 3, 1952.

Starr, Jimmy. "Chas. McGraw, Marie Windsor in *Target*." *Los Angeles Evening Herald & Express*, May 29, 1950.

Starr, Jimmy. "The Other Lunch time at Lucey's, I Met Charles McGraw…" *Los Angeles Evening Herald and Express*, October 21, 1949.

"*The Story of Molly X*." Review. *Los Angeles Express*, October 3, 1949.

"Street Scene at the Pasadena Playhouse," *L.A. Examiner*, September 20, 1954.

"Television Is a Lot Tougher Than Regular Motion Picture Work," *Hagerston Daily Mail*, February 8, 1955.

"Theatre, Flesh and Shadow," Edward Carberry, *Cincinnati Post*, February 4, 1955.

"*The Threat*." Review. *Daily Variety*, October 26, 1949.

"*The Threat*." *Hollywood Reporter*, October 26, 1949.

"*The Threat*." Review. *Today's Cinema*, October 1949.

"*The Threat*." *Showmen's Trade Review*, 1949.

"*The Threat*." Review. *Variety*, October 24, 1949.

"*The Threat*—McGraw Wins Big Fan Following." *Valley Times*, May 3, 1950.

"*Threat* Vivid Action Film, Looks Like Sleeper Hit." *Hollywood Reporter*, October 26, 1949.

"*T-Men.*" Pressbook, Eagle-Lion Studios, 1947.

"*Twilight's Last Gleaming* — No Star." *New York Times,* February 10, 1977.

"Watch That McGraw," *Long Island Press,* February 8, 1955."Weighty Dialogue Slows Up Action." *The Hollywood Reporter,* September 29, 1947.

Williams, Dick. "This Piece of Villainy Might Pay Off." *The Los Angeles Mirror,* December 12, 1949.

Wilson, Earl. "Gravel-voiced Charles McGraw: Akron Actor No Hero to Daughter." February 14, 1955.

Winter, Norman. "George Breakston Has Contacted Agent Paul Wilkins for Services of Charles Mc-Graw." *Los Angeles Examiner,* November 30, 1950.

"*The Undying Monster.*" Review. *The Hollywood Reporter,* 1942.

"Youths Sign for Freighter Duty." *Akron Beacon Journal,* January, 12, 1932.

Documents

Actor's Equity Association contract for *The Survivors* for Charles McGraw, May 5, 1948.

Aldrich, Robert. Letter to Charles McGraw, February 21, 1976.

Artist's Manager and Agency Contract, Paul Wilkins Agency, June 18, 1946.

Bratton, William J. Letter to author, November 9, 2006.

Breen, Joseph I. Letter to Mark Hellinger, December 20, 1946.

Breen, Joseph I. Letter to Mark Hellinger, May 9, 1947.

Breen, Joseph I. Letter to RKO, January 6, 1950.

Butters, Charles C. Boy Scouts of America, Membership Card, February 1927.

Butters, Charles C. United States Shipping Board, Sea Service Medical Exam Record.

Butters, Frank. Letter to parents, November 10, 1907.

County of Los Angeles. Coroner Report, Case No. 80–9706, Death of Charles McGraw.

County of Los Angeles. Final Dissolution, Marriage, Case Number, NCD7824, Freda and Charles McGraw, October 3, 1968.

County of Los Angeles. Property Assessor Report for 3751 Reklaw Drive, Los Angeles CA 91604, 2005.

Crisp, Charles. British Actor's Equity Association Equity Association, Visiting Member Card #VA154.

Dassin, Jules. Letter to author of January 15, 2006.

Fenady, Andrew J. Letter to Charles McGraw, October 2, 1967.

FOIA Request Response from Social Security Administration: ICO Freda McGraw. February 11, 2003.

FOIA Request Response from the Federal Bureau of Investigation: ICO Charles McGraw. June 2, 2006.

FOIPA No. 1049790–00 Charles McGraw FBI File Documents, File No. 100–22316 with cover letter. February 9, 2007.

Gordon, Michael. Note to Charles Crisp, (undated) 1937.

Hellinger, Mark. Letter to Fred Brown, "My two new script enterprises..." May 18, 1946.

Hellinger, Mark. Telegram to John Huston, January 2, 1946.

Hellinger, Mark. Telegram to Joseph I. Breen, May 7, 1947.

Hellinger, Mark. Telegram to Burt Lancaster, July 19, 1949.

Henshaw, Jere. Memorandum."*The Birds*: Charles McGraw." April 30, 1962.

Henshaw, Jere. Memorandum to Alfred Hitchcock, Peggy Robertson, Joe Reich. "*The Birds*, Cast Suggestions." February 9, 1962.

Henshaw, Jere. Memorandum to Alfred Hitchcock. "Film for Casting: *The Birds.*" February 14, 1962.

Hughes, Howard. Memorandum to Jim Wilkinson. "Cutting Instructions — *Target.*" November 29, 1950.

Lang, Fritz. Letter to Mark Hellinger, August 12, 1946.

Mazurki, Mike. Letter to Charles McGraw, January 27, 1975.

McGraw, Charles. Letter of February 3, 1953.

McGraw, Charles. Letter to Freda McGraw, January 6, 1947.

McGraw, Charles. Personal diary of February-March 1932.

Miller, John V. (Director of Archival Services, University of Akron). Email of November 8, 2006.

Montgomery, Robert. Universal-International publicity release, August 18, 1949.

National Personnel Records Center FOIA response: Butters, Charles C., December 26, 2005.

Overman, Jack. Letter to Mark Hellinger, August 13, 1946.

Professional Ambulance Service, Inc. Invoice #31091, December 28, 1977.

"*Railroads on Parade.*" Program from the 1940 New York World's Fair.

Registration of Lease. 6424 Yucca Street, Apartment 107, August 18, 1947.

Riverside Hospital, North Hollywood. Ca Statement, November 7, 1980.

Sherrell, Lew. Letter to Charles McGraw, October 30, 1975.

Side Street (Pressbook). MGM, 1950.

Steranko, Jim. Email: "Richard Brooks," October 21, 2006.

Universal-International publicity release, October 17, 1949.

Universal-International publicity release, October 25, 1949.

Universal-International internal financial report on *The Killers,* November 16, 1947.

Universal-International publicity release, September 30, 1949.

Veiller, Anthony. Letter to Mark Hellinger, December 2, 1945.

Wasatch County Hospital, Heber City, Utah statement, September 30, 1976.

Youngstein, Max E. Telegram to Edward Small, November 25, 1947.

RKO Flash Weekly Newsletters

January 7, 1950: "McGraw Signs for *Code 3*..."

January 21, 1950: "Sid Rogell Appointed Executive

Producer..." "McGraw Signs Seven Year Con-
tract..."
February 4, 1950: "Stanley Rubin Signed..."
March 18, 1950: "*Target* Purchased..."
April 1, 1950: "315 Actors Under Contract Against a
Total of 742 in 1947..."
June 10, 1950: "Charles McGraw, Jacqueline White and
Marie Windsor Draw Stellar Roles in *Target*"
June 24, 1950: "Jerry Wald to RKO $150,000 Transfer
Cost from WB."
July 8, 1950: "*Target* has a Breathless Pace and Novel
Setting by Perry Leiber.
August 19, 1950: "Hughes Signs Wald and Krasna.
Independent Production Deal Involves More than
$50,000,000. Twelve Top Budget Features a Year
for Five Years."
November 10, 1951: Ann Blyth Replaces Colbert in
"*The Korean Story.*"
January 12, 1952: "Wald-Krasna Deal Extended
Another year."
May 10, 1952: "Wald Buys out Krasna."
May 17, 1952: "*Narrow Margin* Big Second Week..."
June 21, 1952: "*The Narrow Margin*. Seventh week at
the Trans-Lux New York Topped the Sixth and
Marathon Run Continues."
August 23, 1952: "*The Narrow Margin* has Gone into
a Fourth Week at the Kimo, Kansas City with
Grosses Holding Steady."
November 15, 1952: "Lewis Rachmil Resigns."

Studio Biographies

Biography of Charles McGraw. Paramount Studios,
November 1966.
Charles McGraw Biography. Universal-International,
June 28, 1956.

Studio Production Files including Daily Call Sheets, Production Notes, Cutting Continuity, Story Treatments, Scripts, and Memoranda for the following films

Angel Face (1953)
Armored Car Robbery (1950)
Berlin Express (1948)
The Birds (1963)

Blood on the Moon (1948)
Border Incident (1949): scripts only
Brute Force (1947)
The Devil Thumbs a Ride (1947)
Double Crossbones (1950)
His Kind of Woman (1951)
In Cold Blood (1967)
The Killers (1946)
Ma and Pa Kettle Go to Town (1950)
Macao (1952)
The Narrow Margin (1952)
One Minute to Zero (1952)
Raw Deal (1948)
The Story of Molly X (1949)
Roadblock (1951)
T-Men (1947)

Internet and Other Media Sources

The Academy of Motion Picture Arts and Sciences
www.oscars.org
American Film Institute (AFI) Catalog of Feature
Films www.afi.com
Archive of American Television Interviews—Abra-
ham Polonsky www.video.google.com
The Authentic History Center www.authentichistory.
com
Estimated Blood Alcohol Content Calculator www.beer
town.org
Evanier, Mark. "*It's a Mad Mad Mad Mad World.*"
POV Online, 2006. www.povonline.com
Frances Farmer Tribute (Opening night program and
cast of 'Golden Boy'). www.geocities.com
Historical Movie Box Office information www.box
officemojo.com
The Internet Broadway Database www.ibdb.com
The Internet Movie Database www.imdb.com
Newspaper archives www.newspaperarchive.com
Silver, Alain. *Senses of Cinema: Robert Aldrich.* www.
sensesofcinema.com
Summit County, Ohio Property Assessor www.mega
tron.summitoh.net
Thompson, R.J. Robert Aldrich. "An Independent
Career." June 30, 2000. www.latrobe.edu.au
TV Guide www.tvguide.com
The Valley Observed: History of the San Fernando
Valley. www.americassuburb.com
Wilson, Mark. "*A Boy and His Dog.*" Classic Science
Fiction Reviews. www.sensesofcinema.com
Spartacus. DVD set. The Criterion Collection, 2001.

Index

Abbott, Philip 147
Abbott & Costello 54
Accardo, Tony "Joe Batters" 38
Act of Violence 35
Adam-12 167, 173, 198
Adams, Edie 143
Adams, Gerald Drayson 71
Adams, Julie 124
Adam's Rib 43
Adkins, Vance 24, 143
Adler, Jay 126
Adler, Luther 13
The Adventures of Falcon 107, 108, 109, 197
The Adventures of Robin Hood 60
After Dark, My Sweet 176
Agar, John 125
Airplane! 104
Aldrich, Robert 176, 177, 178
Alexander, Ben 167
Alfred Hitchcock Presents 141, 197
Alien's World 180
Allen, Barclay 184
Allied Artists 35, 39, 105, 116
Altman, Robert 147
Alton, John 36, 37, 46, 50, 54, 61
American Cavalcade 24
The Andersonville Trial 197
Andes, Keith 115
Angel Face 101, 102
Angus, Robert 71
Ankrum, Morris 107
Apache 176
Arbuckle, Roscoe "Fatty" 144
Argosy Productions 101
Armendariz, Pedro 130
Armored Car Robbery 4, 6, 7, 73–76, 159, 187, 193
Armstrong, Robert 108
Arnaz, Desi 103
Ashby, Hal 174
The Asphalt Jungle 10, 44, 90
The Atomic City 50
Attack! 176
Autry, Gene 69, 149, 154
Away All Boats 113, 114, 115, 119, 194

Babe 91
Backus, Jim 143
Baer, Max 150, 152
Ball, Lucille 66, 103
Ballard, Lucien 41

Banyon 198
Barker, Lex 114, 115
Barnaby Jones 92
Barry, Don "Red" 168
Bartell, Harry 166
Barton, Charles 54
Basehart, Richard 55
Battleground 43, 78
Baxter, Anne 156
Baylor, Hal 175
The Beautiful Blonde from Bashful Bend 71
Beddoe, Don 83, 89, 106
Bedoya, Alfonso 46
Begley, Ed 163
Bel-Air Productions 104
Bel Geddes, Barbara 78
Belita 36, 39
Bellaver, Harry 50
Ben Casey 197
Ben-Hur 132
Bend of the River 133
Bennet, Spencer Gordon 154
Benny, Jack 144
Benton, Suzanne 175
Berg, Gertrude 164
Bergman, Ingrid 55
Berle, Milton 143
Berlin Express 40, 41, 192
Bernhard, Jack 39
Berry, John 35
The Best Years of Our Lives 29
Betty Boop 71
The Beverly Hillbillies 53
Bickford, Charles 33
The Big Combo 107
The Big Fix 35, 192
The Big Heat 50
Big House U.S.A. 72
The Big Knife 176
Big Sister 24
The Big Steal 92
The Bikelodore 126
Binns, Edward 141
The Birds 140, 141, 142, 143
The Birth of a Nation 66
Bischoff, Sam 100
Bissell, Whit 32, 50
Black, Mildred "Millie" 5, 12, 69, 147–154, 155, 170, 179–185, 187
Black, Stanley 152, 184
The Black Book 55

Black Tuesday 50
Blackboard Jungle 158
Blair, Janet 167
Blake, Robert 4, 158, 161, 165
Blanchard, Mari 110, 118
Blood on the Moon 59, 61, 62, 193
Bloomgarden, Harold 15
Blue, Ben 143, 156
Blyth, Ann 32, 33, 48, 49, 96, 97
Boardner, Steve 153
Bob Hope presents the Chrysler Theatre 197
Body and Soul 113, 165
Boehm, Sydney 50
Boetticher, Budd 105
Bogdanovich, Peter 142, 174
Bohnen, Roman 13, 14
Bonanza 105, 197
Bondi, Beulah 55
Boone, Richard 114, 115
Boots and Saddles Productions 116
Border Incident 43, 45–48, 187, 193
Border Patrol 45
Borgnine, Ernest 147
The Boston Strangler 91
The Bottom of the Bottle 50
Bottoms, Timothy 168
Bowery Boys 116
A Boy and His Dog 175, 196
Boy Meets Girl 13
Brady, Scott 20, 52, 56
Brahm, John 19, 59
The Brain That Wouldn't Die 116
Brand, Neville 125
Brand, Phoebe 13, 14
Bratsberg, Henry (Morgan, Harry) 14, 15, 20, 36, 167
Bratton, William J. 183
The Brave One 168
Bredell, Woody 30
Breen, Joseph I. 32, 33, 34, 75, 76, 173, 174
Brennan, Walter 61
Brice, Fanny 82
The Brick Foxhole 157
Bricker, George 92
The Bridges at Toko-Ri 4, 116, 145, 194
The Briskinodore 94, 102
Britton, Barbara 108
Broadway Bill 27
Brocco, Peter 89, 93, 94, 108, 168

209

Broccoli, Albert 146
Brodie, Steve 118
Brooks, Richard 5, 157–160
The Brothers Karamazov 158
Brown, James 35
Brown, Phil 30
Brute Force 32, 34, 35, 157, 192
Bryna Corporation 132
Bunco Squad 94
Burns, George 144
Burr, Raymond 73, 80
Burstein, "Burbey" 16
The Busy Body 22, 145, 156, 195
Butters, Frank 7, 8, 26, 70, 184

Caesar, Sid 143, 156
Caged 54, 100
Cagney, James 27, 66
Cain's Hundred 197
Cambridge, Godfrey 156
Camelot 146
Cannon 92
Canon City 38
Canova, Judy 154
Canutt, Joe 137
Canutt, Tap 137
Canutt, Yakima 137
Capote, Truman 157, 158, 159
Capra, Frank 60
Carey, Macdonald 42
Carnovsky, Morris 13, 14, 168
Caron, Leslie 169
Carradine, John 176
Carroll, Richard 71
Carson, Jack 100
Carter, Helena 52, 53
Carter, Jack 139
Carter, Lynne 72
Caruso, Anthony 130, 131
Casablanca (movie) 19, 60
Casablanca (television series) 110,
    111, 147, 149, 197
Cassavetes, John 126, 138
Castle, Peggie 56
Castle, William 145, 156
Cat on a Hot Tin Roof 158
Cat People 59
Caught 44
Cavalcade of America 197
CBS 154
Challenge to Be Free 172
Chandler 169, 196
Chandler, Jeff 52, 115
Chandler, Raymond 49, 175
Chaplin, Charlie 49
Chapman, Lonny 142
Charisse, Cyd 126
Cheyenne 110
China Smith 107
Chinatown 174
Christmas Holiday 29
El Cid 138
Cigarette Girl 177
Cimarron 138, 139, 195
Citizen Kane 29, 58, 101
City Detective 107

City That Never Sleeps 72, 92
Clark, Fred 42
Clark, Susan 165
Clarke, David 84, 85, 89
Cleopatra 146
Clurman, Harold 13
Clutter, Herb 158
Cobb, Lee J. 13, 14, 20
Code 3 71
Coffin, Tristram 108
Cohen, Mickey 150
Cohen, Ronald 177
Cohn, Harry 146
Colbert, Claudette 95, 96
Colby, Anita 32
Collier, William "Buster," Jr. 108
Collins, Ray 53
Columbia Studios 146, 157, 158
Compulsion 91
Conflict 197
Connors, Chuck 68
Conrad, William 30, 141
Conroy, Frank 62
Consolidated Film Laboratories 154
Constantine, Michael 141
Convict Molly X 48
Conway, Bert 14, 171, 172, 173, 186
Conway, Curt 39
Conway, Tim 68
Conway, Tom 107
Cook, Elisha, Jr. 36, 91, 104
Cooper, Merian C. 101
Coppola, Francis Ford 174
Corby, Ellen 53
Corey, Jeff 14, 20, 31, 159
Cornero, Tony 37
Cortez, Stanley 58
Corvette K-225 20, 62, 191
Costello, Frank 102
Cotten, Joseph 150, 151, 177
Coup du Torchon (Pop. 1280) 176
Cowl, Jane 48
Craig, James 49, 50
Crashout 73
Crawford, Joan 96
The Crimson Pirate 30
Crisis 157
Crisp, Beatrice (Butters) 7, 26, 70,
    184
Crisp, Donald 19
Criss Cross 30, 33
Cronyn, Hume 33, 34
Crosby, Bing 9
Crossfire 84, 101, 157
Crossroads 197
The Cruel Tower 116, 117, 118, 194
Cry of the City 30
Cukor, George 146
Cummings, Robert 55
Curtis, Tony 52, 56, 126, 134
Curtiz, Michael 60, 128, 129
Custer of the West 30

The D.A. 167
Daheim, Johnny 13, 84, 85, 136,
    137, 149, 165, 189

Dahl, Arlene 55
Daiei 101
Dalio, Marcel 110
Daly, James 163
Daniels, Harold 92, 94
Dano, Royal 141, 176
Dark Passage 100
Da Silva, Howard 13, 14, 20, 32, 46,
    143, 168
Dassin, Jules 32, 176
Davis, Bette 18, 27
Davis, Sammy, Jr. 146
Dead End 13
Dead Reckoning 92
Deadman's Tale 180
Dean, James 107
Dear Ruth 100
Death on the Turnpike 147
Death Valley Days 138
De Carlo, Yvonne 32, 35
De Corsia, Ted 108
Decoy 39
The Defiant Ones 126, 195
De Havilland, Olivia 64
Dehner, John 176
DeLuise, Dom 156
Denning, Richard 108
The Deputy 105, 197
De Rochemont, Louis 37
Destination Gobi 91
Destroyer 20, 191
Destry 197
The Detectives 197
De Toth, Andre 104
The Devil and Miss Jones 100
The Devil and Miss Sarah 197
The Devil Thumbs a Ride 62
Diagnosis: Danger 141
Dial 1119 44
The Dick Powell Theatre 138, 197
Dietrich, Noah 77
Dillinger 152
Dillinger, John 152
The Dirty Dozen 176
Dirty Harry 172
Diskant, George 58
Disney, Walt 91, 101
Dixon, Ivan 126
Dixon, Jean 93, 94, 102
Dmytryk, Edward 58, 60, 157
Dr. Kildare 197
Dorsey, Jimmy 150
Double Crossbones 24, 48, 53, 54,
    193
Double Indemnity 57
Doucette, John 104, 141
Douglas, Kirk 3, 4, 5, 63, 132–135,
    137
Douglas, Melvyn 177
Douglas Fairbanks Jr. Presents 104
Dow, Tony 116
Dragna, Jack 150
Dragnet 24, 29, 90, 107, 124, 166
Drake, Charles 52
Duff, Howard 32
Dummy 91

Duncan, Pamela 108
Durante, Jimmy 143
Durbin, Deanna 54
Durfee, Minta 144
Durning, Charles 177
Duryea, Dan 124, 125

Eagle-Lion Studios 36–38, 45, 49, 54, 55, 61, 146
Eastwood, Clint 110, 114, 154, 163
Easy Rider 164
Egan, Richard 124
The Egg and I 53
87th Precinct 138, 197
Eisenhower, Dwight D. 49, 105
Ekberg, Anita 110, 111
Ellery Queen 24
Ellroy, James 4, 90
Elmer Gantry 158
Emergency! 167, 197
Emerson, Hope 54
Erdman, Richard 126
Erickson, Leif 36, 126, 177
Ericson, John 118
Exodus 168

Factor, Jake "The Barber" 37
Fahey, Joseph 92
Fairbanks, Douglas, Jr. 104
The Falcon (film series) 59
Fall of the Roman Empire 138
Family Affair 146
The Far Country 133
Farmer, Frances 13, 20
The Farmer's Daughter 192
Farnsworth, Richard 137
Farrow, John 59, 79, 80
Fast, Howard 132
Faylen, Frank 61, 125
Fedderson, Don 167
Federal Telefilms 107
Feist, Felix E. 62, 76
Felton, Earl 71, 74, 76, 80, 82, 83, 91, 92
Female on the Beach 114
Fenady, Andrew 163
Ferber, Edna 138
Ferguson, Charles 8, 10
Ferguson, Donald 8, 10
Fields, W.C. 66, 160
The File on Thelma Jordon 30
The Filmmakers 101
Fisher, Steve 92
Fitts, Buron 90
Flavin, James 72, 108, 143, 159, 161
Fleischer, Max 71
Fleischer, Richard 61, 71, 78, 80, 81, 82, 83, 84, 90, 91, 92, 95, 152, 176
Flood, James 35
Follow the Sun 197
Fonda, Henry 20, 72, 167, 168
For a Few Dollars More 163
Force of Evil 165
Ford, Glenn 20, 138, 167
Ford, John 48, 101
Ford, Wallace 37, 38, 126

Foreign Correspondent 41
Foreign Legion 104, 197
Forsythe, John 159, 161
Foster, Preston 39
Fowley, Douglas 74, 108
Foy, Bryan "Brynie" 18, 36–38
Francis the Talking Mule 54
Frank, Nino 57
Freed, Arthur 43
Freed, Bert 53
Freeman, Mona 56
Freund, Karl 158
Fuchs, Daniel 36
The Fugitive 147
Fury 100

Gable, Clark 65, 66
Gallaudet, John 50, 159
Gangbusters 24
The Gangster 35, 36, 192
Gann, Ernest 126
Gardner, Ava 16, 28, 31
Garfield, John 13, 14, 18, 165
Garner, James 116
Garnett, Tay 96, 98, 172
Garrett, Betty 17
Gates, Nancy 108
Gato de Sol 184
G.E. Theatre 91, 197
Gebert, Gordon 83, 84, 88
Geer, Will 54, 159
Geiger, Wilson Bridges (Willie) 121
Geisler, Jerry 78, 79
Geray, Steven 48
The Getaway 176
Ghost 104
The Ghost and Mrs. Muir 91
Gillie, Jean 39
Gilmore, Lowell 94
Glad, Gladys 28, 35
Goddard, Paulette 42
The Godfather 174
Goetz, William 28
Golden Boy 13, 14, 15, 28, 36, 48, 168, 171
The Golden Gloves Story 76
Goldsmith, Martin 82
Goldwyn, Samuel 49, 58, 101
Golonka, Arlene 156
Gone with the Wind 54
The Good Humor Man 76
The Good, the Bad and the Ugly 163
Gordon, Michael 13, 48, 49
Grahame, Gloria 169
Grainger, Edmund 96, 138
Granger, Farley 49, 50
Granger, Stewart 101, 141
Grant, Cary 24, 150
Grant, Johnny 146
The Grapes of Wrath 72
Graves, Robert 104
The Great Gildersleeve (film series) 59
Green Acres 53
Greenstreet, Sydney 8, 60, 110
Greer, Jane 137

Gregg, Virginia 166
Gregory, James 141
Gregson, Eddie 184
Grey, Virginia 62, 63
The Grief Shooters 92
Griffies, Ethel 142
Griffith, D.W. 66
The Grifters 176
Grindl 197
Group Theatre 5, 13, 14, 20, 172
Gunfight at the O.K. Corral 125
Gunga Din 101
Gunsmoke 105, 154, 197, 198

Hackett, Buddy 143
Hadley, Reed 37, 45
Hagen, Jean 50
Hague, Frank "I am the Law" 37
Hale, Alan, Jr. 118, 163, 171
Hale, Barbara 59
Half Pint Buccaneer 54
Hall, Conrad 158, 165
Hamilton, Murray 116
Hammett, Dashiell 175
Hang 'Em High 163, 196
The Happy Time 91
Hardy, Oliver 144
Harry O 167
Hart, Dolores 53
Harvey, Paul 52
Hatton, Raymond 159
Havoc, June 51–53
Hawkins on Murder 197
Hawks, Howard 60, 101
Hayden, Sterling 10, 174
Haydn, Richard 126
Haymes, Dick 152
Hayward, Chuck 143
Hayward, Lillian 61
Hayworth, Rita 184
Hazard 42, 193
He Walked by Night 38, 166
Healey, Myron 108
Hecht, Ben 82
Hecht, Harold 30
Hell on Frisco Bay 50
Hellinger, Mark 27–29, 31–35, 50, 71, 157
Hell's Angels 77
Hell's Half Acre 92
Helmore, Tom 129
Helton, Percy 108
Hemingway, Ernest 28, 29
Henshaw, Jere 141
Heydt, Louis Jean 94
Higgins, John C. 45
High Sierra 27
The High Wall 50
Hill, Howard 101
Hilton, Paris 113
Hingle, Pat 163
Hirsch, Foster 57
His Kind of Woman 78–81, 91, 166, 194
Hitchcock, Alfred 5, 29, 4, 55, 84, 91, 95, 140, 141, 142, 143

The Hitchhiker 72
Hitler, Adolf 91
Holden, William 3, 112, 115, 116, 117
Holliman, Earl 113
Hollywood Radio Theatre 180
Holmes, Taylor 48
Homes, Geoffrey 92
Hondo 163, 197
Hood, Darla 172, 173, 174
Hoodlum Empire 107
Hopalong Cassidy 26
Hope, Bob 67, 105, 144
Hopper, Hedda 103
The Horizontal Lieutenant 138, 140, 195
Horvath, Charlie 114, 127, 137, 189
Hotel de Paree 197
The House on 92nd Street 37
How Green Was My Valley 19
Howard, Moe 35
Howard, Peter (Peter the Hermit) 120, 122, 186
Howard, Ron 167
Hoy, Bobby 12, 69, 79, 114, 126, 127, 135, 137, 139, 171, 185, 189
Hoyt, John 32
Hudson, Rock 56, 127
Huebsch, Edward 177
Huggins, Roy 147
Hughes, Howard 5, 43, 59, 61, 65, 76, 77–82, 86, 87, 88, 89, 90, 91, 94, 96, 98, 100–104
Hughes, Mary Beth 106
Humphries, Murray "Curly" 38
The Hunchback of Notre Dame 66, 101
Hunnicutt, Arthur 46
Hunt, Marsha 168
The Hunted 39, 40, 192
Hunter, Evan 138
Hush Money 68
Hush … Hush, Sweet Charlotte 176
Huston, John 29, 157, 158
Hutton, Jim 138, 139, 140

I Remember Mama 101
I Wake Up Screaming 92
I Was a Shoplifter 56, 193
The Imposter 20, 191
In Cold Blood 4, 157–162, 196
Independent Motion Picture Production Association 35
International Alliance of Theatrical Stage Employees 38
Ireland, John 36
Ironside 198
Israel, Peter 68
It's a Mad Mad Mad Mad World 143, 144, 145, 156, 195
It's a Wonderful Life 66

Jaffe, Sam 10
James, Harry 152
Janssen, David 114, 167
Jarrico, Paul 101
Jaws 174

The Jazz Age 13
Jeff Regan, Private Investigator 24
Jergens, Adele 49, 50, 51, 73, 75, 76, 92
Jessel, Georgie 156
Jet Pilot 101
Joan of Arc 55
Joe Butterfly 12, 42, 119, 124, 194
Joe Dakota 195
The Johnny Broderick Story 76
Johnny Got His Gun 168, 196
Johnny Staccato 107, 138, 197
Johnson, Ben 163
Johnson, Don 175
Johnson, Lyndon B. 146
Johnson, Nunnally 20
Jolson, Al 66
Jones, Carolyn 128
Jones, Jennifer 150
Jones, L.Q. 110, 116, 138, 163, 175
Judd for the Defense 163, 197

Kaiser, Harry J. 59
Karlson, Phil 52, 65
Kazan, Elia 13, 14, 15, 166
Keach, Stacy 176
Keaton, Buster 144
Kefauver Crime Commission 107
Keith, Robert 139
Keith-Albee-Opheum Theatres 58
Kelley, Barry 90, 108
Kellin, Mike 130
Kelly, Ed 37
Kelly, Grace 112
Kelly, Paul 49, 50
Kennedy, Arthur 126
Kennedy, Burt 175, 176
Kennedy, John F. 146
Kennedy, Joseph 38, 58
Kennedy, Robert 154, 182
Kerkorian, Kirk 146
Key Largo 100, 157
Kilbride, Percy 53
Kiley, Richard 164
The Kill-Off 176
Killens, John O. 165
The Killer Inside Me 175, 176, 177, 178, 196
The Killers 4, 28–32, 34, 35, 48, 71, 157, 159, 160, 192
The Killing 91, 176
King, Andrea 56
The King Brothers 35
King Kong 72, 101
King of the Zombies 116
Kiss of Death 63
Knotts, Don 143
Knox, Mickey 39, 95, 110
Koch, Howard W. 104
Koerner, Charles 59
Koolish, Abe 102
The Korean Story 95
Korshak, Sidney 38, 94, 102
Kosinski, Frank 35
Kosinski, Herman 35
Kosinski, Maurice 35

Kraft Suspense Theatre 147, 197
Kramer, Stanley 5, 126, 143, 144
Krasna, Norman 100
Krim, Arthur 36, 146
Kruschen, Jack 166
Kubrick, Stanley 133, 134, 137, 176
Kyser, Kay 59

Ladd, Alan 127, 128, 129
Lady in the Lake 28, 48, 92
The Lady Vanishes 41
Lambert, Jack 46
Lancaster, Burt 3, 5, 28–32, 63, 137, 158, 176, 177
Landau, Richard 92
Landers, Lew (Friedlander) 118
Lang, Fritz 59
Laramie 138, 197
Laredo 105
Larkin, John 141
La Rue, Jack 119, 185
The Las Vegas Story 101
The Last Detail 174
Laughton, Charles 133, 134, 153
Laura 57
Laurel, Stan 144
Lawrence, Marc 26
Lawton, Harry 165
Lay, Beirne, Jr. 115
Lea, Tom 131
Le Borg, Reginald 104
Lederer, Francis 66
Lee, Canada 17
Lee, Gypsy Rose 53
Lee, Harper 157
Leeds, Robert 71
Leighton, Michael 176
Leith, Virginia 116
Leonard, Jack 82
Leonard, Sheldon 36
Leone, Sergio 163
LeRoy, Mervyn 115
Leslie, Joan 36
Lesser, Julian 101
Levene, Sam 30, 124
Lewis, Edward 133, 135
Lewis, Elliott 52
Lewis, Jerry 144
Lewis, Joseph H. 60
Lewis, Robert 20
Lewton, Val 59
Liberty Pictures 154
The Lieutenant 197
The Life and Legend of Jesse James 197
Life and Times of Grizzly Adams 179
Lipton, Peggy 166
London, Julie 126, 130
The Long Night 192
The Longest Day 146
The Longest Night 197
The Longest Yard 176
Loo, Richard 169
Loophole 105, 106, 194
Losey, Joseph 176

Love Me or Leave Me 36
Lovsky, Celia 126
Low Company 36
Lucas, George 174, 175
Lukas, Paul 41
Lupino, Ida 59, 101
Lyons, Leonard 28

M-Squad 107
Ma and Pa Kettle Go to Town 48, 53, 193
Macao 82
The Mad Ghoul 21, 191
The Magnificent Ambersons 58
Main, Marjorie 53
Mainwaring, Daniel 92
Malden, Karl 13
Malone, Dorothy 105, 106
The Maltese Falcon 8, 57
The Man and the City 198
A Man Called Shenandoah 197
The Man from Blackhawk 197
The Man from Homicide 24
The Man from Laramie 133
The Man from U.N.C.L.E. 163, 197
The Man He Found 91
The Man in the Net 127, 128, 129, 130, 195
Man of a Thousand Faces 114
The Man with the Golden Arm 174
The Manchurian Candidate 104
Mann, Anthony 7, 36, 37, 45, 46, 49, 50, 54, 55, 61, 132, 133, 134, 138
Manning, Knox 45
Mannix, Eddie 146
Manpower 27
Mantell, Joe 142
March, Fredric 112
Marshall, George 42
Martin, Dick 68, 97, 98, 119
Marx, Groucho 144
Mason, Laura 109
Matt Lincoln 197
Matthau, Walter 124
Max, Ed 50
Maxey, Paul 88
Mayer, Louis B. 32, 43–45, 65
Mazurki, Mike 143, 172
MCA 132
McCarthy, Joseph 106
McClure, Don 74
McCullum, David 163
McGivern, William P. 147
McGrath, Frank 47
McGraw, Charles: Anthony Mann's professional regard for 46; anxiety and struggle to support family 20, 39, 65; anxiety, nervousness of being an actor 95, 129, 169; assumed Irish ancestry 7, 19, 160; attendance at University of Akron 10; being cast by Alfred Hitchcock 141; being cast in *The Killers* by Mark Hellinger 28; birth of daughter 17; bit parts

in war films 20; boxing career 4, 12; boyhood trip to India 8; bringing wife and daughter to film locations 97, 114, 119, 125; career transition to supporting player 32; casting by Richard Brooks 160; change of surname to McGraw 19; childhood in Akron, Ohio 7, 8, 9, 10, 11; colleagues who were blacklisted 13, 14, 168, 172; comedy acting 48, 53, 54, 140, 143; comment on Robert Mitchum's character 98; comments on changes in Hollywood 113; concept for television series 9; contract with RKO 64, 65; craftsmanship as an actor 5, 14, 83; cruelty of selected performances 38, 69 93; death of 3, 180–183; departure from RKO Studios 104; descriptions of movie roles 19, 20, 21, 30, 35, 36, 37, 38, 39, 41, 46, 47, 50, 51, 52, 55, 61, 62, 71, 76, 104, 105, 106, 112, 116, 118, 124, 125, 126, 128, 130, 134, 135, 137, 138, 139, 142, 156, 161, 162, 163, 165, 168, 169, 175, 176, 177; direction from Richard Fleischer 83; distinctive facial profile 4, 37, 46, 62, 104, 153; distinctive voice 4, 24, 62, 122, 170; divorce 147, 148, 155; drinking, alcoholism of 79, 95, 105, 114, 120–123, 126, 131, 145, 147, 155, 156, 170, 179, 180, 182, 187, 188, 189; drinking on the set 85, 110; elementary and high school education 8; enigmatic personality of 5, 116, 126, 170, 171, 180; episodic television appearances 104, 138, 145, 147, 163, 166, 167; FBI file, investigation as alleged Communist 14, 24, 25, 143; film debut 18; film noir visual icon 4, 37; finances 123; formation of Collier-McGraw Enterprises 108; friendship with Bert Conway 14, 171, 173, 189; friendship with Bobby Hoy 12, 69, 126, 135, 140, 143, 189; friendship with Charlie Horvath 114, 127, 137, 189; friendship with Darla Hood 172, 173; friendship with Dick Martin 97, 98; friendship with Frank Van 160, 161; friendship with Fred Clark 42; friendship with John Mitchum 79, 98, 172; friendship with Johnny Daheim 13, 85, 136, 137, 149, 165, 189; friendship with Mickey Knox 39; friendship with Robert Mitchum 62, 79, 98, 130; generosity with friends 123; gratitude towards Mark Hellinger 31; having jaw broken by Kirk Douglas 135; health and physical

problems 166, 177, 179, 180, 181; helping Michael McGreevey 130; helping out with scripts 164; historical perspective of film career 5; Hollywood Walk of Fame Star 147; home movies of 125; incident on airplane with Chuck Roberson 131; incident with Michael Curtiz 129; initial exposure to New York City 8, 9, 12; inspirational comeback for *In Cold Blood* 160, 161; involvement in barroom brawl with Mitchum 98; keeping an eye on Spencer Tracy 144; kissing episode with Anita Ekberg 110; lack of screen credit and studio contract 20; leaving Akron, Ohio 10, 11; legacy of, 185–189; living in Hollywood 39; luck in landing roles 140; marriage to Freda Choy Kitt 16; married life in New York City 16; military service and discharge during World War II 22, 23, 24; missed opportunities to become a movie star 3, 94, 95; missing family while on location 32, 39, 42, 97; missing plane crash 140; movie roles missed out on 76, 125; nihilism and self-destructiveness 6, 187–189; omission by modern directors 174, 175; on-set jokester 117, 118; payment for acting and film roles 17, 30, 62, 64, 65; performing jobs other than acting 12, 17, 20, 39, 65; personal and social life 69, 70, 119, 120, 122, 125, 170, 171; personal opinion of Kirk Douglas 135; personality traits and personal habits 5, 12, 15, 39, 85, 104, 116; philosophy of becoming an actor 26, 128; playing opposite Dan Duryea 124; playing "straight" parts 41; politics of 14; predilection for frequenting bars 15, 38, 69, 119–122, 172; professional relationship with Michael Gordon 13, 48; professional relationship with Paul Wilkins 26, 28, 32, 42; public comment on *The Narrow Margin* 91; purchase of house in Studio City 65, 66; quasi-adoption of Peter the Hermit 119, 122; radio work 24, 180; reason for becoming an actor 11; reciting terse noir dialogue 72, 74, 83, 84; relating fictional stories about himself 4, 22, 112, 183; relationship with daughter 38, 119, 122, 123, 145, 147, 155, 162; relationship with Hitchcock 142, 143; relationship with Joseph Pevney 115; relationship with Marie Windsor 83, 85, 87; relationship with Millie Black 5, 148,

149, 153, 170, 171, 172, 180; relationship with parents 12; relationship with wife 39, 119, 122, 123, 145, 147, 153; remembered by L.Q. Jones 175; reputation as a brawler 12, 13, 160; reputed "last rites" administered 160; reviews and accolades for performances 15, 30, 38, 42, 63, 76, 83; role in *The Adventures of Falcon* television series 107, 108, 109; role in *Casablanca* television series 108; role in *The Smith Family* television series 167; rumored Academy Award nominations 112; sale of house 187; scenes with Frederic March 112; screen persona 3, 4, 38, 105, 187; self-promotion of virility 39; social gaffe in Germany 177, 178; stage acting at Pasadena Playhouse and in Hollywood 42; stage debut in *Golden Boy* 13; on tour in England with *Golden Boy* 15, 16; transition out of film noir roles 118; using professional name of *Charles Crisp* 13; victim of practical jokes 47, 114; views on typecasting as a heavy 62, 63; war record and military service exaggerations 5, 22, 23, 24; work and associations with Group Theatre 5, 13, 14, 15, 20, 168; work as a dancer 14; work at New York World's Fair 16, 17; working class demeanor and outlook as an actor 5, 68, 69, 128; working with Nancy Reagan 138

McGraw, Freda (Kitt, Freda Choy) 5, 15, 16, 17, 18, 20, 24, 26, 31, 39, 42, 65, 85, 87, 97, 98, 114, 119, 120–123, 125, 131, 145, 147, 155, 170, 182, 183, 184, 186

McGraw, Jill 7, 17, 19, 22, 24, 26, 31, 38, 39, 66, 87, 97, 114, 119–123 135, 137, 145, 147, 155, 183, 184, 185

McGreevey, Michael 128
McIntire, Tim 175
McQueen, Steve 158
Mechanized Patrolling 23, 191
Menzies, William Cameron 54, 55, 89
Mercury Theatre 58
Meredith, Burgess 125
Merrill, Gary 130
Metro Goldwyn Mayer 42, 43, 45, 49, 60, 146
Metty, Russell 134
The Mexican Spitfire (film series) 59
Michener, James 112
The Midnight Story 114
Mildred Pierce 100
Milestone, Lewis 176
Miller, Patrick 129

Minton, Terry 181, 182, 183
Mirisch Brothers 146
Mission: Impossible 198
Mr. and Mrs. North 108, 197
Mr. and Mrs. Smith 100
Mitchell, James 110
Mitchum, John 79, 98, 172
Mitchum, Robert 5, 12, 26, 46, 61, 62, 78–82, 86, 95, 96, 97, 98, 99, 100, 102, 130, 131, 152
The Mod Squad 166, 197
Money to Burn 197
Monkey Island 66
The Monklonious 4
Monogram Studios 35, 39, 104, 116, 128, 154
Monroe, Marilyn 102, 182
Montalban, Ricardo 45
Montgomery, Robert 28, 48, 49
Monty Nash 198
The Moon Is Blue 173
The Moon Is Down 20, 191
Moss, Arnold 46, 55
Muller, Eddie 187
Munro, Nancy 98
Murder and Mr. Malone 24
Murder My Sweet 57
Murphy, Audie 124, 125
Musuraca, Nicholas 58, 59, 61, 93
My Fair Lady 146
Mystery Street 44, 50

Nader, George 115, 125
The Naked City 33, 50
The Naked Spur 133
The Name of the Game 197
The Narrow Margin 4, 83, 89, 90, 91, 92, 146, 160, 173, 187, 194
National Velvet 66, 186
Native Son 17
Nayfack, Nicholas 45
NBC 108, 167
The Necklace 82
Neptune Productions 49
The New Breed 197
New York Confidential 107
Newman, Paul 158
Nichols 198
Night and the City 36
Night Court 27
Night of January 16th 16
The Night of the Hunter 130, 153
The Night Stalker 197
Night Waitress 168
Nightmare in Chicago 147, 197
Nitti, Frank 38
Nocturne 113
Noguchi, Thomas 182
Nolan, Lloyd 116
North by Northwest 141
Notorious 95
Novak, Kim 146

Oakie, Jack 130
Oakland, Simon 141
Oates, Warren 169

Oberon, Merle 41
O'Brien, Edmund 29, 30
O'Connor, Donald 53, 54
The Odd Couple 104
Odds Against Tomorrow 165
Odets, Clifford 12, 14
O'Donnell, Cathy 49, 50
Office of Alien Property (OAP) 18
Office of Strategic Services (OSS) 164
O'Hara, United States Treasury 166, 167, 197, 198
O'Keefe, Dennis 20, 37, 38
Olivier, Laurence 133, 135
O'Loughlin, Gerald 159
On the Old Spanish Trail 40, 42, 44, 192
On the Town 43
On the Waterfront 124
Once More My Darling 48–49, 193
Once Upon a Savage Night 147, 197
One Minute to Zero 94, 95, 96, 97, 98, 99, 194
Orr, William T. 110
O'Shea, Michael 62
O'Sullivan, Maureen 79
Out of the Past 92, 101, 137
The Outcasts 197
Outside the Wall 114
Overman, Jack 33
The Ox-Bow Incident 163

Paige, Leroy "Satchel" 130
Pam, Jerry 163
Paramount Studios 5, 4, 107, 113, 185
Parker, William H. 90, 150, 166
Parrish, Robert 126, 130
Parsons, Lindsley, Jr. 105, 117, 118
Parsons, Lindsley, Sr. 105, 106, 116
Pasternak, Joe 138
Pathe Studio 58
Paths of Glory 133, 176
Patton, General George S. 22, 23, 126
Peary, Harold 59
Peckinpah, Sam 105
Peet, Charles 71
Pendergast, Thomas 38
Pendulum 164, 196
Peppard, George 164
Perilous Voyage 197
Perrin, Vic 166
Perry Mason 73, 107
Pevney, Joseph 12, 113, 114, 115, 126, 127
Phantom Lady 29
Pichel, Irving 20
Pillow Talk 48
Poitier, Sidney 126
Police Story 173, 198
Pollack, Sydney 141
Polonsky, Abraham 164, 176
Popeye the Sailor 71
The Postman Always Rings Twice 96

Powell, Dick 11
PRC Studios 36
Preminger, Otto 49, 101, 102, 146
Prentiss, Paula 138, 139, 140
Preston, Robert 61
Price, Vincent 79, 81, 166
The Professionals 158
Pryor, Richard 156
Psycho 141, 174
Puglia, Frank 33

The Quiet Man 154
Quinn, Anthony 150
Quo Vadis 94

The Racket 77
Raft, George 154
Railroaded 45
Railroads on Parade 16, 17
Raines, Ella 32
Rains, Claude 110
Ralston, Vera Hruba 154
Rand, Ayn 16
Rank, J. Arthur 36, 101
Ratoff, Gregory 49
Raw Deal 45
Rawhide 154, 163
Ray, Nicholas 59
Reagan, Nancy Davis 138
Reagan, Ronald 138
The Real McCoys 53
Rear Window 140
Redford, Robert 68, 165
Reich, Joe 141
Reign of Terror 54, 55, 193
Reilly, Hugh 52
Renoir, Jean 176
Repeat Performance 36
Republic Studios 12, 69, 153, 154, 186
Revenge of the Zombies 116
Reynolds, Bernard 98
Reynolds, William 114
Richard Diamond, Private Detective (television) 107
Richard Diamond, Private Detective (radio) 24
Richards, Paul 104
Rickles, Don 144
Ride the High Country 104, 105
Ride the Pink Horse 49
Riffraff 95
Ritt, Martin 13, 14
River of No Return 91, 102
RKO Studios 4, 5, 41, 56–65, 68, 70, 71, 75, 76–81, 82, 84, 85, 87, 88, 90, 91, 92, 94, 95, 98, 99, 100–104, 108, 112, 119, 130, 185, 186
Roadblock 4, 92, 93, 94, 160, 194
The Roaring Twenties 27
Robards, Jason 168, 175
The Robe 132
Roberson, Chuck 130, 131, 137
Robert Montgomery Presents 49
Robertson, Peggy 141

Robin and the 7 Hoods 156
Robinson, Dewey 94
Robson, Mark 58, 59, 112
Rogell, Sid 61, 62, 80, 100
Rogers, Ginger 52
Rogers, Roy 42
Rogue Cop 50
Roman Holiday 168
Rooney, Mickey 44, 112, 143
Roosevelt, Franklin Delano 18
Rope 141
Rose, Reginald 128
Roselli, Johnny 37, 38
Roses Are Red 192
Ross, Katharine 165
Rossen, Robert 176
Route 66 141, 197
Rowan, Dan 68
Royal Productions, Inc. 101
Rozsa, Miklos 28, 84
Rubin, Stanley 39, 82, 83, 84, 86, 87, 90, 91, 92, 102
Run for Your Life 147, 156, 197
Runyon, Damon 15
Russell, Jane 78, 79, 81, 82, 86
Russell, John 52
Ruttenberg, Joseph 50
Ryan, Edmon 49
Ryan, Ray 102
Ryan, Robert 41, 46, 145, 156
Ryan, Sheila 35
Ryder, Alfred 37, 38

Saddle the Wind 125, 126, 195
The Saint (film series) 59
Sakall, S.Z. 110
Sanders, George 20
Sands of Iwo Jima 154
Sarnoff, David 58
Savalas, Telly 141
Scarface 77
Scene of the Crime 44
Schaefer, George S. 58, 59
Schary, Dore 41, 43–45, 6, 78, 146
Schell, Maria 138
Schenck, Aubrey 37, 104
Schenck, Nick 38, 43, 44
Scorsese, Martin 60, 174
Scott, Adrian 164
Scott, Lizabeth 116
Scott, Randolph 104
Scott, Vernon 160
The Sea Wolf 60
Seberg, Jean 164
Second Chance 50
Secret Mission 20
Selznick, David O. 49, 55, 150
Sennett, Mack 89, 153
Serie Noire (A Hell of a Woman) 176
The Set-Up 78
Seven Thieves 50
The Seventh Cross 192
77 Sunset Strip 167, 197
Seymour, Dan 110
Shakedown 114
Shamley Productions 141

Shaw, Frank 38, 90
Shaw, Irwin 42
Sherry, Robert 113
Shirley Temple's Storybook 197
Sholem, Lee 104
Side Street 44, 48, 49–5, 193
Siegel, Benjamin "Bugsy" 150
Silvera, Darrell 58
Silvers, Phil 143
Simmons, Jean 101, 102, 134, 135, 137
Simon, Robert 141
Since You Went Away 149
Siodmak, Curt 29, 40
Siodmak, Robert 29, 30, 35, 59
Siren Song 110
Six Bridges to Cross 50, 114
Slaughter on Tenth Avenue 124, 194
Small, Edward 36, 37
Smiler with a Gun 78
Smith, Art 13, 14, 33, 34
The Smith Family 167, 168, 197
Sokoloff, Vladimir 126
Solt, Andrew 96
The Son of Dr. Jekyll 177
Spartacus 4, 119, 132–135, 137, 168, 195
Spielberg, Steven 174, 175
The Spiral Staircase 29
Stack, Robert 104
Stalag 17 125
Stark, Ray 82
Stein, Jules 18, 38
Steinbeck, John 20
Steiner, Max 84
Sterling, Jan 124
Stevens, George 60
Stevens, Inger 163
Stevens, Warren 166
Stevenson, Edward 58, 62
Stevenson, Robert 80
Stewart, James 65, 167
Stewart, Paul 159
Stone, Lewis 44
Stone, Milburn 21, 94
The Story of G.I. Joe 26
The Story of Molly X 51–53, 193
Stossel, Ludwig 110
Straight No Chaser 4
The Strange Door 114
Stranger on the Third Floor 59
Strangers on a Train 141
The Street with No Name 113
Strode, Woody 134, 135
Sullivan, Barry 35, 105, 106, 134, 165
Sunset Boulevard 3
The Survivors 42
The Suspect 29
Sutherland, Donald 168
Swenson, Karl 142
Switzer, Carl (Alfalfa) 126, 172

T-Men 4, 37, 38, 45, 187, 192
Taft, William Howard 165
Talman, William 72–74, 76

Tamblyn, Russ 55
Tamiroff, Akim 36
Tandy, Jessica 163
Tarantino, Quentin 152
Target 82
Tate, Sharon 182
Taylor, Elizabeth 101, 186
Taylor, Joan 104, 105
Taylor, Robert 126
Taylor, Rod 142
Teahouse of the August Moon 124
Tehachapi — The Story of Molly X 51
Tell Them Willie Boy Is Here 164, 165, 166, 196
10 *Rillington Place* 91
Tension 44
Terror 48
Terry-Thomas 143
Tetzlaff, Ted 95, 96
Thalberg, Irving 43, 44
Thaxter, Phyllis 61
Theasquare Productions 101
They Came to Blow Up America 20, 191
They Drive by Night 27
They Live by Night 49
They Were Expendable 48
The Thief of Baghdad 54
Thieves Highway 113
The Thin Man 44
Thirty Seconds Over Tokyo 26, 84
This Is Your F.B.I. 24
This World, Then the Fireworks 176
Thompson, Jim 175, 176
Thorpe, Richard 138
The Threat 4, 62, 63, 64, 71, 193
The Three Stooges 35, 144
Thriller 197
Thunder Over The Plains 104, 105, 194
Thurman, Sammy 159, 161
Ticket to Anywhere 9
Tierney, Lawrence 46, 62, 150, 151, 152
Tight Spot 52
To Kill a Mockingbird 157
Toland, Gregg 58
Tomack, Sid 50
Tonight We Raid Calais 20, 191
Toomey, Regis 35
Top Hat 101
Tora! Tora! Tora! 91
Totter, Audrey 28
Tourneur, Jacques 41, 59
Toward the Unknown 113, 115, 116, 194
Tracy, Don 35
Tracy, Spencer 90, 143, 144
Tramp Freighter 9
The Travels of Jamie McPheeters 197
The Treasure of the Sierra Madre 158

Trilling, Steve 110
Troubleshooters 197
True Grit 164
Truman, Harry 38
Trumbo, Dalton 35, 132, 134, 164, 168
Tucker, Sophie 150
Turner, Lana 96
The Turning Point 100
TV's Reader's Digest 197
20,000 Leagues Under the Sea 91
Twentieth Century Fox Studios 18, 27, 36, 60, 71
Twilight for the Gods 119, 126, 127, 195
Twilight's Last Gleaming 176, 177, 196
2001: A Space Odyssey 164
Two Tickets to London 20, 191

Uffner, George 102
Under the Gun 95
The Undying Monster 18.191
United Artists 104, 130, 146
Universal, Universal International, U-I Studios 24, 28, 32, 48, 49, 51–54, 65, 68, 132, 154, 186
The Untouchables 138, 197
Ustinov, Peter 133, 134

Valenti, Jack 174
Van, Frank 160
Van Sickel, Dale 70, 137, 186
Van Zandt, Philip 108
Veiller, Anthony 29
Velez, Lupe 150
Vera Cruz 176
Vertigo 140
Viertel, Peter 42
The Vikings 91, 132, 133
Violent Saturday 50
The Virginian 14, 105, 197
Von Stroheim, Eric 3
Voyage to the Bottom of the Sea 197
Vuolo, Tito 108

Wagon Train 104, 138, 197
Wald, Jerry 100, 101
Walk a Crooked Mile 92
Walker, Robert 150
Wallis, Hal B. 19, 27, 60, 100
Walsh, Raoul 69
Walter, Charles 138
Wang, Gene 108
Wanger, Walter 36, 37, 55
War Paint 104, 194
Warden, Jack 129
Warner, Harry 66, 110, 111
Warner, Jack L. 19, 27, 36, 65, 100, 110, 111, 146
Warner Brothers Studios 18, 23, 27, 60, 110, 111, 116, 179

Wasserman, Lew 38, 65, 96, 141, 174
Wayne, John 154, 163, 164
The Web 48
Webb, Jack 90, 166, 167
Webber, Peggy 166
Weill, Kurt 16
Welles, Orson 17, 49, 58
Wellman, William 176
Westerfield, James 108
What Ever Happened to Baby Jane? 176
The Whip Hand 89, 91
The Whistler 24, 197
White, Jacqueline 83, 84, 85, 87, 88, 89, 91
White, Pearl 51
White Heat 63
Whitney, Peter 118
Widmark, Richard 36, 63, 177
Wilbur, Crane 51–53
Wild, Harry J. 58
The Wild, Wild West 154, 197
Wilder, Billy 3, 125, 146
Wilke, Robert J. 80, 104
Wilkins, Paul 26, 28, 32, 42, 63
Wilkinson, Jim 88
Willie Boy: A Desert Manhunt 165
Wilson, Earl 122
Wilson, Scott 158
Winchell, Walter 27
Winchester Productions 101
Winchester '73 65, 133
The Window 95
Windsor, Marie 83, 84, 85, 86, 87, 88, 89, 91, 104, 173
Winters, Roland 48
Winters, Shelley 52, 53
Wise, Robert 58, 49, 61, 152
Witney, William 14
The Woman from Tangier 92
The Woman in the Window 57
The Woman on Pier 13 72
The Wonderful Country 130, 13, 195
Woodstock 164
Woolrich, Cornell 175
Wyler, William 29, 60, 132
Wynn, Keenan 50, 176

Yankee Doodle Dandy 60
Yates, Herbert J. 154
You Are There 164
Young, Collier 101
Young, Robert R. 36
Youngstein, Max E. 37

Zanuck, Darryl F. 19, 146
Zinnemann, Fred 176
Zucco, George 21
Zuckerman, George 45